BIBLE STUDY NOTES:

21:25 *There will be signs ...*
Heavenly portents were thought to predict earthly events, and disruption of regular heavenly patterns would mean disaster on earth. Such apocalyptic imagery was popular in late OT and NT times. See Isaiah 13:10–11 for one of the earliest examples. ***roaring of the sea.*** The sea was seen as symbolic of evil in the apocalyptic imagery of the day.

21:27 *the Son of Man coming ...*
The title "Son of Man" was the title Jesus most frequently used for himself. This reference to him coming on a cloud is a reference to the prediction of Daniel 7:13.

21:28 *stand up and raise your heads.* This is a posture of expectation, hope and courage (Ps. 24:7; 83:2). The terror these signs inspire in the world is contrasted with the hope they provide for Jesus' followers. ***redemption.*** This is the only occurrence of the word in the Gospels. Paul uses the word in association with Jesus' second coming.

21:29–30 *Look at the fig tree.* Fig trees were the most common trees in Palestine and produced leaves only in late spring, thus making them a harbinger of summer.

21:31–32 *the kingdom of God is near.* Was Jesus saying that his second coming was near, within the life span of this ***generation***? Clearly that did not happen, at least in the sense that it is traditionally conceived. Several resolutions have been proposed. One is that it is only the kingdom of God that is near. That kingdom started with Christ's victory over death and the subsequent coming of the Holy Spirit. Its full fruition will not be realized until much later. Another possible resolution is that this passage was a later interpretation of the church, which while undergoing intense persecution, reinterpreted a saying of Christ to promise his immediate return and redemption for their suffering. In any case, the teaching is that while such signs produce fear and panic in the lives of many, believers can have the confidence that these very things are indicators *not* that God has lost control of world events, but that the kingdom of God is pushing its way into human history.

21:34–36 *catch you unexpectedly.* We must be constantly aware of and ready for God's action in our world. This is also the teaching of the parables Jesus told of the lamps and the homeowner who was away (Luke 12:35–40 and Matt. 25:1–13).

CARING TIME AND PRAYER REQUESTS:

 This time is for developing and expressing your caring for each other as group members. We do this by sharing our needs and praying for each other's needs.

Each group member should answer the question,

How can this group help you in prayer this week?

Then join together in group prayer.

 SERENDI  D0125893

Small Group
HANDOUT

WEEK 1: ADVENT 1
Expectations of Deliverance
Luke 21:25–36

 GATHERING 10 min.   STUDY 30 min.   CARING 20–40 min.

Leader: The agenda has three parts. In the Gathering time you'll be getting to know each other through an "ice-breaker." This will be for your total group. The Study time has two parts: (1) Story and (2) Scripture. If you are short of time, skip the Story and move to the Scripture. Begin by reading out loud the Story or the Scripture to the whole group. Then divide into groups of 4 for the Study time. Finally, regather the total group for the Caring time. Keep to this agenda: (1) Gathering—10 minutes, (2) Study—30 minutes, and (3) Caring—20–40 minutes.

 Places in the Heart. Most of us have places we think of from our childhood that have a special place in our heart. Think of when you were in grade school and the neighborhood you lived in at the time. Share a place you remember from each of the categories below.

THE PLACE OF COMFORT: This was where you went to feel at peace or to repair from injuries to your psyche.

THE PLACE OF CHALLENGE: This was the difficult tree to climb, the challenging hill, the scary house—the place where kids went to test their bravery or skill.

THE PLACE OF COMMUNITY: This was where the kids gathered to be together, the heart of the neighborhood.

¹Corrie ten Boom, *The Hiding Place* (Minneapolis, MN: World Wide Publications, 1971), pp. 222–223.

INTRODUCTION STORY:

 Corrie and Betsie ten Boom Are Released. As a punishment for sheltering Jews from the Nazis, Corrie and Betsie ten Boom were sent to a series of concentration camps, eventually ending up in Ravensbruck. There Betsie in particular got physically weaker and weaker. But the ten Booms' faith got stronger and stronger. One day Betsie, though obviously near death, predicted that both she and Corrie would be released from prison by the first of the next year. Not long after that Betsie died. But Corrie realized shortly after her own release, that in a profound sense Betsie's prediction had come true. Corrie tells the story in her book, *The Hiding Place:*

"The heavy iron doors swung open; at the heels of a woman guard we marched through. We climbed the little hill: now I could see the lake, frozen from shore to shore. The pines and the distant church steeple sparkled in the winter sun like an old-fashioned Christmas card.

"I could not believe it. Perhaps we were only going to Siemens factory; tonight we would march back to camp. But at the top of the hill we turned left, toward the center of the small town. ...

"At the small train station the guard turned and left us without a backward glance. Apparently we were all traveling as far as Berlin, then each pursuing her separate route home. There was a long wait on cold iron benches.

"The feeling of unreality persisted. Only one thing seemed familiar, the hungry hollow in my stomach. ...

"At last a train pulled into the station and we crowded eagerly to it but it was for military personnel only. Late in the afternoon we were allowed aboard a mail train, only to be put off two stops farther on to make room for a food shipment. The trip became a blur. We reached the huge, bomb-gutted terminal in Berlin sometime after midnight.

"It was New Year's Day, 1945. Betsie had been right: she and I were out of prison. ..."[1]

1. How do you react to the idea that Betsie ten Boom had "correctly" predicted what happened?
   - ❒ That's cheating!—dying is not really being released.
   - ❒ It was coincidence.
   - ❒ Her insight came from observing what happened around her.
   - ❒ Her insight came from God.
   - ❒ other:_____

2. When has something good happened to you that seemed unreal, either because it was unexpected or because it was such a relief from what had gone before?
   - ❒ I don't remember this happening.　❒ when I fell in love
   - ❒ when I finally got a job　　　❒ other:_____
   - ❒ when I received an award or honor
   - ❒ when I came home from a war or military action

SCRIPTURE:

 Praying for Time? Popular singer George Michael sang a song a few years ago called "Praying for Time," in which he bemoaned the fact that there was "so much to hate" about what was going on in the world—particularly the lack of generosity people showed in the presence of so much hunger and need. He wondered if "God stopped keeping score," and even declared that God wasn't coming back because "he had no children to come back to" anymore. He concluded by saying that maybe we should all be "praying for time." Cynical?—certainly. But he was also expressing something which many today wonder about. Our Scripture for this week assures us that God hasn't "stopped keeping score." The God who sent Jesus Christ for redemption will also send him for judgment. His hope and expectation is that those he is coming back for will be found faithful when he returns—he indeed has children "to come back home for." The task of his disciples is to make sure as many as possible are in that category, working for and expecting God's deliverance.

Have someone in your group read the following passage out loud. Then go around on each question and let each person share their answer. Take advantage of the Study notes following the questionnaire. Be sure to save the last 20–40 minutes for the Caring time.

25"There will be signs in the sun, the moon, and the stars, and on the earth distress among nations confused by the roaring of the sea and the waves. 26People will faint from fear and foreboding of what is coming upon the world, for the powers of the heavens will be shaken. 27Then they will see 'the Son of Man coming in a cloud' with power and great glory. 28Now when these things begin to take place, stand up and raise your heads, because your redemption is drawing near."

29Then he told them a parable: "Look at the fig tree and all the trees; 30as soon as they sprout leaves you can see for yourselves and know that summer is already near. 31So also, when you see these things taking place, you know that the kingdom of God is near. 32Truly I tell you, this generation will not pass away until all things have taken place. 33Heaven and earth will pass away, but my words will not pass away.

34"Be on guard so that your hearts are not weighed down with dissipation and drunkenness and the worries of this life, and that day catch you unexpectedly, 35like a trap. For it will come upon all who live on the face of the whole earth. 36Be alert at all times, praying that you may have the strength to escape all these things that will take place, and to stand before the Son of Man."

Luke 21:25–36

QUESTIONS:

1. When you were a teenager, what connection were you most likely to have with heavenly bodies?
   - ❒ sun-worshiping—out on the beach
   - ❒ stargazing—through my telescope
   - ❒ stargazing—while camping at night
   - ❒ moon-gazing—with a certain someone at night
   - ❒ chasing after "heavenly bodies"!—or is that what you meant?

2. What event in your adolescence most disrupted your "universe"?
   - ❒ the divorce of my parents　　❒ when we moved
   - ❒ the death of a friend or loved one　❒ other:_____
   - ❒ when a friend moved
   - ❒ when I broke up with a boyfriend/girlfriend

3. Finish this sentence: "Jesus told his disciples the things in this passage so that ..."
   - ❒ they could amaze their friends with their insight into the future
   - ❒ they could warn people to repent
   - ❒ they could be comforted during times of persecution
   - ❒ they could be alert to what God was doing in the world
   - ❒ they would keep their life "in order"

4. What is your favorite sign that summer is coming?
   - ❒ baseball players at spring training
   - ❒ the sales on swimming suits and summer clothes
   - ❒ the budding of trees and greening of the grass
   - ❒ the rain gets warmer (for those in Washington and Oregon!)
   - ❒ the days get longer
   - ❒ sun-worshiping—out on the beach
   - ❒ other:_____

5. What signs do you see in your life or the world around you of frightening things ahead?

6. What signs do you see in your life or the world around you of the redeeming power of God?

7. What do you need to do in response to the teaching of this passage?
   - ❒ really look at those frightening signs and stop ignoring them
   - ❒ remember to look at God's signs of redemption—and take hope!
   - ❒ stop getting weighed down by the "worries of this life"
   - ❒ get my life in order
   - ❒ witness to Christ's coming
   - ❒ other:_____

BIBLE STUDY NOTES:

3:1 *the fifteenth year ...* Following the manner of ancient historians, Luke dates the appearance of John the Baptist. The fifteenth year of the reign of Tiberius Caesar was about A.D. 28. Before his death in 4 B.C., Herod the Great divided his territory between three of his sons: **Herod** (Antipas) and **Philip** ruled as tetrarchs (a term used to describe the ruler of a minor domain) over their areas until 39 and 33 A.D. respectively. The third son, Archelaus, was given Judea, Samaria and Edom. The Jews thoroughly hated him and petitioned Rome for his removal. This resulted in the establishment of a Roman governorship over Judea. Pilate held this post from 26–37 A.D. **Abilene** was the district centering around Abila, a town in Lebanon, northeast of Mount Hermon. This area was ruled by a king named **Lysanias** from 40 to 36 B.C. But, according to *The Intepreter's Bible,* various extrabiblical references "lend plausibility to the hypothesis that another Lysanias with the title of tetrarch governed Abilene at some period in the first century of the Christian era before A.D. 37."[2]

3:2 *the high priesthood of Annas and Caiaphas.* The high priest was the civil and religious heart of the Jewish community.

While the Jews regarded this as a lifelong office, the Romans, seeking people who would administer in a way they approved, appointed men to that office at will. Annas, who served as high priest until 14 or 15 A.D., was removed from office and replaced first by his son Eleazor and then by his son-in-law, Caiaphas, who held this position from 18–37 A.D. Luke recognizes that while Caiaphas held the position, Annas still held the power (see John 18:13). *the word of God came to John.* A common way of referring to the calling of a prophet (Jer. 1:1,4; Hos. 1:1; Joel 1:1).

3:3 *a baptism of repentance.* While converts to Judaism were baptized as a sign of washing away their "Gentile filth," John was radical in his call to Jews to be baptized as a sign of their turning from sin and toward God. To do so implied that being born Jewish was not sufficient to be considered the people of God, a reality made blatantly clear in verse 8.

3:4–6 Isaiah 40:3–5 provides the background for John's work. Before a king would visit a city, a herald was sent to urge people to literally prepare the roads so that the king's journey would be smooth.

CARING TIME AND PRAYER REQUESTS:

 This time is for developing and expressing your caring for each other as group members. We do this by sharing our needs and praying for each other's needs.

Each group member should answer the question,

> *How can we help you in prayer this week?*

Then join together in group prayer.

WEEK 2: ADVENT 2
Expecting to Hear God's Word
Luke 3:1–6

GATHERING 10 min.	STUDY 30 min.	CARING 20–40 min.

Leader: The agenda has three parts. In the Gathering time you'll be getting to know each other through an "ice-breaker." This will be for your total group. The Study time has two parts: (1) Story and (2) Scripture. If you are short of time, skip the Story and move to the Scripture. Begin by reading out loud the Story or the Scripture to the whole group. Then divide into groups of 4 for the Study time. Finally, regather the total group for the Caring time. Keep to this agenda: (1) Gathering—10 minutes, (2) Study—30 minutes, and (3) Caring—20–40 minutes.

No Man Is an Island. The famous poem declares, "No man is an island, apart to himself." While that is true, some of us have sought to live an "island-like" lifestyle by separating ourselves from others. Which of the following land formations or natural phenomena most resemble the way you have sought to live your life?

ISLAND—I am a loner who likes my private time.

MOUNTAIN—I see myself as seeking to rise above the mediocrity around me.

ISTHMUS—I am one who joins others together.

OASIS—I seek to be an island of life and refreshment in a dry world.

GROVE OF TREES— I live best in community.

JUNGLE—Full of life, but with my dark, scary side too.

FLOWERY MEADOW—I am colorful and inviting.

BLACKBERRY PATCH—I have good fruit, but watch my thorny side!

[1]Mary Bosanquet, *The Life and Death of Dietrich Bonhoeffer* (New York: Harper & Row, 1968), pp. 119–120.
[2]S. MacLean Gilmour, "Luke," *The Interpreter's Bible,* Vol. VIII (New York: Abingdon Press, 1952), p. 70.

INTRODUCTION STORY:

Dietrich Bonhoeffer Warns Against Embracing Nazis. When the Nazis rose to power in Germany, the young theologian Dietrich Bonhoeffer was one who warned against the dangers of this movement. At first, however, he was heeded so little that he must have felt like a "voice crying in the wilderness." Later Bonhoeffer's opposition became more active and he even cooperated in a plot to kill Hitler, a major struggle for a man of peace. Eventually he was imprisoned and executed just days before the end of World War II. Bonhoeffer's early reservations about the Nazis are discussed in his biography by Mary Bosanquet, *The Life and Death of Dietrich Bonhoeffer*:

"While the psychiatrists were discussing Hitler with clinical detachment, the Bonhoeffers watched with anxiety and distaste as one repressive measure followed another. ...

"The boycott [of Jewish businesses] was followed a week later by an order whose purpose was said to be 'the Restoration of the civil service.' This was the notorious 'Aryan Paragraph' which required that the civil service should be purged of all those who were of Jewish or partly Jewish descent. Dietrich Bonhoeffer was among the first to see the implication of this for Christians, and possibly for the Church. A number of factors combined to make him quickly sensitive to the central importance of the situation with which the Christians were now faced. One was the presence of a non-Aryan in his own family, his twin sister's husband, Gerhard Leibholz; another was his friendship with Franz Hildebrandt, whose future would now be in jeopardy, and a third was his intimate knowledge of another suffering minority, the coloured people of America. Thus it was on behalf of the Jewish Christians that his first serious protest was made. It took the form of an address given somewhere in Berlin before the end of April.

"After an attempt to define the functions of Church and State, which he based upon Luther's doctrine of the two spheres, the one spiritual and the other temporal, he went on to denounce the theory that membership of a Church can ever be based on race. ..."[1]

1. What qualifies a person to be a "prophet" in your eyes?
   ❏ There are no modern prophets—prophecy ended in Bible times.
   ❏ Only the passage of time can verify legitimate prophets from pretenders.
   ❏ willingness to stand up for what God has proclaimed through Scripture
   ❏ a vision from God for the future that captures popular imagination
   ❏ a vision from God for the future that is independent of what is popular
   ❏ other:_____

2. Was Dietrich Bonhoeffer a "prophet"? Why?

SCRIPTURE:

A Non-Prophet Society. We have become quite familiar in our day with "nonprofit organizations." These are organizations, in contrast to most of our society, that exist to serve instead of to make a financial profit. Normally, we are very concerned with profits. We are much less concerned with prophets. Prophets are either people in robes from the Old Testament, or the crazy guy with the Bible who accosts people on the street. The word "prophet" literally means "speak for" and means one who speaks for God. We worry about people who think they can speak for God. We conjure up images of Jim Jones and David Koresh, and people being led to do crazy acts in the name of God. But on the other hand more and more people are realizing they have a hunger for spiritual direction which they cannot seem to find. We are like the people of Amos' time when God said through him: "The time is surely coming, says the Lord God, when I will send a famine on the land; not a famine of bread, or a thirst for water, but of hearing the words of the Lord" (Amos 8:11).

Only when we get past our cynicism and *expect* God to speak to us today as God has in the past will our famine end, and only then will we find the spiritual guidance we hunger for.

Have someone in your group read the following passage out loud. Then go around on each question and let each person share their answer. Take advantage of the Study notes following the questionnaire. Be sure to save the last 20–40 minutes for the Caring time.

3 In the fifteenth year of the reign of Emperor Tiberius, when Pontius Pilate was governor of Judea, and Herod was ruler of Galilee, and his brother Philip ruler of the region of Ituraea and Trachonitis, and Lysanias ruler of Abilene, ²during the high priesthood of Annas and Caiaphas, the word of God came to John son of Zechariah in the wilderness. ³He went into all the region around the Jordan, proclaiming a baptism of repentance for the forgiveness of sins, ⁴as it is written in the book of the words of the prophet Isaiah,

"The voice of one crying out in the wilderness:
'Prepare the way of the Lord,
     make his paths straight.
⁵Every valley shall be filled,
     and every mountain and hill shall be made low,
and the crooked shall be made straight,
     and the rough ways made smooth;
⁶and all flesh shall see the salvation of God.' "

Luke 3:1–6

QUESTIONS:

1. If we didn't number years like we do, how would you date the time when you really felt you had become an adult and had "come out" into the world? Who was president at the time? What were some of the major events you remember happening in the world?

2. Share one "mountain" experience (when the world seemed to be "at your feet") and one "valley" experience (when you were "down so far the bottom looked like up") in your life.

3. What person has "prepared the way" for you in your life, by making the rough places a little smoother?
   ❏ my father   ❏ my mentor,_____
   ❏ my mother   ❏ my spouse
   ❏ a grandparent   ❏ other:_____

4. Why do you think God needed to send John the Baptist to prepare the way for Jesus?
   ❏ It was prophesied.
   ❏ to bring a spirit of expectation
   ❏ to correct some misconceptions before Jesus came
   ❏ to get their attention
   ❏ They had to repent of the past before they could be open to the future.
   ❏ other:_____

5. Which of the following modern songs do you think might make a good theme song for John the Baptist's ministry?
   ❏ "Show Me the Way" (Styx)
   ❏ "The Wind Beneath My Wings" (Bette Middler)
   ❏ "The Man in the Mirror" (Michael Jackson)
   ❏ "Be Prepared" (from *The Lion King*)
   ❏ "Change the World" (Eric Clapton)
   ❏ "The Age of Aquarius" (The Fifth Dimension)

6. When did the coming of Jesus Christ start making sense in your life?

7. What "rough places" do you see ahead of you right now for which you would like to have God send someone to "make them smooth"?

QUESTIONS (cont.) and BIBLE STUDY NOTES:

5. At what time in your life did you feel the greatest sense of expectation about what was ahead?
   - ❑ when I graduated from high school
   - ❑ when I graduated from college
   - ❑ when I was engaged to be married
   - ❑ when I was pregnant (or my wife was)
   - ❑ when I was nearing retirement
   - ❑ other:_____

6. What are you expecting God to do through Jesus right now (check as many as apply)?
   - ❑ to save me from my sins
   - ❑ to make the world better
   - ❑ to help us make the world better
   - ❑ to deliver me from the things I get so worried about
   - ❑ to help make me a stronger, more loving person
   - ❑ to stay out of my way and not bring anything bad
   - ❑ to direct my life
   - ❑ to come again soon
   - ❑ nothing

7. What is the next step for you in your spiritual pilgrimage?

3:7 baptized. There is no clear pre-Christian parallel to John's baptism, as other known types of baptism in that era were self-baptisms. The Jewish sect at Qumran practiced frequent baptism as a cleansing from sin. When Gentiles were converted to Judaism they were required to bathe in a river as part of the ceremony. John's call to baptism was a radical act highlighting that simply having the ethnic background of a Jew was no assurance of being one of God's people. **You brood of vipers!** The image painted by these words is of snakes slithering through the undergrowth trying to escape an oncoming fire—the wrath to come, the final judgment of God.

3:8 Abraham as our ancestor. John warns that they cannot retreat to an easy assumption that just because they are members of God's chosen race that they will be spared judgment. Paul later writes that the true heirs of Abraham are those who have faith in the promise given to him, not those who are merely physical descendants of him (Rom. 9:6–8).

3:11 Following the thought common in the OT and anticipating that seen later on in the NT epistles, John taught repentance was to be shown by concrete acts of compassion for the needy (Isa. 58:7; Ezek. 18:7; James 2:14–17). Unlike some rabbinic teaching which taught such actions are to be done so as to gain favor with God, the NT emphasizes that this change of lifestyle should be the natural result of a heart that has turned to God.

3:12 tax collectors. Considered to be as vile as robbers or murderers, these were Jews who were seen as traitors because they collabo-

BIBLE STUDY NOTES (cont.) and CARING TIME:

rated with the Roman power in order to become wealthy. Since only the tax collector knew the tax rate required by Rome, he was free to charge whatever the market would bear. Once he paid what he owed Rome, the rest was his to keep.

3:14 Soldiers. These are probably not Roman legionnaires, but men employed by Herod Antipas for police duty and to assist the tax collectors in their work. Their intimidating power to accuse people of non-payment was used to extort payoffs which would enhance their relatively meager pay. While John does not insist that repentance means leaving these jobs, he does assert such jobs need to be carried out with honesty and integrity.

3:16 not worthy to untie the thong of his sandals. The task of removing the master's sandals was that of the lowest-ranking slave in the household. **baptize you with the Holy Spirit.** It was expected the Messiah would be filled with the Spirit of God (Isa. 11:2), but that was not necessarily connected with the expectation of that time wherein God would pour out his Spirit upon the nation, such that it would permanently become a community of righteousness, justice, peace and security (Isa. 32:15–20; 44:3; Ezek. 37:14). John links together these two strands of OT prophecy in that it is through the Messiah that this community of the Spirit will be established. **fire.** This is a symbol of judgment. The OT anticipates a time of judgment upon Israel before the coming of the age of the Spirit (see Isa. 4:4; 32:9–14; Zech. 13:9; Mal. 3:2–4). The fire that comes during these last days will bring not just destruction, but cleansing.

3:17 Drawing from the practice involved in harvesting wheat, John presents a dramatic image of the anticipated messianic judgment. In order to separate wheat grain from straw, the mixture is tossed up into the air by a winnowing fork. The heavier kernels of wheat fall to the ground while the straw and chaff blow away to be burned.

 This time is for developing and expressing your caring for each other as group members. We do this by sharing our needs and praying for each other's needs.

Each group member should answer the question,

How can this group help you in prayer this week?

Then join together in group prayer.

¹Corrie ten Boom, *The Hiding Place* (Minneapolis, MN: World Wide Publications, 1971), pp. 220–221.

SERENDIPITY

Small Group
HANDOUT

WEEK 3: ADVENT 3
Expectations of the Messiah
Luke 3:7–18

 GATHERING
10 min.

 STUDY
30 min.

 CARING
20–40 min.

Leader: The agenda has three parts. In the Gathering time you'll be getting to know each other through an "ice-breaker." This will be for your total group. The Study time has two parts: (1) Story and (2) Scripture. If you are short of time, skip the Story and move to the Scripture. Begin by reading out loud the Story or the Scripture to the whole group. Then divide into groups of 4 for the Study time. Finally, regather the total group for the Caring time. Keep to this agenda: (1) Gathering—10 minutes, (2) Study—30 minutes, and (3) Caring—20–40 minutes.

Meal Time! Have everyone in the group respond to the first question, and then go on to the second, etc. If time is limited, choose two out of the three questions.

1. If you were to compare this past week to a meal, what kind of meal would it be?
   - ❑ down-home cookin'—filling and good for the soul
   - ❑ pheasant under glass—full of elegance, a rare treat
   - ❑ pizza with a hot fudge sundae for dessert—lots of fun, but lots of guilt
   - ❑ dinner at a health food restaurant—probably good for me, but some parts were hard to "get down"
   - ❑ greasy spoon special—lots of heartburn and a bad taste in my mouth

2. What part of your week was so delectable you just wanted to savor it for a while?

3. What part of your week do you wish you could have "sent back to the chef"?

INTRODUCTION STORY:

Corrie ten Boom Experiences Christmas. Corrie ten Boom helped shelter Jews from the Nazis during World War II, and for this act of courage was sent to the Nazi concentration camps, eventually ending up at Ravensbruck. There she experienced horrid conditions and eventually had to watch her beloved sister Betsie die. One day she received the unbelievable news of her release, but even that was not easy. A doctor doing a prerelease physical noticed her bad case of edema, and sent her back to the camp hospital until it was better. She writes of her experience there in her book, *The Hiding Place:*

" ... I was assigned a place on an upper bunk next to a woman whose body was covered with erupting pustules. But at least it was near a wall where I could keep my swollen legs elevated. That was what mattered now: to get the swelling down, to pass the inspection.

"... The suffering was unimaginable. Around me were survivors of a prison train which had been bombed on its way here. The women were horribly mutilated and in terrible pain, but at each moan two of the nurses jeered and mimicked the sounds.

"Even in the other patients I saw that stony indifference to others that was the most fatal disease of the concentration camp. I felt it spread to myself: how could one survive if one kept on feeling! The paralyzed and the unconscious kept falling off of the crowded narrow cots; that first night four women fell from upper bunks and died on the floor. It was better to narrow the mind to one's own need, not to see, not to think.

"But there was no way to shut out the sounds. All night women cried out a German word I didn't know. 'Schieber!' Over and over from rasping throats: 'Schieber!'

"Finally I realized that they were calling for bedpans. It was out of the question for most of the women in this room to make it to that filthy latrine next door. At last, reluctant to lower my legs, I climbed down from my cot and set about the chore. The gratitude of the patients was heart-wrenching. 'Who are you? Why are you doing this?'—as though cruelty and callousness were the norm, ordinary decency the marvel.

"As a wintry dawn crept through the windows, I realized it was Christmas Day."[1]

1. When do you remember going through a Christmas in less-than-ideal circumstances? How did you react? Was there a way in which God seemed to "come to you" even then?

2. Corrie ten Boom risked delaying her own release from a concentration camp to give sick women a special Christmas present of service. What similar act of service can you think of to do for someone this Christmas season?

SCRIPTURE:

Messiah-of-the-Month. Every four years in our country we hold auditions for our next Messiah—it's called a "presidential election"! Backers of each candidate are convinced that if we just elect their candidate, everything that is wrong in the country will suddenly be solved. Of course, after we elect this person, it doesn't happen. So we "crucify" that one and go off looking for another. In between elections we look to other than presidential candidates to fulfill the function of Messiah—sometimes it's a popular self-help author, sometimes a radio or television talk show host, or sometimes an entertainment figure. But one thing all of these have in common in the end is that they are all just human beings. That's why they all fall short. Things were no different in New Testament times. They were always looking for a Messiah. John the Baptist was a candidate for the position at one time. He said himself very clearly that he wasn't qualified. But he also had some good news, and his good news is *our* good news—a Messiah *was* coming into the world. He was Jesus of Nazareth. Even today he is the only one who can deliver on what we are expecting—one who can rise above the limitations of humanity to save us and our world. If we as his followers could get behind him with the enthusiasm and sense of expectation that the strongest followers of a presidential candidate do, there would be no limit to what difference that would make in our world.

Have someone in your group read the following passage out loud. Then go around on each question and let each person share their answer. Take advantage of the Study notes following the questionnaire. Be sure to save the last 20–40 minutes for the Caring time.

[7]John said to the crowds that came out to be baptized by him, "You brood of vipers! Who warned you to flee from the wrath to come? [8]Bear fruits worthy of repentance. Do not begin to say to yourselves, 'We have Abraham as our ancestor'; for I tell you, God is able from these stones to raise up children to Abraham. [9]Even now the ax is lying at the root of the trees; every tree therefore that does not bear good fruit is cut down and thrown into the fire."

[10]And the crowds asked him, "What then should we do?" [11]In reply he said to them, "Whoever has two coats must share with anyone who has none; and whoever has food must do likewise." [12]Even tax collectors came to be baptized, and they asked him, "Teacher, what should we do?" [13]He said to them, "Collect no more than the amount prescribed for you." [14]Soldiers also asked him, "And we, what should we do?" He said to them, "Do not extort money from anyone by threats or false accusation, and be satisfied with your wages."

[15]As the people were filled with expectation, and all were questioning in their hearts concerning John, whether he might be the Messiah, [16]John answered all of them by saying, "I baptize you with water; but one who is more powerful than I is coming; I am not worthy to untie the

SCRIPTURE (cont.) and QUESTIONS:

thong of his sandals. He will baptize you with the Holy Spirit and fire. [17]His winnowing fork is in his hand, to clear his threshing floor and to gather the wheat into his granary; but the chaff he will burn with unquenchable fire."

[18]So, with many other exhortations, he proclaimed the good news to the people.

Luke 3:7–18

1. What future reality do you wish someone would have warned you about more when you were in high school?
   - ❏ the hard work it takes to make a good marriage
   - ❏ how quickly time flies and you find that you are old!
   - ❏ how precious health is and the need to protect it
   - ❏ how important it is to learn the things needed to get a good job
   - ❏ the need to look to God for guidance all life long
   - ❏ It makes no difference what they warned me about—I wouldn't have listened!

2. Finish this sentence with the choice that best fits for you: "When it comes to being warned, I generally ..."
   - ❏ try whatever it is people warn me not to do
   - ❏ have to learn by my own mistakes
   - ❏ catch on after a few warnings
   - ❏ respond immediately when warned
   - ❏ am so cautious I don't need to be warned!

3. What would you say would be a good modern equivalent of "Bear fruits worthy of repentance"?
   - ❏ "Put your money where your mouth is."
   - ❏ "Walk your talk."
   - ❏ "Grace is free, but not cheap."
   - ❏ "Your actions speak louder than your words."
   - ❏ " 'Sorry' doesn't change a thing."

4. What would you say is the best way to describe the relationship between repentance and expectation of the Messiah in John's eyes?
   - ❏ If people didn't repent, the Messiah would come in judgment.
   - ❏ Ready or not, the Messiah was coming!
   - ❏ The Messiah would come to deliver people from judgment.
   - ❏ The Messiah would give us the spiritual resources we need to make repentance real.

QUESTIONS (cont.) and BIBLE STUDY NOTES:

7. When you think about the future, what causes you a sense of "joy"?
- ❏ seeing my kids take that next step—graduation, getting married, etc.
- ❏ seeing accomplishment of the goals I have worked for in life
- ❏ hearing those words from God, "Well done, good and faithful servant!"
- ❏ when I retire and can spend more time with my spouse
- ❏ when my kids make a meaningful commitment to Christ
- ❏ being reunited with loved ones in heaven

:39 *a Judean town.* We are not told what town this is, but such a journey would have been 80–100 miles from Nazareth!

1:40 *greeted Elizabeth.* Elizabeth had been identified in verse 36 as a relative of Mary's who had become pregnant in her old age.

1:41 *leaped in her womb.* At six months, such movement would not have been unusual. However, the timing of this most certainly was to say that, even in the womb, the unborn child who was to become John the Baptist was prophesying Jesus' coming role as Messiah. ***filled with the Holy Spirit.*** While the New Testament asserts that the Holy Spirit came in a special way after Jesus' resurrection and ascension, that is not to say that the Holy Spirit was totally inactive previous to that time. In the Old Testament era, the Spirit came upon people from time to time to inspire prophecies or prepare them for special deeds.

1:42 *Blessed are you among women.* We think of the "beatitudes" being those sayings in Matthew 5:3–11 or Luke 6:20–23;

but there are in reality many beatitudes throughout Scripture, and this is one of them. Like with the other beatitudes, what is blessed is the believing, expectant heart. In most cases, women of this time were anything but "blessed." They had few rights, and were most often treated as property. But in the person of Mary, women down through the ages have found a figure with whom they can identify. As people seek to emulate Mary's belief, the blessedness is spread.

1:43 *why has this happened to me ... ?* All too often we ask this question when bad things happen. Here Elizabeth asks it of an unexpected blessing. Unless we think of all the times we have been blessed in unexpected, undeserved ways, the question of "Why has this happened to me?" when tragedy strikes is at best inappropriate.

1:45 *she who believed.* Mary's reaction of belief to a seemingly-impossible promise can be contrasted with Zechariah's skepticism (1:18) or, in the Old Testament, such figures as Abraham (Gen. 17:17) and Sarah (Gen. 18:12).

CARING TIME and PRAYER REQUESTS:

 This time is for developing and expressing your caring for each other as group members. We do this by sharing our needs and praying for each other's needs.

Each group member should answer the question,

How can this group help you in prayer this week?

Then join together in group prayer.

¹Victoria Lincoln, *Teresa: A Woman* (Albany, NY: State University of New York Press, 1984), p. 103.

SERENDIPITY
Small Group
HANDOUT

WEEK 4: ADVENT 4
Joyful Expectations
Luke 1:39–45

 GATHERING 10 min.

STUDY 30 min.

 **CARING** 20–40 min.

Leader: The agenda has three parts. In the Gathering time you'll be getting to know each other through an "ice-breaker." This will be for your total group. The Study time has two parts: (1) Story and (2) Scripture. If you are short of time, skip the Story and move to the Scripture. Begin by reading out loud the Story or the Scripture to the whole group. Then divide into groups of 4 for the Study time. Finally, regather the total group for the Caring time. Keep to this agenda: (1) Gathering—10 minutes, (2) Study—30 minutes, and (3) Caring—20–40 minutes.

 TV Identifications. Most of us occasionally find ourselves identifying with famous television characters. In each of the following pairs, which one are you more like?

IN TERMS OF "HIGH CULTURE":
Frasier Crane_____Roseanne

IN MECHANICAL ABILITY:
Bob Vila _____Tim Taylor

IN PHYSICAL GRACE:
Fred Astaire _____Kramer

IN EXPRESSING EMOTION:
Bob Newhart_____Lucille Ball

IN DOMESTIC INTEREST (WOMEN):
June Cleaver _____Murphy Brown

IN MACHO ATTITUDE (MEN):
John Wayne _____Al Borland

INTRODUCTION STORY:

Teresa of Avila Affirms Laughter. Teresa of Avila was a Christian mystic who lived in Spain in the sixteenth century. She is known for reforming the Carmelite order by restoring spiritual discipline, and in the process helping to reform the church as a whole. She wrote much on the spiritual disciplines, and her writings have inspired many. She was canonized in 1622, and in 1970 she became the first woman to be proclaimed a Doctor of the Church. But while some think of the residents of a convent as being especially somber, that was not how Teresa saw things. Her biographer Victoria Lincoln gives her perspective in *Teresa: A Woman:*

"Maria Bautista recalls that on a day when there was nothing to eat but the Bishop's bread, they marched into the chapel carrying a statue of the Infant Jesus and singing *coplas.* Teresa wrote their *coplas,* songs for all sorts of occasions, including one that dealt with an infestation of lice. One verse and the chorus came down to us from the pen of a sister who dared to remember that 'La Santa' liked a little fun:

> Daughters, since you bear the Cross,
> Be valorous.
> Turn to Jesus your own light
> To favor us.
> He will bring defense to us
> In this fix, as in all. ...

"Teresa also wrote some seasonal plays whose authorship is generally denied her because, as you might say, they laughed in Church: as when the bumbling shepherds at the Nativity express their bewilderment.

" 'What's such a fine lady doing out in a stable with her baby? Why, look at her—she must be the mayor's daughter!'

"Teresa knew that sanity demands some laughter. ..."[1]

1. In which of the following life situations do you remember singing songs about somewhat silly things (e.g. "The Old Lady Who Swallowed a Fly"!), as when Teresa sang about lice?
   - ❏ as a child, with our family
   - ❏ at camp as a youth
   - ❏ in college—at parties!
   - ❏ as an adult, with my children
   - ❏ other:_____

2. In what recent life stress have you rediscovered what Teresa taught, that "sanity demands some laughter"?

SCRIPTURE and QUESTIONS:

Beyond "Murphy's Law." Most of us are familiar with "Murphy's Law": "Anything bad that can happen, will happen." People doing planning are often wise to remember this "law" so that they will plan for what to do when things start to go awry. But Murphy's Law is only part of the truth, and Scripture reminds us of another law that takes us beyond Murphy— "Anything bad that can happen, won't defeat us!" The bottom line in Jesus Christ is that joy and victory have the last word! The redemption God has planned for this world will not fail because we have not planned ahead for "Murphy's Law." Our bungling will never cancel the kingdom's arrival in its fullness. This is true, because while God acts through us he is also acting over and above our abilities to assure his promises will not fail. That is why what we preach is called "good news." That is why Christ's coming was "good news of great joy." We can have joyful expectations of the future because of these assurances of God's action.

Have someone in your group read the following passage out loud. Then go around on each question and let each person share their answer. Take advantage of the Study notes following the questionnaire. Be sure to save the last 20–40 minutes for the Caring time.

> ³⁹*In those days Mary set out and went with haste to a Judean town in the hill country,* ⁴⁰*where she entered the house of Zechariah and greeted Elizabeth.* ⁴¹*When Elizabeth heard Mary's greeting, the child leaped in her womb. And Elizabeth was filled with the Holy Spirit* ⁴²*and exclaimed with a loud cry, "Blessed are you among women, and blessed is the fruit of your womb.* ⁴³*And why has this happened to me, that the mother of my Lord comes to me?* ⁴⁴*For as soon as I heard the sound of your greeting, the child in my womb leaped for joy.* ⁴⁵*And blessed is she who believed that there would be a fulfillment of what was spoken to her by the Lord."*
>
> *Luke 1:39–45*

1. When something exciting happened to you as an adolescent, who was the first person you wanted to tell it to?
   - ❏ my father
   - ❏ my mother
   - ❏ a brother or sister
   - ❏ a grandparent
   - ❏ another adult, namely_____
   - ❏ my best friend, _____

QUESTIONS (cont.):

2. Why did Mary go to Elizabeth's house?
   - ❏ for a little "female bonding"
   - ❏ to get away from the neighbor's talk about her pregnancy
   - ❏ to share in the joy of another pregnant woman
   - ❏ to get some advice from an older and wiser female relative
   - ❏ just to spread the exciting news

3. What thing that Mary and Elizabeth shared is most important to you in a friendship?
   - ❏ a common experience—but it doesn't have to be pregnancy!
   - ❏ really sharing in another person's joy
   - ❏ taking time to visit each other
   - ❏ talking about our feelings
   - ❏ encouraging each other in the faith
   - ❏ noncompetitiveness—like when Elizabeth wasn't jealous of who Mary's son would be

4. What do you need to share with an "Elizabeth" right now?
   - ❏ a joy that I have been wanting to share with someone
   - ❏ a burden, where I need to talk with someone who knows what it's like
   - ❏ just someone to have fun and celebrate with
   - ❏ someone to share my faith with
   - ❏ other:_____

5. What is the biggest barrier keeping you from sharing your joys with others right now?
   - ❏ I have no joys to share!
   - ❏ No one seems interested.
   - ❏ If I shared my joys it would sound like I was bragging.
   - ❏ There are no barriers—I do it easily!
   - ❏ other:_____

6. What has God done recently for you that caused something inside of you to "leap for joy"?
   - ❏ He answered a prayer.
   - ❏ He gave me peace in a time of turmoil.
   - ❏ He reassured me of forgiveness after I had been torn with guilt.
   - ❏ He slowed me down enough to get me to enjoy his world.
   - ❏ He healed someone close to me.
   - ❏ He reminded me of the precious people he's given to love me.
   - ❏ He gave me his presence when I really needed it.
   - ❏ other:_____

QUESTIONS (cont.) and BIBLE STUDY NOTES:

6. What is the major concern you have right now as a parent (or a future parent) for your children?

2:41–52 Luke is the only Gospel that includes a scene from Jesus' boyhood. Later on writers of non-canonical Gospels wrote fanciful tales, such as one that described Jesus transforming clay birds into living ones. By contrast, Luke's story has no miraculous elements, but simply sets the context of Jesus' growing realization of his identity and his relationship to God.

2:41 went to Jerusalem. While Jews were supposed to go to Jerusalem three times a year for the feasts of Passover, Pentecost and the Feast of Booths, in practice most only attended the annual Passover celebration.

2:42 when he was twelve years old. At age 13, a Jewish boy was expected to take his place in the religious community of Israel. Age 12 would be a time of preparation for assuming the responsibilities of adulthood. It is unclear whether this was Jesus' first visit to the temple, or whether he might have accompanied Mary and Joseph on earlier pilgrimages.

2:43–44 Jewish pilgrims from outside Jerusalem traveled to and from the feast in large caravans. Typically, the women and children would be up front while the men and older boys traveled along behind. In the evenings, when the caravan stopped for the night, families would regroup. It would have been easy during the day for Mary and Joseph to each assume that Jesus was with the other parent or with friends.

2:46 After three days. This does not mean they spent three days in Jerusalem looking for Jesus. Day one was the trip out of the city with the caravan—probably a walk of about 25 miles. Day two was their trip back to the city. Day three was when they found him in the temple.

2:47 This seems to be the main reason why Luke included this story. Jesus' insight into the Law drew the respect and wonder of his elders, even at this early age.

2:49–50 I must be. Luke records several statements which reflect Jesus' sense of the absolute necessity of his mission and the steps required to fulfill it (4:43; 9:22; 24:7). Mary and Joseph's inability to comprehend what he meant is paralleled later on by his family's misunderstanding of him (8:19–21). **my Father's house.** This is a second reason why Luke included this story. Mary referred to Joseph as "your father" (v. 48). Jesus' answer to Mary shows his growing realization of his true Father and of his identity as the Son of God.

CARING TIME AND PRAYER REQUESTS:

 This time is for developing and expressing your caring for each other as group members. We do this by sharing our needs and praying for each other's needs.

Each group member should answer the question,

How can this group help you in prayer this week?

Then join together in group prayer.

¹Frances Gies, *Joan of Arc: The Legend and the Reality* (New York: Harper & Row, 1981), pp. 14–15.
²James Fowler, *Becoming Adult, Becoming Christian* (San Francisco: Harper & Row, 1984), p. 88.

SERENDIPITY

Small Group

HANDOUT

WEEK 5: CHRISTMAS 1

Expectations of Our Youth

Luke 2:41–52

 GATHERING
10 min.

 STUDY
30 min.

CARING
20–40 min.

Leader: The agenda has three parts. In the Gathering time you'll be getting to know each other through an "ice-breaker." This will be for your total group. The Study time has two parts: (1) Story and (2) Scripture. If you are short of time, skip the Story and move to the Scripture. Begin by reading out loud the Story or the Scripture to the whole group. Then divide into groups of 4 for the Study time. Finally, regather the total group for the Caring time. Keep to this agenda: (1) Gathering—10 minutes, (2) Study—30 minutes, and (3) Caring—20–40 minutes.

 I'm a Classic. If you were to write the story of your life, which of the following classic titles would fit that story best?

THE DEERSLAYER—because hunting has been my life

WAR & PEACE—because my life has been one battle after another

PRIDE & PREJUDICE—because I've tried to maintain my pride in the face of much prejudice

PILGRIM'S PROGRESS—because in my travels I have progressed through many adventures

THE GRAPES OF WRATH—because I have struggled with anger

GREAT EXPECTATIONS—because the ones I have had to live up to have been pretty high

OF MICE & MEN—or, "What are two things that make me scream?"

ANIMAL FARM—because livestock have been my life

INTRODUCTION STORY:

Joan of Arc Shows Precocious Piety. Joan of Arc was convinced that God was speaking to her to lead the armies of France to fight for their freedom against England. But her role in history was more than a political one. She led through a spiritual vision and a courage that lifted a people who had lost heart. Her spiritual qualities had their birth at an early age. Her biographer Frances Gies tells her story in the book, *Joan of Arc: The Legend and the Reality:*

"She was intensely pious—'so pious,' her childhood friend Mengette declared, 'that her comrades and I said she was too much so.' When she heard the bell sound for mass, and she was in the fields, she would immediately return and go to church in order to hear the service said. When evening came, she listened keenly for the compline bell, and, if she was still in the fields, would fall to her knees and say her prayers. On occasion the churchwarden Perrin Drappier would forget to ring for compline. Joan, though normally gentle, would then become perturbed and would scold him. She even offered to give him some wool if he would be more conscientious about his duties in this respect. Within the church she could sometimes be seen prostrated before the crucifix; or with her hands joined and her face and eyes lifted towards the image of Christ and that of the Holy Virgin.

"Every Saturday she would go on a pilgrimage to the little chapel of Notre Dame de Bermont, which lay above the road between Domremy and Neufchateau. ... Later, Joan developed the habit of slipping away to this chapel on her own, at a time when her parents thought she was busy ploughing or working elsewhere in the fields. ...

"Perhaps the most significant sign of the crisis through which Joan was passing was the frequency with which she went to confession ...

"... A modest estimate was that she 'confessed at Easter and at the other solemn feasts.' Others thought she confessed whenever she got the opportunity, and that opportunities were not lacking. ..."[1]

1. How do you react to the youthful piety of Joan of Arc?
   ❑ She should have just enjoyed being a teenager!
   ❑ It's a whole lot better than drugs.
   ❑ It was probably just a stage she was going through.
   ❑ She was a little extreme, but she had the right idea.
   ❑ We need more young people like this!

2. If you had known Joan of Arc in your teenage years, how would you have related to her?
   ❑ avoided her like the plague
   ❑ thought of her as a curiosity
   ❑ sought to learn from her
   ❑ sought to learn from her while trying to get her to "lighten up"
   ❑ other:_____

SCRIPTURE:

Spiritual Prodigies. Much has been written about such musical prodigies as Mozart, who not only played concert quality music as a child, but composed it as well. Others have described prodigies in math and science—children who can do complicated mathematical problems in their head, and who end up getting into exclusive colleges while others their age are being weaned off *Sesame Street*. But even as there are musical and mathematical prodigies, there are also spiritual prodigies in our world, and much less is written of them. James Fowler, a respected authority in the field of faith development, does write of one such child in his book, *Becoming Adult, Becoming Christian*. This was a 12-year-old boy who was raised in a family that was so militantly atheistic that the older brother (age 15) named his parrot "God" so that when it squawked, he could say, "Shut up, God!" In this context, this boy developed what Fowler called "the most remarkably pure and strongly held theism I had ever encountered in a person of this age." The boy likened God's role to his own in taking care of his aquarium. Although the aquarium was designed to be a self-contained ecological system, he still had to do things periodically to "restore the balance." He reasoned that was the role God takes in our world.[2] Jesus was certainly also this kind of spiritual prodigy as a youth. He was probing the deepest questions about his Father's world at an age when many youth today are enmeshed in video games. The existence of such prodigies especially reminds us that we can learn from people of every age.

Have someone in your group read the following passage out loud. Then go around on each question and let each person share their answer. Take advantage of the Study notes following the questionnaire. Be sure to save the last 20–40 minutes for the Caring time.

41Now every year his parents went to Jerusalem for the festival of the Passover. 42And when he was twelve years old, they went up as usual for the festival. 43When the festival was ended and they started to return, the boy Jesus stayed behind in Jerusalem, but his parents did not know it. 44Assuming that he was in the group of travelers, they went a day's journey. Then they started to look for him among their relatives and friends. 45When they did not find him, they returned to Jerusalem to search for him. 46After three days they found him in the temple, sitting among the teachers, listening to them and asking them questions. 47And all who heard him were amazed at his understanding and his answers. 48When his parents saw him they were astonished; and his mother said to him, "Child, why have you treated us like this? Look, your father and I have been searching for you in great anxiety." 49He said to them, "Why were you searching for me? Did you not know that I must be in my Father's house?" 50But they did not understand what he said to them. 51Then he went down with them and came to Nazareth, and was obedient to them. His mother treasured all these things in her heart.

SCRIPTURE (cont.) and QUESTIONS:

52And Jesus increased in wisdom and in years, and in divine and human favor.

Luke 2:41–52

1. When you were a teenager, what episode caused your parent(s) or guardian(s) "great anxiety"?

2. Had you been Joseph or Mary, what would you have done when you found Jesus in the temple?
   ❑ grounded him for a month!
   ❑ cried and hugged him
   ❑ cried and hugged him—and *then* grounded him for a month!
   ❑ blamed myself for the miscommunication
   ❑ blamed my spouse for the miscommunication
   ❑ acted politely around the authorities in the temple, and then "laid into him" when we got him alone
   ❑ called a family meeting to talk about communication

3. How would you describe Jesus' attitude when his parents shared their concern?
   ❑ typical preteen—blaming his parents!
   ❑ naive—He didn't know how parents worry.
   ❑ coolly logical—An adolescent "Mr. Spock"!
   ❑ controlled—"I wasn't lost—you were!"
   ❑ confused—He thought he was doing what he was supposed to be doing.
   ❑ mildly rebuking—"You should have known!"
   ❑ other:_____

4. What expectations might you have had of Jesus after this incident, had you been one of his parents? (Check all that apply.)
   ❑ that we would have to keep a constant eye on him
   ❑ that he would always have "a mind of his own"
   ❑ that we would progressively be losing control of him
   ❑ that he would continue to pursue spiritual interests
   ❑ that we'd be learning more from him than he would from us

5. What expectations did your parents have of you when you were around 12?
   ❑ that I just stay out of trouble
   ❑ that I get mostly "A's" in school
   ❑ that I excel at music
   ❑ that I excel at everything
   ❑ that I be a "good kid" like Jesus or Joan of Arc
   ❑ that I excel at sports
   ❑ none at all!
   ❑ other:_____

6. As you look at your future, what do you need for God to be with you?

❑ peace as I face my aging and mortality

❑ direction as I face some hard decisions

❑ assurance of his presence and love in my situation

❑ to see I am needed and have a purpose

❑ other:_____

1:1 In the beginning. John's version of the "New Testament" begins with the same phrase that begins the Old Testament. This underlines the fact that the coming of Jesus inaugurates a new creation. **the Word.** This is the translation of the Greek word *Logos,* a word with multiple meanings from both Greek philosophy and the OT. A popular form of Greek thought taught that the *Logos* was an impersonal force or principle that gave order and meaning to the universe. The OT spoke of the *Logos* as the divine wisdom active in creation and human affairs (Prov. 8:12–36). This term, therefore, builds a bridge of understanding between the author and his readers, be they Jewish or Gentile.

1:4 life. This word also has a double meaning, referring to both physical life and the supernatural illumination that brings life to all people.

1:5 light / darkness. A Jewish sect called the Essenes, who separated themselves from the rest of Jewish society, had a book called, *The War of the Sons of Light Against the Sons of Darkness,* and this was apparently a popular theme of the day.

1:6 John. John the Baptist's influence was felt from Egypt to Asia Minor (Acts 18:24–26; 19:1–5). Some scholars think the emphasis on John's role as a witness to the coming of the Messiah was because even after Jesus many of John's followers still saw John as the Messiah.

1:11 to what was his own. Israel, God's own people (Gen. 17:7), especially failed to see who Jesus was. But in a larger sense, we are all "God's own" and have failed to see who Jesus was.

1:12 power to become children of God. In one sense we are all children of God from birth, for God created us all. But spiritually, when we rebel against God, we renounce our family and become children of the world. Only by finding forgiveness through Christ do we find power to become children of God again.

1:14 the Word became flesh. This is a repudiation of the doctrine of the Gnostics (a popular philosophy of the time), which disparaged humanity's physical nature, and said that Christ could not have really taken on human flesh, since flesh is inherently evil. "Flesh," while sometimes used by John in contrast to "spirit," does not carry any derogatory sense. **and lived among us.** The Greek word used for "lived" here literally meant "tented." John may have been thinking of the tabernacle in the wilderness where the Lord dwelt with Israel.

1:15 he was before me. The *Logos,* here identified with Christ, was seen as a preexistent agent of creation.

1:18 who has made him known. As a person can often see a child's parent in the child, so Christ, as the perfect child, perfectly reflected his Parent.

 This time is for developing and expressing your caring for each other as group members. We do this by sharing our needs and praying for each other's needs, as well as by affirming the strengths we see in each other.

Think about the others in your group. What attributes do each of them have which you have learned to appreciate in these sessions? Focus on one group member at a time, and have the others share what attributes they see in that person. Make sure everyone has a chance to be affirmed. Then, remembering what people shared, close in prayer, thanking God for each other and what you are experiencing as a group.

¹John Pudney, *John Wesley and His World* (London: Thames & Hudson, Ltd., 1978), p.114.

SERENDIPITY

Small Group

H A N D O U T

WEEK 6: CHRISTMAS 2

Expectations of God's Presence

John 1:1–18

 **GATHERING** 10 min.

STUDY 30 min.

 CARING 20–40 min.

Leader: The agenda has three parts. In the Gathering time you'll be getting to know each other through an "ice-breaker." This will be for your total group. The Study time has two parts: (1) Story and (2) Scripture. If you are short of time, skip the Story and move to the Scripture. Begin by reading out loud the Story or the Scripture to the whole group. Then divide into groups of 4 for the Study time. Finally, regather the total group for the Caring time. Keep to this agenda: (1) Gathering—10 minutes, (2) Study—30 minutes, and (3) Caring—20–40 minutes.

 And Now, the News! How we read a newspaper says much about who we are and what we enjoy. Look at the following list of things that often appear in a newspaper and rank them in order from 1 (what you are most likely to read) to 10 (what you are least likely to read):

_____ the national headline story

_____ the local headline story

_____ the business section

_____ the "human interest" section

_____ the arts and entertainment section

_____ the personal advice column

_____ the "funnies"

_____ the sports section

_____ the horoscope

_____ the want ads

INTRODUCTION STORY:

 John Wesley Faces His Death. John Wesley was not only the founder of Methodism, but he also led the Western world of the eighteenth century in a spiritual revival. His teachings and influence extend far beyond the denomination he founded. But like with many, his faith is shown more clearly in how he died than in what he taught. John Pudney tells the story in his book, *John Wesley and His World:*

"A week before the end came, in 1791, he wrote what is believed to be his last letter—to the young abolitionist William Wilberforce: '... Go on, in the name of God and in the power of His might, till even American slavery, the vilest that ever saw the sun, shall vanish before it.' The next day he grew weaker, and it became clear that his life was beginning to slip away. His last hours were as serene and peaceful as one might have expected. Towards the end he said in a clear voice: 'The best of all—God is with us.' And this message he repeated with special emphasis, so that it has become one of the rallying cries of Methodism. *'The best of all—God is with us!'* He died on the morning of 2 March 1791."[1]

1. Rank the following factors as to how important you think they are in facing death with the serenity that John Wesley faced it (with 1 being most important, and 6 being least important):

    ___ having lived a productive life

    ___ having lived a long life

    ___ having faith in Jesus Christ and his resurrection

    ___ being surrounded with friends

    ___ having sensed God's presence throughout life

    ___ the ability to accept the reality of where you are at in life

2. Who do you know personally who faced death with the serenity that John Wesley did?

SCRIPTURE:

 God With Skin on Him. The story is told of a little girl who was frightened by a sudden thunderstorm at night. The mother came into the bedroom to comfort her. "Don't worry, honey," her mother said, "you know that God is with you." "I know that, Mommy," the girl replied, "but I want somebody with skin on them." That's what Jesus came into this world to be—"God with skin on him." Today Jesus is not here with us in the flesh. That's why *we* have to be God's presence for people sometimes. For people who need something more solid-feeling than a simple assurance that God and Jesus are with us in all of life's circumstances, our presence with them in those circumstances is to say that God cares. But whether in the form of one of God's children, or in the form of a more mystical experience, we are reminded that we are never alone in what we face. God is that Parent who comes in during the darkest thunderstorm, and tells us that everything is going to be all right.

Have someone in your group read the following passage out loud. Then go around on each question and let each person share their answer. Take advantage of the Study notes following the questionnaire. Be sure to save the last 20–40 minutes for the Caring time.

1 *In the beginning was the Word, and the Word was with God, and the Word was God. ²He was in the beginning with God. ³All things came into being through him, and without him not one thing came into being. What has come into being ⁴in him was life, and the life was the light of all people. ⁵The light shines in the darkness, and the darkness did not overcome it.*

⁶There was a man sent from God, whose name was John. ⁷He came as a witness to testify to the light, so that all might believe through him. ⁸He himself was not the light, but he came to testify to the light. ⁹The true light, which enlightens everyone, was coming into the world.

¹⁰He was in the world, and the world came into being through him; yet the world did not know him. ¹¹He came to what was his own, and his own people did not accept him. ¹²But to all who received him, who believed in his name, he gave power to become children of God, ¹³who were born, not of blood or of the will of the flesh or of the will of man, but of God.

¹⁴And the Word became flesh and lived among us, and we have seen his glory, the glory as of a father's only son, full of grace and truth. ¹⁵(John testified to him and cried out, "This was he of whom I said, 'He who comes after me ranks ahead of me because he was before me.' ") ¹⁶From his fullness we have all received, grace upon grace. ¹⁷The law indeed was given through Moses; grace and truth came through Jesus Christ. ¹⁸No one has ever seen God. It is God the only Son, who is close to the Father's heart, who has made him known.

John 1:1–18

QUESTIONS:

1. If you were the special effects and music or sound track director, what sound, music or special effects would you use for making this Scripture passage into the beginning of a movie?

2. Of the various teachings of this passage, which is most important to you personally?
    - ❑ Jesus has been part of the picture from the beginning (vv. 1–3).
    - ❑ The darkness has not overcome the light Jesus brought (v. 5).
    - ❑ All who believe in Jesus become children of God (v. 12).
    - ❑ We have all received much from the fullness of God (v. 16).
    - ❑ Though we have never seen God, we can know him through Jesus Christ (v. 18).

3. What is the most important thing you have learned recently about God?
    - ❑ God isn't distant and remote, but was willing to come and be with us.
    - ❑ God is a God of righteousness and justice.
    - ❑ God is a God of grace and mercy.
    - ❑ God is a powerful God who will not be defeated, even by death.
    - ❑ God is the God of all people.
    - ❑ God is the Creator who continues to care for creation.

4. What is the greatest "darkness" you have had to experience in your life?
    - ❑ financial or business failure
    - ❑ divorce
    - ❑ being personally assaulted
    - ❑ death of a loved one
    - ❑ being publicly insulted or libeled
    - ❑ a tumultuous relationship with a child or parent
    - ❑ other:_____

5. How does God usually break into your own life in times of darkness?
    - ❑ through bringing me supportive friends
    - ❑ through giving me some new understandings
    - ❑ through bringing me forgiveness and/or self-acceptance
    - ❑ through a miraculous intervention

6. Where could you use a little help from God right now in your life?
- ❑ help in dealing with a crisis I am facing in my life / career
- ❑ help in dealing with a painful relationship in my family / office
- ❑ help in knowing what to do about the future
- ❑ help in a struggle I am dealing with in my personal / spiritual life

2:1 *King Herod.* Herod the Great was a shrewd but cruel monarch who was appointed by Rome to rule over Palestine. He reigned from 40 B.C. to 4 B.C. *Bethlehem.* Bethlehem was some 90 miles from Nazareth, a three- or four-day journey. Luke's Gospel tells us that the family had to go from Nazareth to Bethlehem for a census, possibly because that is where Joseph's clan originated, and he may have had property there. *wise men.* Also known as "Magi," these were astrologers who probably came from Babylon—modern Iran or Iraq.

2:2 *his star.* Attempts have been made to correlate the presence of this star with a variety of natural phenomena, including an unusual conjunction of Jupiter and Venus in 7 B.C., but little can be said with certainty. What is obvious, however, is that these astrologers saw in it a sign of a special messenger from God. Magi believed that a star could be a "fravashi" (a counterpart or angel) of a great person. *at its rising.* Some translations of this passage say "in the east." A rising star would be a good omen. It's significant that God used a foreign philosophy (astrology) to speak to non-Jewish people. It's significant also that while a Jewish

king (Herod) would later plot to kill this new king, Gentile kings worship him, a parallel to how the Gentiles were later more receptive to the Gospel.

2:3 *he was frightened.* Toward the end of his reign Herod became paranoid that people were plotting to take over his throne. He actually had his favorite wife, her mother, two of her sons, and his oldest son murdered.

2:6 A comparison with Micah 5:2 shows that Matthew was not so much quoting the original as interpreting its meaning.

2:8 *pay him homage.* This was a cynical statement on the part of Herod which contrasts with the genuine worship of the wise men (v. 11). By allowing the wise men to search for the child he may have thought he had a better chance of finding him than if he were to send in troops.

2:9 It is not clear whether Matthew means that the star led them in the sense of physical movement or that it led them in the sense that the interpretation of this sign allowed them to find the child.

2:11 *the house.* Luke's narrative

pictures Jesus' parents as temporary visitors to Bethlehem. In Matthew, it seems to be the place where they lived. Whatever the case, time has elapsed since Jesus' birth, since Jesus is no longer in a stable, but a house. He is also called a "child" *(paidion)* and not a "baby" *(brephos).* *they knelt down and paid him homage.* The first people to worship Jesus in Matthew's account were Gentiles, hinting at the fact that Jesus had come not just for the Jews but for all nations. *offered him gifts.* Matthew no doubt thinks of Isaiah 60:6, where "those from Sheba," i.e. south Arabia, bring gold and incense. *gold.* Gold was the curren-

cy of kings. *frankincense.* It was a sweet-smelling gum that was burned during worship. *myrrh.* Myrrh was another gum, used as a perfume, as a medicine, and to embalm bodies. Taken together, the gifts could represent the identity of Jesus as the royal Son of God who gave his life for his people.

2:12 *a dream.* For the second time in this account, a dream plays a crucial role in the childhood of Jesus. The Magi are obedient to this vision and return home another way so as not to have to reveal to Herod the whereabouts of the child.

 This time is for developing and expressing your caring for each other as group members. We do this by sharing our needs and praying for each other's needs.

Each group member should answer the question,

> *How can this group help you in prayer this week?*

Then join together in group prayer.

¹Frances Gies, *Joan of Arc: The Legend and the Reality* (New York, NY: Harper & Row, 1981), p. 118.

SERENDIPITY
Small Group
HANDOUT

WEEK 1: EPIPHANY OF OUR LORD
Acts of Intervention
Matthew 2:1–12

 GATHERING 10 min.   **STUDY** 30 min.   **CARING** 20–40 min.

Leader: The agenda has three parts. In the Gathering time you'll be getting to know each other through an "ice-breaker." This will be for your total group. The Study time has two parts: (1) Story and (2) Scripture. If you are short of time, skip the Story and move to the Scripture. Begin by reading out loud the Story or the Scripture to the whole group. Then divide into groups of 4 for the Study time. Finally, regather the total group for the Caring time. Keep to this agenda: (1) Gathering—10 minutes, (2) Study—30 minutes, and (3) Caring—20–40 minutes.

Nostalgia Auction. Imagine that you have been given $5,000 to spend on the following items. You can spend it all on one item or divide it between several. Whoever was born earliest in the year is the auctioneer. Auction off one item at a time and on the line put the name of whoever has the winning bid for each item.

_____ an autographed picture of Elvis Presley

_____ an original movie poster of *Gone With the Wind*

_____ a poodle skirt worn by Olivia Newton-John in *Grease*

_____ an original Glen Miller 78 rpm album

_____ an autographed Lou Gehrig baseball card

_____ mouse ears worn by Annette Funicello

_____ a leather jacket worn by "the Fonz" on *Happy Days*

_____ a football jersey worn by Joe Montana

INTRODUCTION STORY:

Joan of Arc and a "Sign From God." Joan of Arc is one of history's great stories of female courage. She was convinced that God was speaking to her to lead the armies of France to fight for their freedom against England. But her role in history was more than a political one. She led through a spiritual vision and a courage that lifted a people who had lost heart. When her people saw this teenage young woman grab her standard and fearlessly charge into battle, believing strongly that it was God's leading that impelled her, how could they fear? Neither was Joan much slowed by the wounds that come in such a fray. In fact, one she saw as a sign from God that victory was sure. Her biographer Frances Gies tells the story in *Joan of Arc: The Legend and the Reality:*

"Before she came to Orleans, Joan had predicted that she would be wounded in this way. She told her judges, when they inquired about it, that she had had it revealed to her by St. Catherine and St. Margaret, and that she had 'told her king about it.' Evidently, he was not the only one she told, as the prophecy is recorded in a letter written from Lyons on 22 April 1429—that is to say, before Joan had even arrived at the siege, and more than a fortnight before the attack on the Tourelles. It is perhaps the best attested example of Joan's prophetic gifts; and it is not something for which we can provide a rational explanation. Though she was expecting the wound, the reality came as a shock. ... The consolation may have been the fact that her prediction had been so exactly fulfilled. One chronicle actually asserts that she was 'more joyful than troubled,' and that, after removing the bolt herself, she remarked: 'Now the English have no further power, this wound is the sign of their confusion and misfortune, a sign God has revealed to me, and that I have not made known till now.' [Joan returned within hours to rally her troops to victory.]"[1]

1. Finish this sentence: "If Joan of Arc lived today, she would ..."
   - ❏ be the president of NOW
   - ❏ be put away in a padded cell
   - ❏ be working with revolutionaries in Latin America
   - ❏ be poster-girl for the army's female recruitment program
   - ❏ other:_____

2. What do you see as the continuing lesson of this story?
   - ❏ It's one's spirit, not one's age or sex, that makes a good leader.
   - ❏ God does give us signs, if we just see them with the right attitude.
   - ❏ God may not take sides—but even thinking he does can make a difference!
   - ❏ Everyone gets "wounded" in one way or another—but we can't let it stop us from doing what we are called to do.

SCRIPTURE:

Chance Happenings? Most of us have heard the stories—a man was planning on taking a certain flight, and then something happened—he was delayed, a conflicting appointment came up, or he just had a "funny feeling" he shouldn't go—and that very flight crashed, killing most everyone on board. Was this person saved by some kind of divine intervention, or was it just a chance happening? Even as Christians we debate this back and forth. If God would save one, why not all? But on the other hand, hasn't God down through history intervened in certain circumstances to save people? In our Scripture for this week, didn't God warn the wise men in order to save the infant Jesus? How and in what ways God intervenes in this world will be something people may debate forever, but *that* God sometimes intervenes is something that the Bible is bold to proclaim. The coming of Jesus Christ into the world was itself God's most significant intervention. Through such acts of intervention God seeks to make himself known, and the most vital thing he makes known about himself is that he cares what is happening to us in this world. God may not rescue us from all disasters, but in the midst of every disaster he is there, watching and caring.

Have someone in your group read the following passage out loud. Then go around on each question and let each person share their answer. Take advantage of the Study notes following the questionnaire. Be sure to save the last 20–40 minutes for the Caring time.

2 In the time of King Herod, after Jesus was born in Bethlehem of Judea, wise men from the East came to Jerusalem, ²asking, "Where is the child who has been born king of the Jews? For we observed his star at its rising, and have come to pay him homage." ³When King Herod heard this, he was frightened, and all Jerusalem with him; ⁴and calling together all the chief priests and scribes of the people, he inquired of them where the Messiah was to be born. ⁵They told him, "In Bethlehem of Judea; for so it has been written by the prophet:
⁶"And you, Bethlehem, in the land of Judah,
   are by no means least among the rulers of Judah;
for from you shall come a ruler
   who is to shepherd my people Israel.' "
⁷Then Herod secretly called for the wise men and learned from them the exact time when the star had appeared. ⁸Then he sent them to Bethlehem, saying, "Go and search diligently for the child; and when you have found him, bring me word so that I may go and pay him homage." ⁹When they had heard the king, they set out; and there, ahead of them, went the star that they had seen at its rising, until it stopped over the place where the child was. ¹⁰When they saw that the star had stopped, they were overwhelmed with joy. ¹¹On entering the house, they saw the child with Mary his mother; and they knelt down and paid him homage. Then, opening their treasure chests, they

SCRIPTURE (cont.) and QUESTIONS:

offered him gifts of gold, frankincense, and myrrh. ¹²And having been warned in a dream not to return to Herod, they left for their own country by another road.

Matthew 2:1–12

1. Where were you born? What do you know about the circumstances surrounding your birth?

2. In comparison to the wise men, where are you right now in your spiritual journey?
   - ❏ seeing the "rising star" and making the commitment to start searching
   - ❏ making the long journey, feeling tired and discouraged
   - ❏ getting nearer in my quest by asking questions of those around me
   - ❏ feeling overwhelmed with joy because I have found the object of my search
   - ❏ "sharing my gifts" to pay homage to my king

3. What do you think is the most important reason why Matthew decided to include this story?
   - ❏ to make a more colorful beginning to his Gospel
   - ❏ to show how Gentiles were responsive to Christ from the start
   - ❏ to show how God intervened on behalf of this child from the very start
   - ❏ to affirm that Christ was indeed king
   - ❏ other:_____

4. What "Herod" did you find most threatening as a child?
   - ❏ "the bogeyman"
   - ❏ my parent(s) when they were angry
   - ❏ a bully at school or in the neighborhood
   - ❏ a mean teacher I had
   - ❏ other:_____

5. What "Herod" do you find most threatening now?
   - ❏ an oppressive boss
   - ❏ an oppressive government official
   - ❏ my own demanding self
   - ❏ "the grim reaper"
   - ❏ other:_____

QUESTIONS (cont.) and BIBLE STUDY NOTES:

7. If a voice from heaven came to you at this point in your life, what do you think it would say?
- ❏ "You are also my beloved child, and I am pleased with you."
- ❏ "You are also my beloved child, but I'm not so pleased!"
- ❏ "Hey! Remember me? Why don't we ever talk?"
- ❏ "It's going to be okay!"
- ❏ other:_____

3:15 questioning in their hearts concerning John ... Apparently quite a few of the followers of John the Baptist thought that he might be the Messiah. Some remained as John's disciples for some time even after Jesus had come on the scene, indicating that they weren't overly receptive to switching allegiances (see Matt. 9:14; 11:2; Luke 5:33).

3:16 not worthy to untie the thong of his sandals. The task of removing the master's sandals was that of the lowest-ranking slave in the household. **baptize you with the Holy Spirit.** It was expected that the Messiah would be filled with the Spirit of God (Isa. 11:2), but that was not necessarily connected with the expectation of that time wherein God would pour out his Spirit upon the nation, such that it would permanently become a community of righteousness, justice, peace and security (Isa. 32:15–20; 44:3; Ezek. 37:14). John links together these two strands of OT prophecy in that it is through the Messiah that this community of the Spirit will be established. **fire.** This is a symbol of judgment. The OT anticipates a time of judgment upon Israel before the coming of the age of the

Spirit (see Isa. 4:4; 32:9–14; Zech. 13:9; Mal. 3:2–4). The fire that comes during these last days will bring not just destruction, but cleansing.

3:17 Drawing from the practice involved in the harvesting of wheat, John presents a dramatic image of the anticipated messianic judgment. In order to separate the wheat grain from the straw, the mixture is tossed up into the air by a winnowing fork. The heavier kernels of wheat fall to the ground while the straw and chaff blow away to be burned.

3:21–22 Unlike Matthew's longer account with its conversation between Jesus and John (Matt. 3:13–17), Luke's stress is that the importance of this event lay in Jesus' reception of the Spirit and the divine declaration of his Sonship. **like a dove.** According to *The Interpreter's Bible,* "In early rabbinical literature the sound of a voice ... from heaven ... is likened to the cooing of a dove, and Luke may have been employing familiar symbolism in his simile."[3]

CARING TIME AND PRAYER REQUESTS:

 This time is for developing and expressing your caring for each other as group members. We do this by sharing our needs and praying for each other's needs.

Each group member should answer the question,

How can this group help you in prayer this week?

Then join together in group prayer.

[1]Julien Green, *God's Fool: The Life and Times of Francis of Assisi* (San Francisco: Harper & Row, 1983), pp. 158–159.
[2]Harvey Cox, *God's Revolution and Man's Responsibility* (Valley Forge, PA: Judson Press, 1965), p. 42.
[3]S. MacLean Gilmour, "Luke," *The Interpreter's Bible,* Vol. VIII (New York: Abingdon Press, 1952), p. 79.

SERENDIPITY

Small Group
HANDOUT

WEEK 2: EPIPHANY 1
Spirit-Powered Acts
Luke 3:15–17,21–22

 GATHERING 10 min.　　 **STUDY** 30 min.　　 **CARING** 20–40 min.

Leader: The agenda has three parts. In the Gathering time you'll be getting to know each other through an "ice-breaker." This will be for your total group. The Study time has two parts: (1) Story and (2) Scripture. If you are short of time, skip the Story and move to the Scripture. Begin by reading out loud the Story or the Scripture to the whole group. Then divide into groups of 4 for the Study time. Finally, regather the total group for the Caring time. Keep to this agenda: (1) Gathering—10 minutes, (2) Study—30 minutes, and (3) Caring—20–40 minutes.

 A Day in the Life ... There would probably be no better way to get to know a person than to follow them around for a day. Since we cannot do that very easily with each other, we'll do the next best thing—share what a typical day in our life is like. Do so by completing the following sentences:

1. Generally it's best to not talk to me in the morning before ...
- ❏ I've had my cup of coffee.
- ❏ noon!
- ❏ No problem—I'm a morning person.
- ❏ I've read my paper.
- ❏ I've had my shower.
- ❏ other:_____

2. The high point of my day is when ...
- ❏ I eat (I need to get a life!).
- ❏ I get to delve into my pet project.
- ❏ my spouse comes home.
- ❏ I talk to my friend(s).
- ❏ my kids go to school.
- ❏ I come home.
- ❏ my kids come home.
- ❏ other:_____

3. An important part of ending my day is ...
- ❏ watching a favorite TV show.
- ❏ prayer and quiet time.
- ❏ reflecting on the day with my spouse.
- ❏ watching the sunset.
- ❏ reading.
- ❏ other:_____

INTRODUCTION STORY:

 Francis of Assisi, a Medieval John the Baptist. In many respects, Francis of Assisi was a medieval John the Baptist. Like John the Baptist he stepped out of the shallow religiosity of his day to proclaim something more radical: total-life discipleship. He gave away all he had and served the church and the poor. He dressed in plain and "humble" clothing, and while other people proclaimed their allegiance and admiration, he pointed to another "greater than he" as the true source of his life and power. Julien Green tells the story of Francis and his followers in the book, *God's Fool: The Life and Times of Francis of Assisi:*

"... They left the world behind and traveled in pairs, one behind the other, praying as they walked along. ... It should not be forgotten that Francis was a man who lived in the open air. He was never locked up in a convent cell for very long. The road, the highways, the word of God borne like a seed on all the winds ... Contemplation couldn't be put aside, of course: It found its place in the heart of the night. But in the day they had to act. ...

"A natural scene with such a gently spiritual appeal drew the man who lived close to heaven to make him listen one day to the ecstatic song of the earth. Francis glanced around him like a lover who is forever wonderstruck. ...

"And so Francis carried within him the land of Umbria, borrowing its color for the clothes he and his brothers wore. It was a far cry from the days when the crowds threw mud and rocks at them. Now when he came to a town, he was welcomed by cries of joy; and as the bells rang out he was led in procession by people singing psalms and bearing leafy branches in their hands. He preached of returning to God and obedience to the Church. He was never a reformer. The throng surrounding him cut off so many pieces of his tunic he was left almost naked.

" 'The saint! There's the saint!' they shouted. What did he think of these cheers? We know very well. 'Don't canonize me too soon,' he said once during a triumph of that sort. 'I am still perfectly capable of fathering children.' ..."[1]

1. What do you think was the most important key to Francis of Assisi's spirituality?
    - ❏ his willingness to sacrifice the riches of the world
    - ❏ his emphasis on action
    - ❏ the time he took for contemplation and prayer
    - ❏ his closeness to the natural world
    - ❏ his passion for bringing people back to God
    - ❏ his humility

STORY (cont.) and SCRIPTURE:

2. Why do you think Francis told the people, "Don't canonize me too soon ... I am still perfectly capable of fathering children"?
    - ❏ He knew they would love him all the more if he seemed humble.
    - ❏ He didn't want to get a swelled head and forget his own humanity.
    - ❏ He didn't want them to put him on a pedestal from which he might fall.
    - ❏ He knew he was still susceptible to sexual temptation.
    - ❏ other:_____

 Beyond Cold Logic. Much of our society today seems to be led by a cold kind of logic. That is especially true in business. What enhances the "bottom line"? Forget what is best for society or what is most humane—what raises our profit level? In government, it's what do the regulations say? Forget what will do the most good! We need to get beyond these issues and be led by a Spirit-filled passion. Theologian Harvey Cox a number of years ago compared people to Adolph Eichmann, and his observations still hold some truth. He described Eichmann, the Nazi convicted for his role in the attempted genocide of the Jewish people, as "overpoweringly-ordinary." Cox writes, "Incapable of Luciferian evil, we would all commit genocide just by getting to work on time and keeping our noses clean."[2] Certainly Cox was overstating the case, but it is true that passionless logic *can* make Eichmanns of us all. In contrast, Christ came to "baptize us with the Holy Spirit and fire." There's nothing cold or passionless about that! The phrase speaks of being led by a kind of love that isn't always logical. That is what set Christ apart from the Pharisees following their logical regulations. If we are going to make a difference in our world, we must be set apart by the same Spirit.

Have someone in your group read the following passage out loud. Then go around on each question and let each person share their answer. Take advantage of the Study notes following the questionnaire. Be sure to save the last 20–40 minutes for the Caring time.

[15]As the people were filled with expectation, and all were questioning in their hearts concerning John, whether he might be the Messiah, [16]John answered all of them by saying, "I baptize you with water; but one who is more powerful than I is coming; I am not worthy to untie the thong of his sandals. He will baptize you with the Holy Spirit and fire. [17]His winnowing fork is in his hand, to clear his threshing floor and to gather the wheat into his granary; but the chaff he will burn with unquenchable fire."

... [21]Now when all the people were baptized, and when Jesus also had been baptized and was praying, the heaven was opened, [22]and the Holy Spirit descended upon him in bodily form like a dove. And a voice came from heaven, "You are my Son, the Beloved; with you I am well pleased."

Luke 3:15–17,21–22

QUESTIONS:

1. When your were in high school, what were your parents "well pleased" with in your life?
    - ❏ how I did in school
    - ❏ how I did in sports
    - ❏ my moral choices
    - ❏ my performance in music or drama
    - ❏ the friends I chose
    - ❏ almost nothing I did!
    - ❏ other:_____

2. What were your parents least likely to be "well pleased" about?

3. When in your life have you felt yourself to be "baptized with fire"?
    - ❏ during a rough childhood
    - ❏ when I went through divorce or a time of marital stress
    - ❏ during the time of a serious health difficulty
    - ❏ during a time of financial stress
    - ❏ other:_____

4. What does it mean to you to be "baptized with the Holy Spirit"?
    - ❏ to speak in tongues or feel strong spiritual emotions
    - ❏ to feel especially close to God
    - ❏ to be filled with God's power in what I am doing
    - ❏ to be part of a community knit together by the Spirit
    - ❏ I'm not sure.
    - ❏ other:_____

5. Why did the Holy Spirit descend on Jesus at his baptism?
    - ❏ He was just starting his ministry and he was going to need it.
    - ❏ The Holy Spirit comes at those special times when we feel close to God.
    - ❏ It was God's way of affirming Jesus for his obedience.
    - ❏ because that's when the Holy Spirit comes—at baptism
    - ❏ to witness to those around that this truly was God's Son
    - ❏ other:_____

6. What would need to happen for you to feel like the Holy Spirit was present and active in your life?
    - ❏ A dove and a voice from God would be convincing!
    - ❏ I would need to feel more joy.
    - ❏ I would need to feel more of his direction in my life.
    - ❏ My witness would have to be more effective.
    - ❏ I would need to feel closer to God.
    - ❏ I would need to see more success in what I do for God.
    - ❏ I feel the Holy Spirit is present and active in me right now.

QUESTIONS (cont.) and BIBLE STUDY NOTES:

6. What is the closest you have come to seeing God work a miracle?

7. If God could perform a miracle in your life right now, what would you ask him to do?

2:1 On the third day ... This was on the third day after the call of Philip and Nathanael. **a wedding in Cana.** Nathanael, whom Jesus had just called as a disciple, is described in John 21:2 as being from Cana in Galilee. A marriage feast traditionally lasted seven days, and new guests arrived each day. Since this was quite an exuberant celebration, much wine was consumed.

2:3 the mother of Jesus. Mary's concern for the situation as well as her relationship to the servants (v. 5) indicates she may have been active in planning the wedding.

2:4 My hour. The "hour" of Jesus in this Gospel is the time when he will reveal himself through his acts of power. Jesus' response communicates that he will not operate on any other time frame than that of the one his Father has assigned to him.

2:6 six stone water jars. Although not required by the Law of Moses, by Jesus' day many Jews, in order to show their devotion to God, practiced purification rituals based on those required of the priests (Ex. 30:19–20; Mark 7:1–4). A large event like this wedding would require a great deal of water for such cleansing.

2:9–10 the steward. This may have been the headwaiter, or perhaps one of the guests chosen to preside through the seven days of feasting. The steward's protest to the bridegroom refers to the custom of many hosts to reserve inferior wine until the time when the somewhat inebriated guests were less capable of judging the quality of the wine.

2:11 first of his signs. John uses the term for "signs" frequently to describe Jesus' miracles in order to encourage his readers not to see them simply as acts of power, but as pointers to God's presence in Jesus. In contrast to this, in other Gospels Jesus discounts the people's request for a "sign" (see Matt. 12:39; Mark 8:12; Luke 11:29). **glory.** While the steward of the banquet may have been so overjoyed at the abundance of the wine that he failed to consider by whom it came, the disciples saw the reality behind the sign.

CARING TIME AND PRAYER REQUESTS:

 This time is for developing and expressing your caring for each other as group members. We do this by sharing our needs and praying for each other's needs.

Each group member should answer the question,

How can this group help you in prayer this week?

Then join together in group prayer.

[1]Corrie ten Boom, *The Hiding Place* (Minneapolis, MN: World Wide Publications, 1971), p. 194.
[2]Daniel T. Wackerman, *America*, April 20, 1996, p. 4.
[3]Nancy Gibbs, "The Message of Miracles," *Time*, April 10, 1995, p. 64.

SERENDIPITY
Small Group
HANDOUT

WEEK 3: EPIPHANY 2
Miraculous Acts
John 2:1–11

 GATHERING
10 min.

STUDY
30 min.

CARING
20–40 min.

Leader: The agenda has three parts. In the Gathering time you'll be getting to know each other through an "ice-breaker." This will be for your total group. The Study time has two parts: (1) Story and (2) Scripture. If you are short of time, skip the Story and move to the Scripture. Begin by reading out loud the Story or the Scripture to the whole group. Then divide into groups of 4 for the Study time. Finally, regather the total group for the Caring time. Keep to this agenda: (1) Gathering—10 minutes, (2) Study—30 minutes, and (3) Caring—20–40 minutes.

 And Now, the Weather Report. If you were to give a weather report on how your life has been looking this past week, what report would you give?

❏ sunny and warm, with more of the same on the way
❏ sunny and warm, but with some threatening clouds on the horizon
❏ partly cloudy—could be better, but no complaints
❏ gloomy and overcast, but no real storms
❏ stormy all week, with more to come
❏ stormy all week, but it seems to be clearing
❏ quick-moving fronts—One day it's great, the next the skies open up!
❏ tornadoes and floods!—Where's my disaster aide?

What "weather gear" do you anticipate needing for the coming weeks?
❏ ear muffs and a heavy coat—for the "coldness" of the world
❏ sunglasses and a swimsuit—The horizon looks sunny.
❏ an umbrella and rain boots—A lot of storms are ahead!
❏ a sailboat—The wind of the Spirit may blow me in any direction!

INTRODUCTION STORY:

Corrie ten Boom Gets Past the Guards. Corrie ten Boom helped shelter Jews from the Nazis during World War II, and for this act of courage was sent to Nazi concentration camps, eventually ending up at Ravensbruck. Upon entering that camp, she had to pass through a series of inspections by the guards, in which she feared that her Bible and other precious items she had wrapped in a bundle to preserve would be taken from her. She tells the story of what was to her a miracle in her book, *The Hiding Place:*

"We stood beneath the spigots as long as the flow of icy water lasted, feeling it soften our lice-eaten skin. Then we clustered dripping wet around the heap of prison dresses, holding them up, passing them about, looking for approximate fits. I found a loose long-sleeved dress for Betsie that would cover the blue sweater when she would have a chance to put it on. I squirmed into another dress for myself, then reached behind the benches and shoved the little bundle quickly inside the neck.

"It made a bulge you could have seen across the Grote Markt. I flattened it out as best I could, pushing it down, tugging the sweater around my waist, but there was no real concealing it beneath the thin cotton dress. And all the while I had the incredible feeling that it didn't matter, that this was not my business, but God's. That all I had to do was walk straight ahead.

"As we trooped back out through the shower room door, the S.S. men ran their hands over every prisoner, front, back and sides. The woman ahead of me was searched three times. Behind me, Betsie was searched. No hand touched me.

"At the exit door to the building was a second ordeal, a line of women guards examining each prisoner again. I slowed down as I reached them but the *Aufseherin* in charge shoved me roughly by the shoulder. 'Move along! You're holding up the line!'

"And so Betsie and I arrived at Barracks 8 in the small hours of that morning, bringing not only the Bible, but a new knowledge of the power of Him whose story it was."[1]

1. What would be your explanation for how Corrie ten Boom was able to smuggle her Bible and other contraband into Ravensbruck?
   - ❏ chance
   - ❏ The guards must have been tired.
   - ❏ God miraculously hid these things from them.
   - ❏ Corrie's confident attitude of faith kept her from being suspected by the guards.

2. If you were to smuggle three things into a concentration camp, to help you make it through, what would those three things be?

SCRIPTURE:

Hungering for a Sign. More and more today we seem to be hearing people talk about various kinds of "miracles." In one place the police worried about traffic problems because people were massing beside the road where it was reputed one could see an image of the Virgin Mary in the back of a road sign. Others talk of a picture of Mary that weeps, a statue of Christ that bleeds, or a vision of an angel in the clouds at a place where children died. Such events ignite controversy and have gotten people talking about just what a miracle is, and if in fact they happen today. In the Jesuit publication, *America,* the author contends that the popular hunger for such miracles comes out of a shallow faith that cannot see miracles in the everyday—"... what of such daily natural wonders as a sunset, the birth of a child, the regeneration of salmon in rivers and streams?"[2] In a *Time* magazine article, the reason behind much pastoral caution over miracles is said to be, "The preacher who affirms that miracles do indeed happen must also be prepared to explain why they do not. Why do some cancers vanish while others consume?" Yet the same article contains stories of people from mainline Protestant and Catholic churches, as well as from the more charismatic faiths, who insist they have experienced miracles.[3] It is this variety of experience that necessitates that we listen to each other to come to a fuller understanding of this complex topic.

Have someone in your group read the following passage out loud. Then go around on each question and let each person share their answer. Take advantage of the Study notes following the questionnaire. Be sure to save the last 20–40 minutes for the Caring time.

2 On the third day there was a wedding in Cana of Galilee, and the mother of Jesus was there. [2]Jesus and his disciples had also been invited to the wedding. [3]When the wine gave out, the mother of Jesus said to him, "They have no wine." [4]And Jesus said to her, "Woman, what concern is that to you and to me? My hour has not yet come." [5]His mother said to the servants, "Do whatever he tells you." [6]Now standing there were six stone water jars for the Jewish rites of purification, each holding twenty or thirty gallons. [7]Jesus said to them, "Fill the jars with water." And they filled them up to the brim. [8]He said to them, "Now draw some out, and take it to the chief steward." So they took it. [9]When the steward tasted the water that had become wine, and did not know where it came from (though the servants who had drawn the water knew), the steward called the bridegroom [10]and said to him, "Everyone serves the good wine first, and then the inferior wine after the guests have become drunk. But you have kept the good wine until now." [11]Jesus did this, the first of his signs, in Cana of Galilee, and revealed his glory; and his disciples believed in him.

John 2:1–11

QUESTIONS:

1. What is your first impression of this Scripture story?
   - ❏ I wish we had had Jesus at our wedding!
   - ❏ It looks like Jesus got hassled by his mother too!
   - ❏ I didn't know Jesus was a wine expert!
   - ❏ Jesus enjoyed all the aspects of life that we do.

2. What attitude do you think Jesus had when he said, "Woman, what concern is that to you and to me?"
   - ❏ embarrassed at being put on the spot
   - ❏ angry at being manipulated to do what he didn't want to do
   - ❏ proud that his mother depended on him, but feeling he ought to act humble
   - ❏ put upon—He was having a good time and didn't want to work at a party.
   - ❏ other:_____

3. Had your own mother been in the place of Jesus' mother, what would she have done?
   - ❏ stayed out of the whole situation
   - ❏ let the wine run out, then used it as an item of gossip for the next month
   - ❏ figured it served them right for serving wine in the first place
   - ❏ did what Jesus' mother did—not taken no for an answer
   - ❏ accepted Jesus' refusal, but made him feel guilty for a month
   - ❏ shared her recipe for nonalcoholic punch
   - ❏ other:_____

4. Why do you think Jesus went ahead and performed this miracle?
   - ❏ He couldn't say no to his mother.
   - ❏ He didn't want the wedding celebration to be spoiled.
   - ❏ He wanted to show his disciples what he could do.
   - ❏ It was his way of warming up for more important miracles.
   - ❏ It was symbolic of something spiritual—like his blood poured out for many.
   - ❏ other:_____

5. What is your definition of what a "miracle" is?
   - ❏ Something that cannot be explained by natural law.
   - ❏ Something that is beyond present human understanding.
   - ❏ Something that happens at just the right time to help someone.
   - ❏ All of life is a miracle.
   - ❏ There are no miracles.
   - ❏ other:_____

QUESTIONS (cont.) and BIBLE STUDY NOTES:

7. What is holding you back from taking the initiative to reach out to the people you mentioned in question #6?

4:14 filled with the power ... It is significant that this power of the Holy Spirit came to him only after a time of severe testing in the wilderness. Too often people want the power without the wilderness experience! **returned to Galilee.** From 4:14–9:50 Luke records Jesus' ministry in Galilee, a province about 50 miles long and 25 miles wide in the north of Palestine.

4:15 synagogues. While the temple in Jerusalem was the religious center for all Jews, the community synagogue was the focal point of weekly worship and teaching. Jesus' initial ministry was as a well-received itinerant preacher teaching in synagogues throughout Galilee.

4:16 Nazareth. Nazareth, a town of about 20,000 people, was located in a hollow surrounded by hills. **the Sabbath.** Each Sabbath, Jews would gather at the synagogue for a service of worship and instruction from Scripture. There was a standard order governing which passages of the Law would be read and the same may have been true about the reading from the prophets as well. The synagogue had no formal clergy, so various people read and taught from the Scripture. Given Jesus' emerging reputation, it is not surprising that he was asked to do so. **He stood up to read.** As a sign of reverence

for God, men would stand as they read the Scripture, but sit down to teach.

4:18 The passage Jesus read was from Isaiah 61:1–2 (with the addition of a phrase from 58:6). The OT prophets frequently regarded the poor and oppressed as the only righteous people since their condition was so often caused by the evil perpetrated by those who had forsaken God.

4:19 the year of the Lord's favor. This specifically refers to the Jubilee Year of Leviticus 25. Every fifty years, the Jews were to release their slaves, cancel all debts, and return land to the families of its original owners. While there is no record that the Jews ever kept that command, it became a symbol of the deliverance God intended to bring about when he would right the wrongs suffered by his people.

4:21 Today this scripture has been fulfilled ... The phrase is reminiscent of Mark 1:15 with its announcement that the kingdom of God "has come near." In both cases, Jesus asserts that the new era foretold by Isaiah has begun because he has come to bring it about.

CARING TIME AND PRAYER REQUESTS:

 This time is for developing and expressing your caring for each other as group members. We do this by sharing our needs and praying for each other's needs.

Each group member should answer the question,

How can this group help you in prayer this week?

Then join together in group prayer.

[1]Stephen Oates, *Let the Trumpet Sound: The Life of Martin Luther King, Jr.* (New York: Penguin Books, 1982), pp. 142–143.

SERENDIPITY

Small Group
HANDOUT

WEEK 4: EPIPHANY 3
Acts of Justice
Luke 4:14–21

 GATHERING
10 min.

 STUDY
30 min.

 CARING
20–40 min.

Leader: The agenda has three parts. In the Gathering time you'll be getting to know each other through an "ice-breaker." This will be for your total group. The Study time has two parts: (1) Story and (2) Scripture. If you are short of time, skip the Story and move to the Scripture. Begin by reading out loud the Story or the Scripture to the whole group. Then divide into groups of 4 for the Study time. Finally, regather the total group for the Caring time. Keep to this agenda: (1) Gathering—10 minutes, (2) Study—30 minutes, and (3) Caring—20–40 minutes.

 Games That Tell Our Story. Most of us remember playing games as a child. The titles or themes of some of the games many of us played suggest lifestyles we have lived since. Which of these childhood game titles comes closest to suggesting how you have lived your life?

CLUE: Life's a mystery, and I've been searching for clues to its solution!

MOTHER MAY I: I have spent my life trying to please her.

HIDE AND SEEK: I hide who I really am, and look for people who care enough to try to find out.

CHESS: Life is a game of competitive strategies.

JUMP ROPE: Other people set the rhythm and I jump!

MARBLES: I've lost mine!

CHARADES: I say nothing, and you try to guess what I'm thinking!

SPIN THE BOTTLE: I've gone through a series of seemingly random romantic partnerships.

INTRODUCTION STORY:

 Martin Luther King, Jr. Touched by India's Poverty. Most of us know Martin Luther King, Jr. as one who fought for equal opportunity in our country. But on one occasion he took a trip to India, and was also touched by the victims of poverty and injustice there. He also felt he learned much from them. Stephen Oates tells the story in his book, *Let the Trumpet Sound: The Life of Martin Luther King, Jr.*:

"From New Delhi, the Kings set out on a month-long tour of the country. They rode clattering trains from one city to another and bounced along in jeeps to the more remote villages. 'Everywhere we went,' King recorded, 'we saw crowded humanity—on the roads, in the city streets and squares, even in the villages. ...' Most men, if they had employment at all, toiled at seasonable agricultural jobs. And nearly everyone was impoverished—the average personal income was less than $70 a year. And food shortages were epidemic. 'They are poor, jammed together and half starved,' King said of Indians, 'but they do not take it out on each other. ... They do not abuse each other—verbally or physically—as readily as we do. We saw but one fist fight in India during our stay.' In sharp contrast to the poverty, King saw a lot of opulence, too, riding by great homes on vast landed estates. 'The bourgeoisie—white, black or brown—behaves about the same the world over,' he said. ...

"Soon after, the Kings headed back for New Delhi, having found the spirit of Gandhi very much alive in this sprawling land. On March 9 they left India with King in a pensive mood. He could not forget the contorted faces of all those hungry people he had seen in the towns and villages. He thought how America spent millions of dollars every day to store her surplus food, and he told himself: 'I know where we can store that food free of charge—in the wrinkled stomachs of starving people in Asia and Africa.' And he said so repeatedly on his return to America."[1]

1. Why do you think it was important for King to see what was happening in India?
   - ❏ to realize there were people even worse off than blacks in America
   - ❏ to find a unanimity with other suffering people
   - ❏ to get an idea of how other people dealt with injustice
   - ❏ other:_____

2. When, if ever, have you seen the poverty of a Third World country? How did you react?

SCRIPTURE:

 The Great Equalizer. One of the most important questions any religion must deal with is why, if God is good and powerful, there is injustice in the world. Hinduism says there isn't injustice—what appears to be unfair is really the punishment one receives for sin in previous lifetimes. That is a variation of the same perspective that many had in Old Testament times, who said that people basically got what they deserved. But Christianity is a faith that admits that unjust things happen. The good news is that God can be known as one who comes to the aid of victims of injustice, and calls his followers to do the same. Thus in our lectionary Scripture for this week, Christ's mission is defined as aiding victims of injustice—the poor, those with disabilities, and those suffering from political oppression. Thus, while in the short run injustice exists, in the long run God is "the Great Equalizer" who comes in on the side of the underdog. Perhaps that is why Jesus in another place says, "But many who are first will be last, and the last will be first" (Matt. 19:30).

Have someone in your group read the following passage out loud. Then go around on each question and let each person share their answer. Take advantage of the Study notes following the questionnaire. Be sure to save the last 20–40 minutes for the Caring time.

> [14]*Then Jesus, filled with the power of the Spirit, returned to Galilee, and a report about him spread through all the surrounding country.* [15]*He began to teach in their synagogues and was praised by everyone.*
>
> [16]*When he came to Nazareth, where he had been brought up, he went to the synagogue on the sabbath day, as was his custom. He stood up to read,* [17]*and the scroll of the prophet Isaiah was given to him. He unrolled the scroll and found the place where it was written:*
>
> [18]*"The Spirit of the Lord is upon me,*
> *because he has anointed me*
> *to bring good news to the poor.*
> *He has sent me to proclaim release to the captives*
> *and recovery of sight to the blind,*
> *to let the oppressed go free,*
> [19]*to proclaim the year of the Lord's favor."*
>
> [20]*And he rolled up the scroll, gave it back to the attendant, and sat down. The eyes of all in the synagogue were fixed on him.* [21]*Then he began to say to them, "Today this scripture has been fulfilled in your hearing."*
>
> *Luke 4:14–21*

QUESTIONS:

1. When was the last time you went back to the town where you were raised? How had things changed? What memories came to mind?

2. Why do you think Jesus chose his hometown of Nazareth to make this announcement of his role?
   - ❏ He considered it his "power base."
   - ❏ Getting in touch with your roots helps you get in touch with your future.
   - ❏ He wanted to give them the honor of "launching" their "favorite son."
   - ❏ It just happened to be where he was at the time.

3. What does it say to you that Jesus chose this particular Scripture to describe his mission?
   - ❏ His mission was more political-social than religious.
   - ❏ His mission was to show that true faith in God is shown in caring for those in need.
   - ❏ This was symbolic language—he came to rescue the spiritually poor and blind.
   - ❏ He knew the "down and out" would be the ones most receptive to his message.

4. Choose one of the four key words in this passage and tell how it applies to you in either a literal or figurative way.
   - ❏ poor   ❏ captive   ❏ blind   ❏ oppressed

5. How has Jesus brought you "good news" in the midst of the condition you revealed in question #4 (your poverty, captivity, blindness or oppression)?

6. In light of this passage, what group of people does your heart go out to in your community?
   - ❏ the poor—to share more of my financial abundance
   - ❏ the spiritually poor—to share the Good News of salvation
   - ❏ the captive—those in jail and needing guidance and support
   - ❏ the captive—those held captive to addictions or compulsive behavior
   - ❏ the blind—or those with any physical disability
   - ❏ the blind—those people heading down a "blind alley" in their life
   - ❏ the oppressed—persons abused by the power structures of their society
   - ❏ the oppressed—those suffering the oppression of loneliness or rejection

6. What has God taught you lately as you try to share your faith?
   - ❑ Listen to everyone's thoughts and try not to get angry.
   - ❑ Sometimes the truth is not pleasant to hear.
   - ❑ God's grace is for everyone, even people we may not like.
   - ❑ If you just want everyone to like you, you probably will not say or do much of significance.
   - ❑ It's hard to reach out effectively to people close to you.

7. Where do you need to grow in sharing your faith?

4:21 Today this scripture has been fulfilled ... The phrase is reminiscent of Mark 1:15 with its announcement that the kingdom of God "has come near." In both cases, Jesus asserts that the new era foretold by Isaiah has begun because he has come to bring it about. This is a clear claim Jesus is making that he is God's appointed Messiah (note that "Messiah" means "anointed one" and the Scripture Jesus had just quoted began by saying "... he has anointed me ...").

4:22 All spoke well of him. How are we to understand this phrase in the light of the almost immediate turn to hostility against Jesus? Some contend the problem comes from editing together different accounts, in one of which the people were hostile and in one of which the people were supportive. Others contend that the Greek word *martureo* used here can also be translated "to condemn or speak against" depending on its context (compare Acts 13:22 with Matt. 23:31). The violent response later in the story as well as Mark's record that the reaction to Jesus was decidedly negative (Mark 6:1–6), indicates that "to speak against" may be the better way to understand this word. **the gracious words.** This phrase is used in Acts 14:3 and 20:32 as an idiomatic expression that refers to the Gospel message. **"Is not this Joseph's son?"** Jesus had been raised in Nazareth and they knew his family. It was incomprehensible to them that God's Messiah might come as the son of someone they knew in their little city. This young man must be full of himself!

4:23 This proverb has both Greek and Arabic parallels. The doubt and cynicism of his hometown is seen in that they would not believe the stories they had heard from elsewhere unless they could see further evidence for themselves. **you did at Capernaum.** While Luke had not recorded Jesus as having done anything at Capernaum as yet, Mark does indicate that Jesus did great acts at Capernaum before returning to his hometown (Mark 1:21ff).

4:24 This proverb has Greek parallels. It simply observes that typically the hardest place for a famous person to gain respect is among the people he or she grew up with.

4:25–27 The ministries of Elijah and Elisha included those outside of Israel, just as Jesus' ministry would. (Also, Elijah at one point felt so rejected and alone in what he was trying to say that he wanted to die—see 1 Kings 19.) These stories referred to by Jesus, found in 1 Kings 17:1–18:1 and 2 Kings 5:1–27, illustrate that God has never limited his grace only to Israel. They further accent the point that if Nazareth (and, if by extension, the Jews as a whole) will not receive Jesus with faith, then there are plenty of others, including Gentiles, who will. This was incendiary language! **Sidon ...**

Syrian. Sidon and Syria were neighboring countries and traditional enemies of Israel.

4:28–29 Jesus' strong words, which implied that Gentiles were more worthy of God's grace than the people from Jesus' own hometown, provoked such a strong response that a mob desired to kill him.

4:30 he passed through the midst of them. Similar to an incident recorded in John 7:30, it is implied that Jesus had this miraculous protection because his time had not yet come.

 This time is for developing and expressing your caring for each other as group members. We do this by sharing our needs and praying for each other's needs.

Each group member should answer the question,

How can this group help you in prayer this week?

Then join together in group prayer.

¹John Pollock, *To All the Nations: The Billy Graham Story* (San Francisco: Harper & Row, 1985), p. 131.

SERENDIPITY

Small Group
H A N D O U T

WEEK 5: EPIPHANY 4

Prophetic Acts
Luke 4:21–30

	GATHERING 10 min.		STUDY 30 min.		CARING 20–40 min.

Leader: The agenda has three parts. In the Gathering time you'll be getting to know each other through an "ice-breaker." This will be for your total group. The Study time has two parts: (1) Story and (2) Scripture. If you are short of time, skip the Story and move to the Scripture. Begin by reading out loud the Story or the Scripture to the whole group. Then divide into groups of 4 for the Study time. Finally, regather the total group for the Caring time. Keep to this agenda: (1) Gathering—10 minutes, (2) Study—30 minutes, and (3) Caring—20–40 minutes.

 Now That Would Have Been a Party! If you could have planned for yourself the perfect party for your 12th birthday, what would you have done? Indicate what you would have chosen in each of the following categories:

RECREATION (choose 2):
- ❑ horses to ride
- ❑ a trip to see my favorite team
- ❑ a trip to Disneyland
- ❑ a dance with a live band
- ❑ a great magic show
- ❑ other:_____

FRIENDS:
I would have invited ___ friend(s), including especially_____.

FOOD:
For my birthday dinner, we would have eaten _____ for the main course, and had _____ for dessert.

OTHER:
The thing that too often happened at my real birthday parties, and would *not* happen at this party would be:

INTRODUCTION STORY:

 Billy Graham Takes a Stand. For the most part Billy Graham's ministry has been preaching the straight Gospel message, and in the process avoiding political controversy. But at least on one occasion he decided he needed to speak out on the issue of nuclear armaments, and in the process irritated some followers. His biographer John Pollock tells the story in *To All the Nations: The Billy Graham Story:*

"If Billy Graham influenced Poland, Poland also influenced Billy Graham. It gave him more assurance, and encouragement and experiences in helping Christians in the difficult circumstances of Eastern Europe. It brought him more contacts and friendships towards his further ministry in socialistic countries. And it brought him the profound experience of the visit to Auschwitz.

"He and Ruth had been briefed, back in Montreat, by a senior official of the United States government about the consequences of a nuclear war between the superpowers. The grim facts, expounded in accurate detail five years before the general public were given impressions by a television company, appalled the Grahams. Billy realized as never before that the human race could destroy itself in a matter of hours. 'Man's technology has leaped far ahead of his moral ability to control his technology. As I searched the Scriptures, my responsibilities dawned on me.' He determined to speak out.

"He chose the visit to Auschwitz concentration camp between Kracow and Katowice, preserved as a memorial, to make his first public statement on the need for nuclear disarmament of all nations: 'The very survival of human civilization is at stake ... The present insanity of a global arms race, if continued, will lead inevitably to a conflagration so great that Auschwitz will seem a minor rehearsal.' In a widely reported speech he called on world leaders, whatever their ideology, to put national pride and power second to the survival of the human race. ...["1]

1. How do you react to Billy Graham's decision to speak out on this issue?
   - ❏ He should have stuck to the Gospel.
   - ❏ If he wanted to speak about that, he should have done so in our own country.
   - ❏ He should have had faith that God wouldn't let us destroy his world.
   - ❏ He should have done this more often.
   - ❏ He used a good combination of discretion and courage in saying this.

2. When have you been confronted with the question of whether to speak out on something you knew might make some people angry at you?

SCRIPTURE:

 To Comfort or Afflict? It has been said that the role of the preacher is to "Comfort the afflicted ... and afflict the comfortable!" If the truth were known, most preachers are much more at ease with the role of comforting the afflicted than with afflicting the comfortable. When preachers comfort the afflicted, their people love them, they advocate for higher pastoral pay, and they help the preacher feel needed. But sometimes preachers need also to take on a prophetic role and "afflict the comfortable"—challenging the complacent to change, the apathetic to start caring, and the spiritually blind to open their eyes. Most of the time this does not win the preacher many friends—or many raises. But in such times preachers—and indeed any person seeking to teach the faith in a prophetic way—must pause to consider the action of Christ in our Gospel story for this week. Seeking to be "a prophet in his own country" he tried to knock people off dead center where they had been resting, and he was driven out of town. The prophetic pastor today must occasionally risk the same thing.

Have someone in your group read the following passage out loud. Then go around on each question and let each person share their answer. Take advantage of the Study notes following the questionnaire. Be sure to save the last 20–40 minutes for the Caring time.

[21]Then he began to say to them, "Today this scripture has been fulfilled in your hearing." [22]All spoke well of him and were amazed at the gracious words that came from his mouth. They said, "Is not this Joseph's son?" [23]He said to them, "Doubtless you will quote to me this proverb, 'Doctor, cure yourself!' And you will say, 'Do here also in your hometown the things that we have heard you did at Capernaum.' " [24]And he said, "Truly, I tell you, no prophet is accepted in the prophet's hometown. [25]But the truth is, there were many widows in Israel in the time of Elijah, when the heaven was shut up three years and six months, and there was a severe famine over all the land; [26]yet Elijah was sent to none of them except to a widow at Zarephath in Sidon. [27]There were also many lepers in Israel in the time of the prophet Elisha, and none of them was cleansed except Naaman the Syrian." [28]When they heard this, all in the synagogue were filled with rage. [29]They got up, drove him out of the town, and led him to the brow of the hill on which their town was built, so that they might hurl him off the cliff. [30]But he passed through the midst of them and went on his way.

Luke 4:21–30

QUESTIONS:

1. If the people in the neighborhood where you lived in junior high school would have made a prediction about you from what they knew at the time, what would they have predicted?
   - ❏ I'd be spending a lot of time behind bars!
   - ❏ I'd be spending a lot of time *in* bars!
   - ❏ I'd be more likely to *own* the bars ... and the banks ... and the real estate ...
   - ❏ I'd end up just like them.
   - ❏ I'd never be one to "fit in."
   - ❏ I'd grow up to be a great scientist ... or blow up the world!
   - ❏ I'd grow up to be a proper little wife in a proper little house.
   - ❏ I'd follow in my dad's or mom's footsteps.
   - ❏ I doubt if they had any idea!
   - ❏ other:_____

2. What expectations do you think the people of Nazareth had for Jesus when he was young?
   - ❏ He'd be a carpenter like his daddy.
   - ❏ He'd never be one to "fit in."
   - ❏ He'd become a rabbi who would say lots of wise things and make his mom proud.
   - ❏ He'd be just like them.
   - ❏ They knew God had something special planned for him.

3. What do you think was the biggest reason why people got angry at Jesus?
   - ❏ He sided with their enemies.
   - ❏ He was not being very tactful.
   - ❏ They wanted him to comfort the afflicted, and he was afflicting the comfortable!
   - ❏ He was expecting them to reject him, so they did.
   - ❏ He seemed to think too much of himself.

4. If you could go back and give a message to the people in the neighborhood where you grew up, what message might it be?

5. Had you been in Jesus' shoes in this situation, what would you have more likely done?
   - ❏ declined to speak in the first place
   - ❏ given a nice "politically correct" devotional
   - ❏ found a way to challenge them, but in a way that didn't make them mad
   - ❏ laid it on the line, like Jesus did

6. What are you personally seeking to "catch" at this point in your life?

❏ a sense of life purpose   ❏ financial success
❏ just a happy, secure home life   ❏ other:_____
❏ more excitement in life
❏ more spiritual impact in the lives of those around me

7. Where are you in this effort, in terms of this story?

❏ worn out from trying, "washing my nets"
❏ resting and diverting myself
❏ feeling Christ call me to try one more time
❏ reeling in my "catch," my boat overflowing

8. What needs to happen for you to have a greater spirit of obedience in the face of the possibilities God lays before you?

❏ I need to believe more in myself.
❏ I need to believe more in God.
❏ I need to hear more about the miraculous "harvest" God has given to others.
❏ other:_____

5:1 *lake of Gennesaret.* This is another name for the Sea of Galilee. According to *The Revell Bible Dictionary,* "The northern end of the lake was a rich source of fish in biblical times, and Josephus says that some 330 fishing boats operated on the body of water in the first century."[2]

5:2 *washing their nets.* In the morning fishermen would clean and repair the nets which they dragged along behind the boats while fishing throughout the night.

5:3 *the boats.* While one belonged to Simon, the other boat may have been owned by James and John (Mark 1:19), Simon's partners in his fishing business (v. 10). These would have been open craft about 20 to 30 feet long. The boat served as a speaking platform while Jesus addressed the crowd that amassed on the water's edge.

5:4–5 From any normal perspective, Jesus' command was absolutely foolish since mid-morning was not the time when fish would be feeding. To get the feeling behind the words in verse 5, one must picture tired and hungry men who have worked unsuccessfully all night suddenly wondering why in the world they should listen to a religious teacher when it comes to their fishing business! Still, Simon decides to obey.

5:6–7 In contrast to Simon's initial doubt, Luke underscores the magnitude of the catch.

5:8 Peter's fear and confession

before Jesus is similar to that of people in the OT when they encountered the divine (Isa. 6:5; Dan. 10:15–18). Just what Peter recognized about Jesus' identity at this point is unclear since "Lord" can be the title for God or a title of respect for an esteemed person.

5:10 *Do not be afraid ...* Jesus' words echo those of the divine response seen in Isaiah 6, Daniel 10 and Luke 1. *catching people.* This incident is portrayed as a prediction of the eventual success of the mission of Christ, in which these disciples would play an important part.

5:11 *left everything.* See also 5:28; 9:23; 14:33; 18:22,28. A loyalty to Jesus which takes precedence over anything else in life is Luke's characteristic way of describing what it means to be a Christian.

This time is for developing and expressing your caring for each other as group members. We do this by sharing our needs and praying for each other's needs.

Each group member should answer the question,

How can this group help you in prayer this week?

Then join together in group prayer.

¹John Pollock, *To All the Nations: The Billy Graham Story* (San Francisco: Harper & Row, 1985), pp. 53–56.
²"Galilee, Sea of," *The Revell Bible Dictionary* (Old Tappan, NJ: The Fleming H. Revell Co., 1990), p. 413.

SERENDIPITY

Small Group
HANDOUT

WEEK 6: EPIPHANY 5
Acts of Obedience
Luke 5:1–11

 GATHERING 10 min.   **STUDY** 30 min.   **CARING** 20–40 min.

Leader: The agenda has three parts. In the Gathering time you'll be getting to know each other through an "ice-breaker." This will be for your total group. The Study time has two parts: (1) Story and (2) Scripture. If you are short of time, skip the Story and move to the Scripture. Begin by reading out loud the Story or the Scripture to the whole group. Then divide into groups of 4 for the Study time. Finally, regather the total group for the Caring time. Keep to this agenda: (1) Gathering—10 minutes, (2) Study—30 minutes, and (3) Caring—20–40 minutes.

 Risky Business. There are people in the world who go for all the gusto they can. Others simply try to keep their waters as calm as possible. Where are you on the risk scale? Place an *"X"* on the following lines, and share your responses with the group.

go skydiving _____go bowling
spend my inheritance _____put the money in the bank
take a lap around the track with an Indy driver _____sit in the stands
try new foods _____eat the same thing
go to a party where I don't know anybody _____stay at home
say what I think _____keep my opinions to myself
explore the city_____stay close to home
watch a suspense thriller _____watch a Disney animation
take an African safari_____vacation on my front porch

INTRODUCTION STORY:

Billy Graham's Radio Ministry Begins. In addition to the people he has preached to in tents, stadiums and auditoriums, Billy Graham has reached many people through the media of radio and television. But in spite of his effectiveness through those media, when the idea was first proposed to him to go that way he was resistant. His biographer John Pollock tells of his encounter with Dr. Theodore Elsner, then president of the National Religious Broadcasters, who proposed to him the idea of doing a weekly radio program. We read what happened in *To All the Nations: The Billy Graham Story:*

"On reflection, Billy rejected the idea; a national weekly programme could be almost a full-time occupation. When next month, at a conference in northern Michigan, two well-dressed strangers introduced themselves as Walter Bennett and Fred Dienert of the Walter Bennett Advertising Company, Billy charmingly sent them away. They reappeared at Montreat, and told him that a peak Sunday afternoon time would shortly be available coast-to-coast on the American Broadcasting Company's network, for an initial thirteen week contract at a total of $92,000, a sum which to Graham appeared astronomical.

"Shortly afterward Graham began a six weeks' crusade at Portland, Oregon. ... Bennett and Dienert pursued him by telephone and telegram to explain that the programme cost about $7,000 a week; if he raised $25,000 he could go on the air, for after three weeks the gifts of listeners would certainly maintain it. ...

[Billy prayed that if God wanted him to start such a ministry, he would have to provide. He asked God to make it so they could raise $25,000, a large sum in 1950, by midnight that night. After that night's crusade, however, they had only come up with $23,500, and Billy thought they had failed.]

"A subdued Team returned to the hotel shortly before midnight. Billy went to his room, Grady to the mail desk, where he was given three envelopes delivered by hand.

"In each was a pledge from somebody ... one for $1,000, two for $250. Together they made up the $25,000."[1]

1. When you hear stories like this where God seems to have provided a "miraculous harvest," how do you react?

❏ Oh yeah, how come this never happens to me!

❏ Well, it helps to have rich friends.

❏ Pure coincidence!

❏ When one is obedient, God provides.

❏ Yes, now tell us about the times when the money *didn't* come!

❏ That's why Billy Graham is Billy Graham! (But it wouldn't work for me!)

2. When have you felt like God was calling *you* to step out in a risky venture like this one?

SCRIPTURE:

Unsolicited Advice. For many of us, there is little more irritating than unsolicited advice, especially when it relates to our field and comes from an amateur. What business does this person have telling *us* how to do our job? With all of our training and experience, does this person still think he or she knows more than we? Yet acting on unsolicited advice from an amateur is exactly what the disciples did in our Gospel story for this week. For that is what Jesus was—he had been raised in the family of a carpenter, and knew that profession, but there is nothing to indicate that he had any training in fishing. That the disciples listened to him indicates that even at this stage of his ministry, before they had been called, they respected his authority. They were willing to listen to what they at least suspected might be the call of God, even when it went against their professional instincts. When they obeyed, they found that God provided for them. That is the kind of obedience to God we need today.

Have someone in your group read the following passage out loud. Then go around on each question and let each person share their answer. Take advantage of the Study notes following the questionnaire. Be sure to save the last 20–40 minutes for the Caring time.

5 Once while Jesus was standing beside the lake of Gennesaret, and the crowd was pressing in on him to hear the word of God, ²he saw two boats there at the shore of the lake; the fishermen had gone out of them and were washing their nets. ³He got into one of the boats, the one belonging to Simon, and asked him to put out a little way from the shore. Then he sat down and taught the crowds from the boat. ⁴When he had finished speaking, he said to Simon, "Put out into the deep water and let down your nets for a catch." ⁵Simon answered, "Master, we have worked all night long but have caught nothing. Yet if you say so, I will let down the nets." ⁶When they had done this, they caught so many fish that their nets were beginning to break. ⁷So they signaled their partners in the other boat to come and help them. And they came and filled both boats, so that they began to sink. ⁸But when Simon Peter saw it, he fell down at Jesus' knees, saying, "Go away from me, Lord, for I am a sinful man!" ⁹For he and all who were with him were amazed at the catch of fish that they had taken; ¹⁰and so also were James and John, sons of Zebedee, who were partners with Simon. Then Jesus said to Simon, "Do not be afraid; from now on you will be catching people." ¹¹When they had brought their boats to shore, they left everything and followed him.

Luke 5:1–11

QUESTIONS:

1. Which of the following have you spent your life "fishing" for?

❏ opportunities to get ahead   ❏ recognition

❏ the approval of my parents   ❏ fish!

❏ acceptance and belonging   ❏ other:_____

❏ compliments

2. If Jesus came to your place of employment and wanted to set up a pulpit to preach to the people, how would your coworkers react?

❏ Great, a motivational speaker!   ❏ Save it for Sunday!

❏ Sorry, against union rules!   ❏ Anything for a break!

❏ No way—it might spread dangerously ethical behavior!

❏ That would violate the rights of nonbelievers!

❏ Wonderful! We need some moral direction!

3. Why do you think Simon and the others agreed to have their boats used for preaching?

❏ They figured it was a good advertising opportunity.

❏ Anything for a break!

❏ They needed a lift after a bad day of fishing.

❏ Jesus was someone you couldn't say "no" to.

❏ They had heard him before and wanted to hear more.

❏ other:_____

4. Had you been Simon, how would you have responded when Jesus told you to put out your nets for a catch?

❏ I'd have told him to stick to preaching.

❏ I'd have explained to him how foolish an idea that was.

❏ I'd have done it grudgingly.

❏ I'd have done it just to make him happy.

❏ I'd have done it with a sense of expectation.

5. What would it mean for your church leadership to "put out into the deep water and let down their nets for a catch"?

❏ We'd stop being so afraid of failing.

❏ We'd try things even when someone says, "We already tried that before."

❏ We'd reach out to people who have been said to be unreachable.

❏ We'd expect success instead of expecting failure.

❏ We'd be obedient to God's call wherever it led us.

❏ other:_____

QUESTIONS (cont.) and BIBLE STUDY NOTES:

4. When have you felt rejected or excluded because of your faith?

5. What do you need most in order to better persevere in the face of rejection, poverty or oppression?
- ❑ to make sure I hold true to my faith
- ❑ to stick with a community of faith that can support me
- ❑ to remember the promises of God, like those in this passage
- ❑ I never have to face such things
- ❑ other:_____

6:17 a level place. In Matthew this was the "Sermon on the Mount"— what a contrast in locale! **from all Judea ... Tyre and Sidon.** Luke emphasizes the breadth of Jesus' ministry, geographically and culturally. Judea and Jerusalem, known for Jewish orthodoxy, were to the south, while Tyre and Sidon, Gentile areas, were to the northeast.

6:19 power came out from him. In Mark 5:30 and Luke 8:46, it is also said that when Jesus healed power "had gone forth" or "had gone out" from him.

6:20 poor. Where in Matthew Jesus speaks of "the poor in spirit," in Luke the reference is simply to "the poor." Even so, he is not saying that the poor are blessed simply because they are poor. Rather, it is a spirituality that goes with those not relying on riches that Jesus commends. The Hebrew word for "poor" had come in late Judaism to mean "saintly" or "pious."[2]

6:21 hungry. Once again this differs from Matthew where it takes the more spiritualized form of "hunger and thirst for righteousness" (Matt. 5:6). The overall emphasis here is the same as when Jesus says "some are last who will be first, and some are first who will be last" (Luke 13:30). But again the merit is not in being without the comforts of this world: the merit comes when people who are without such things learn to turn to God for their comfort and hope.

6:22 Like with Jesus himself, the suffering of the disciples will result from the ostracism, insults and slander they will experience at the hands of others, especially the religious authorities, who hate them.

6:23 what their ancestors did to the prophets. Elijah, Jeremiah, Ezekiel and other OT prophets faced consistent rejection, ridicule and abuse from people of their day.

6:24–26 But woe to ... These woes have no parallel in Matthew's

BIBLE STUDY NOTES (cont.) and CARING TIME:

account of the "Beatitudes," but they are the logical antithesis of what Jesus has already said.

6:26 speak well of you. This is a warning against the "people pleasers" of all ages! If everybody likes you, maybe it's because you never stand up for anything that might irritate people. Such was certainly not the pattern of Christ who constantly irritated the religious establishment by opposing their injustice and hypocrisy.

 This time is for developing and expressing your caring for each other as group members. We do this by sharing our needs and praying for each other's needs.

Each group member should answer the question,

How can this group help you in prayer this week?

Then join together in group prayer.

[1] Shirley DuBoulay, *Tutu: Voice of the Voiceless* (London: Hodder & Stoughton, 1988), pp. 168–169.
[2] S. MacLean Gilmour, "Luke," *The Interpreter's Bible,* Vol. VIII (New York: Abingdon Press, 1952), p. 118.

SERENDIPITY

Small Group
HANDOUT

WEEK 7: EPIPHANY 6
Acts of Perseverance
Luke 6:17–26

GATHERING 10 min.   **STUDY** 30 min.   **CARING** 20–40 min.

Leader: The agenda has three parts. In the Gathering time you'll be getting to know each other through an "ice-breaker." This will be for your total group. The Study time has two parts: (1) Story and (2) Scripture. If you are short of time, skip the Story and move to the Scripture. Begin by reading out loud the Story or the Scripture to the whole group. Then divide into groups of 4 for the Study time. Finally, regather the total group for the Caring time. Keep to this agenda: (1) Gathering—10 minutes, (2) Study—30 minutes, and (3) Caring—20–40 minutes.

 Fictional Fantasies. If you had the choice, which of the following situations from these popular movies would you most like to live out?

- ❑ meeting a real-live "extraterrestrial" (*ET*)
- ❑ touring a Jurassic Park (*Jurassic Park*)
- ❑ finding a magical secret that revives my youth (*Cocoon*)
- ❑ riding in a real time machine (*Back to the Future*)
- ❑ cloning myself so I can be several places at once (*Multiplicity*)
- ❑ connecting with a loved one now dead (*Ghost*)
- ❑ playing with baseball stars of the past (*Field of Dreams*)
- ❑ forcing someone to be always truthful (*Liar, Liar*)

INTRODUCTION STORY:

 Desmond Tutu Stands With the Oppressed. Poor, hungry, hated, excluded and reviled—For a long time there has been no people better described by those words than the black people of South Africa. But thanks to the way God has worked through people like Desmond Tutu, they are now "rallying from behind" and finding a greater sense of dignity and freedom. Courage and perseverance by people of faith is starting to win out. Shirley DuBoulay tells of some of the battles Tutu had to fight along the way in her book, *Tutu: Voice of the Voiceless*:

"Though Desmond Tutu's instincts to negotiate rather than confront, to reconcile rather than to attack, have received criticism, there has never been any doubting the courage of both his words and his actions, nor any wavering in his determination to stand with his people ... he has shown the sort of courage that can only come from a deep sense of the rightness of his cause.

"On one occasion in Soweto, seeing two large white policemen beating an elderly black man, he put his small frame between them, holding up his Bishop's cross until they stopped. At another he risked his life at a political funeral in the Ciskei by flinging himself across the body of a black security policeman being stoned by a large and angry mob. Thinking the crowd had desisted, he returned to the rostrum, his clothes soaked with the policeman's blood. They were, however, merely waiting for him to turn his back; later they dragged the policeman away and beat him to death. ...

"... On June 16th, 1982, he was taking a service in the Regina Mundi Church to commemorate the Soweto killings. ... Inside the church Tutu was addressing 5,000 blacks in what Joseph Lelyveld, who later heard a tape recording, called 'an emotionally charged political litany'; 'Is there anyone here who doubts that apartheid is doomed to failure?' he cried. 'No' the crowd shouted back. 'Is there anyone who doubts we are going to be free?' 'No' came the reply. Then Tutu made the crowd chant, 'We are going to be free!' "[1]

1. What do you think made Tutu so sure that apartheid was going to be defeated?
    ❏ He wasn't—he just wanted to make them think positively.
    ❏ He saw the "handwriting on the wall."
    ❏ He believed in God's power.
    ❏ He was confident in his own influence.

2. What would have been the hardest for you had you been in Desmond Tutu' situation?
    ❏ to take the physical risks
    ❏ to speak up on something so controversial
    ❏ to keep on hoping when things looked hopeless

SCRIPTURE:

A Come-From-Behind Victory. There is perhaps nothing more exciting in sports than a come-from-behind victory—the longshot horse comes from back in the pack to win the Kentucky Derby; the baseball team is 10 games behind late in the season, but "refuses to lose" and storms in to take the pennant; the outside shooter gets a hot hand and rallies his basketball team to get into the Final Four with a buzzer-beater. In many respects it was this kind of victory that Jesus promised to his followers. Most of them were definitely "behind" in this life. They were the poor, the hungry, the ones who mourned their low position in life. But Jesus promised to rally them for a "come-from-behind victory." They would laugh, be spiritually filled, and inherit the kingdom of God and a reward in heaven. In order to have this victory they needed to have enough faith in their God to persevere in the face of suffering and opposition. We may not face the same amount of suffering they did, but the promise remains. If we go through trials with the understanding that our God is a God that rallies us from behind, we can persevere in the midst of any situation.

Have someone in your group read the following passage out loud. Then go around on each question and let each person share their answer. Take advantage of the Study notes following the questionnaire. Be sure to save the last 20–40 minutes for the Caring time.

[17]He came down with them and stood on a level place, with a great crowd of his disciples and a great multitude of people from all Judea, Jerusalem, and the coast of Tyre and Sidon. [18]They had come to hear him and to be healed of their diseases; and those who were troubled with unclean spirits were cured. [19]And all in the crowd were trying to touch him, for power came out from him and healed all of them.

[20]Then he looked up at his disciples and said:

"Blessed are you who are poor,
for yours is the kingdom of God.
[21]"Blessed are you who are hungry now,
for you will be filled.
"Blessed are you who weep now,
for you will laugh.
[22]"Blessed are you when people hate you, and when they exclude you, revile you, and defame you on account of the Son of Man. [23]Rejoice in that day and leap for joy, for surely your reward is great in heaven; for that is what their ancestors did to the prophets.

[24]But woe to you who are rich,
for you have received your consolation.
[25]"Woe to you who are full now,
for you will be hungry.
"Woe to you who are laughing now,
for you will mourn and weep.

SCRIPTURE (cont.) and QUESTIONS:

[26]"Woe to you when all speak well of you, for that is what their ancestors did to the false prophets."

Luke 6:17–26

1. When you were in grade school, what was your family rich in, and what were you poor in? Indicate your responses on the scales below:

    MONEY

1	2	3	4	5
Poor				Rich

    LOVE

1	2	3	4	5
Poor				Rich

    LEARNING EXPERIENCES

1	2	3	4	5
Poor				Rich

    SPIRITUALITY

1	2	3	4	5
Poor				Rich

2. Which of the following do think best expresses Jesus' attitude toward poor people? (Choose as many as apply.)
    ❏ He loved them more than rich people.
    ❏ He saw more spirituality in them than he did in rich people.
    ❏ He felt sorry for them.
    ❏ He wanted to help them have opportunities for something better.
    ❏ He wanted them to keep on trying.
    ❏ He assumed they were poor because they were oppressed.

3. What does this passage say to you about how you need to be living your life?
    ❏ I need to share more of my possessions.
    ❏ I need to put my hope in God for a better life beyond this one.
    ❏ I need to put my hope in God for this life being better.
    ❏ I need to stop worrying so much about whether people speak well of me.
    ❏ I need to make sure my laughter and enjoyment of life is not at another's expense.
    ❏ other:_____

7. What would it take for you to behave toward the person you mentioned in question #6 in a way that is consistent with the teaching of this passage?

❐ I'd have to develop a severe case of amnesia!

❐ They would have to meet me halfway.

❐ I would just have to meditate more on how much God has loved and forgiven *me*.

❐ I'd need to give more study to the methods of Martin Luther King and Gandhi.

❐ I'd just have to remember what I said I wanted people to do to me (question #4).

❐ I'd need to ask for special strength from God.

❐ I'd just have to study this passage more and take it seriously.

❐ other:_____

Christians are not to assume that they are capable of passing the ultimate sentence upon other people. Only God is righteous enough to do that. **Forgive, and you will be forgiven.** The Greek word used here (*apoluo*) normally means to loose or release from a burden. This offers a picture of forgiveness as a releasing of someone from the guilt and consequences associated with their wrongdoing.

6:38 A good measure. A poor measure was when someone merely poured corn into a measuring jar so as to fill it up. A good measure meant that the corn was packed down, shaken to remove air spaces, and filled some more to pack in as much as the jar could possibly hold. The point here is that the generosity of Jesus' disciples will be fully matched by God's generosity to them.

6:27 Love your enemies. The traditional Jewish religious leadership only regarded fellow Jews as their neighbors, but Jesus makes it clear that there is no one to whom love is not owed. The word used for love here is *agape*. This type of love is not a matter of feelings, but of actions. *Agape* love is benevolent action done for another without the expectation of reward. It is shown by actively seeking the good of those who hate, blessing those who curse, praying for those who would mistreat, and willingly giving to those who would rob.

6:29 strikes you on the cheek. This was often done as a means of insulting another person.

6:31 Do to others ... The "Golden Rule" sums up what the righteousness of the disciples is to look like in terms of human relationships. The negative form of this rule ("Do not do to others what you do not want them to do to you") is found in Chinese, Jewish, Hindu, Buddhist, Greek and Roman litera-

ture. Jesus, however, alters this statement in a highly significant way. Whereas the negative rule was fulfilled by simply not bothering others, the positive rule requires the active pursuit of love toward others.

6:32–34 credit. This is to say, credit in the eyes of God. **even sinners.** In Matthew's version Jesus says "even the tax collectors do the same" (Matt. 5:46). Certainly we are all sinners, but what is implied here is people who have no desire to follow God's way.

6:35 children of the Most High. A child is one who reflects the character of the parent. While the traditional Jewish religious leadership assumed their relationship with God was based on their physical descent from Abraham, Jesus emphasizes that a lifestyle of love is the true mark of a child of God.

6:37 Do not judge. Moral discernment is not forbidden, but

 This time is for developing and expressing your caring for each other as group members. We do this by sharing our needs and praying for each other's needs.

Each group member should answer the question,

How can this group help you in prayer this week?

Then join together in group prayer.

¹Stephen Oates, *Let the Trumpet Sound: The Life of Martin Luther King, Jr.* (New York: Penguin Books, 1982), pp. 78–79.

SERENDIPITY

Small Group
HANDOUT

WEEK 8: EPIPHANY 7
Peaceful Acts
Luke 6:27–38

 GATHERING 10 min.   **STUDY** 30 min.   **CARING** 20–40 min.

Leader: The agenda has three parts. In the Gathering time you'll be getting to know each other through an "ice-breaker." This will be for your total group. The Study time has two parts: (1) Story and (2) Scripture. If you are short of time, skip the Story and move to the Scripture. Begin by reading out loud the Story or the Scripture to the whole group. Then divide into groups of 4 for the Study time. Finally, regather the total group for the Caring time. Keep to this agenda: (1) Gathering—10 minutes, (2) Study—30 minutes, and (3) Caring—20–40 minutes.

They're Singing My Song! If you could describe how your life has been going recently in terms of a song, which song in each of the following pairs would be more accurate?

IN THE AMOUNT OF ENERGY YOU FEEL

"Runnin' on Empty" _____ *"Feeling Stronger Every Day"*
(Jackson Browne)   (Chicago)

IN HOW YOU ARE FEELING ABOUT THE WORLD

"On the Eve of Destruction" _____ *"It's a Wonderful World"*
(Barry McGuire)   (Louie Armstrong)

IN HOW YOU ARE RELATING TO PEOPLE

"Mr. Lonely" _____ *"We Are Family"*
(Bobby Vinton)   (Sister Sledge)

INTRODUCTION STORY:

 Martin Luther King, Jr. Stands Up for Nonviolence. Martin Luther King, Jr. is known and respected throughout the world because of his campaign to bring justice and equality to African-Americans. But in contrast to how those of white European ancestry often treated blacks, and in contrast to the methods of some other black leaders, King advocated using nonviolence in this fight. His biographer Stephen Oates shares King's perspective in the book, *Let the Trumpet Sound: The Life of Martin Luther King, Jr.*:

" 'One of the great glories of American democracy is that we have the right to protest for rights,' King would say. 'This is a nonviolent protest. We are depending on moral and spiritual forces, using the method of passive resistance.' And this *is* resistance, he would insist, it is not stagnant passivity, a 'do-nothing' method. ... it is not a method for cowards. Gandhi said that if somebody uses it because he's afraid, he's not truly nonviolent. Really, nonviolence is the way of the strong. ...

" 'I want young men and young women who are not alive today but who will come into this world, with new privileges and new opportunities, I want them to know and see that these new privileges and opportunities did not come without somebody suffering and sacrificing for them.'

"But to gain these principles 'within the framework of the American democratic set-up,' we must eschew violence at all costs. For us, violence is both impractical and immoral. Remember that 'he who lives by the sword will perish by the sword.' Moreover, 'to meet hate with retaliatory hate would do nothing but intensify the existence of evil in the universe. Hate begets hate, violence begets violence; toughness begets a greater toughness. We must meet the forces of hate with the power of love; we must meet physical force with soul force. Our aim must never be to defeat or humiliate the white man, but to win his friendship and understanding.' We are asking the white man to open himself to the gift that God has given him for brotherhood."[1]

1. Martin Luther King, Jr. gave two basic reasons for eschewing violence—it doesn't work, and it isn't right. Do you agree? Which of those two reasons do you feel is most important?

2. King spoke of desiring to gain the "friendship and understanding" of people with white European ancestry. On the following scale, indicate to what degree you feel this has now happened:

```
1     2     3     4     5     6     7     8     9     10
Not at all                                      Totally!
```

SCRIPTURE:

 Impractical or Revolutionary? Jesus' teachings about turning the other cheek and loving our enemy are some of his best-known teachings. They are also his teachings that are most likely to be described as naive and impractical. Many people are convinced that the only way to fight oppressive powers is to fight fire with fire. Turning the other cheek is wimpy and impotent. But perhaps we should pause to consider who in human history has done the most to change the world in which we live. Certainly on the list would be the names of Martin Luther King, Jr., Mahatma Gandhi and Jesus Christ. The primary thing these three have in common is that they effected their changes in nonviolent ways. Not that they were passive pushovers! They stood up in powerful ways for what they believed. But their power was in their resolve to change things and their willingness to use love as their weapon. And yet their method still has not caught on. Perhaps that is because it is so much in conflict with popular secular wisdom. "It is not so because it *cannot* be so!" In a world so heavily invested in violence and power, people cannot afford to believe in love and nonviolence. Two thousand years after Christ, these teachings of his are still revolutionary.

Have someone in your group read the following passage out loud. Then go around on each question and let each person share their answer. Take advantage of the Study notes following the questionnaire. Be sure to save the last 20–40 minutes for the Caring time.

27 "But I say to you that listen, Love your enemies, do good to those who hate you, 28 bless those who curse you, pray for those who abuse you. 29 If anyone strikes you on the cheek, offer the other also; and from anyone who takes away your coat do not withhold even your shirt. 30 Give to everyone who begs from you; and if anyone takes away your goods, do not ask for them again. 31 Do to others as you would have them do to you.

32 "If you love those who love you, what credit is that to you? For even sinners love those who love them. 33 If you do good to those who do good to you, what credit is that to you? For even sinners do the same. 34 If you lend to those from whom you hope to receive, what credit is that to you? Even sinners lend to sinners, to receive as much again. 35 But love your enemies, do good, and lend, expecting nothing in return. Your reward will be great, and you will be children of the Most High; for he is kind to the ungrateful and the wicked. 36 Be merciful, just as your Father is merciful.

37 "Do not judge, and you will not be judged; do not condemn, and you will not be condemned. Forgive, and you will be forgiven; 38 give, and it will be given to you. A good measure, pressed down, shaken together, running over, will be put into your lap; for the measure you give will be the measure you get back."

Luke 6:27–38

QUESTIONS:

1. When you were in grade school, who "struck you on the cheek" and took things that belonged to you? How did you respond, and how did you feel about your response?

2. How would you describe your reaction to the teaching of this passage?
   - ❑ Dream the impossible dream.
   - ❑ It makes a lot of sense.
   - ❑ Looks good on paper, but I doubt it will work.
   - ❑ Good advice for oppressed people, but we're not oppressed.
   - ❑ It's too much to take in right now.
   - ❑ Too soft. You have to stand up to bullies!
   - ❑ I'm still confused!
   - ❑ other:_____

3. Why do you think Jesus advises the extreme measures he refers to in verses 27–30?
   - ❑ Maybe he was an undercover agent for a thieves' union!
   - ❑ He figured it would make the perpetrators feel guilty.
   - ❑ He knew the only hope was to teach the perpetrators how to love.
   - ❑ He wanted to remind us that God loves us even when we curse and abuse him.
   - ❑ other:_____

4. Jesus says to "Do to others as you would have them do to you." What is it that you are really needing people to do more to you?
   - ❑ listen to me
   - ❑ tolerate my weaknesses and idiosyncrasies
   - ❑ affirm me and believe in my potential
   - ❑ just give me a hug every now and then
   - ❑ let me be me
   - ❑ other:_____

5. Who is hardest for you to love?
   - ❑ those who curse me (who abuse me verbally)
   - ❑ those who strike me (who abuse me physically)
   - ❑ those who steal from me (who abuse me financially)

6. If you could choose one person who has hurt you so much that you don't see any way you could love him or her, what person would that be? (You don't have to share that person's identity with the group.)

QUESTIONS (cont.) and BIBLE STUDY NOTES:

BEARING GOOD FRUIT (ACTS OF LOVING MINISTRY)

1   2   3   4   5
Struggling   Doing great!

FOUNDING MY LIFE ON DOING WHAT JESUS SAYS

1   2   3   4   5
Struggling   Doing great!

6:39 a parable. Sometimes we think a parable has to be a long story, but here we have a parable told in two pointed sentences. A person who cannot see his or her own fallacies is blind. How could such a person "straighten out" someone else?

6:42 speck. The word refers to something very small like a splinter of wood or a bit of sawdust. **hypocrite.** This is the person who refuses to acknowledge the gulf that exists between their lifestyle and their profession of values. A person is not hypocritical because they fail to reach the high set of standards they have set for themselves: they are hypocritical when they make believe they have reached those standards and stand in judgment on others for not reaching them also. **log.** This is an example of how Jesus reveals a sense of humor through his use of hyperbole. Can you imagine a person walking around with an entire log in his eye, trying to examine other people's eyes?!

6:44 each tree is known by its own fruit. Hypocrites may think they are fooling others by the praise they give to their own moral performance, but the people around them are looking more at what they are doing.

6:45 out of the abundance of the heart. The way we act on the outside eventually reveals what we are on the inside. The key to change then is changing the heart. John tells us that change is brought about by a genuine reaction to the love God has shown us in Jesus Christ: "We love because he first loved us" (1 John 4:19).

6:46 Lord, Lord. "Lord" was a title of respect often used for rabbis by their disciples. The repetition of the title served to show heightened honor. But Jesus' question here shows that true discipleship is not just a matter of verbally honoring him—they must honor him with their lives.

6:47–49 This final parable reflects on the climate of Palestine, which was dry most of the year. However, the autumn heavy rains would turn what appeared to be dry land into a raging river as flash floods swept down the ravines. Only homes built on a solid foundation (obedience to Jesus) will stand when the storm comes (the final judgment).

CARING TIME and PRAYER REQUESTS:

 This time is for developing and expressing your caring for each other as group members. We do this by sharing our needs and praying for each other's needs.

Each group member should answer the question,

How can this group help you in prayer this week?

Then join together in group prayer.

SERENDIPITY

Small Group
HANDOUT

WEEK 9: EPIPHANY 8
Acts of Integrity
Luke 6:39–49

 GATHERING
10 min.

 STUDY
30 min.

 CARING
20–40 min.

Leader: The agenda has three parts. In the Gathering time you'll be getting to know each other through an "ice-breaker." This will be for your total group. The Study time has two parts: (1) Story and (2) Scripture. If you are short of time, skip the Story and move to the Scripture. Begin by reading out loud the Story or the Scripture to the whole group. Then divide into groups of 4 for the Study time. Finally, regather the total group for the Caring time. Keep to this agenda: (1) Gathering—10 minutes, (2) Study—30 minutes, and (3) Caring—20–40 minutes.

Our Tool Chest. In many respects this group is like a "tool chest," with each member being a different kind of "tool" to help build community. Write the name of each group member next to these tools. Then focus on one group member at a time and have the others share what "tool" they see them being like.

_____HAMMER: You drive home your points with power.

_____SAW: You cut "to the heart of the matter."

_____LEVEL: You keep the group on an even keel.

_____EXTRA-FINE SANDPAPER: You "gently polish" people to bring out their best.

_____SCREWDRIVER: You secure the connections that hold us together.

_____CHISEL: You know how to cut away what isn't essential.

_____CROW BAR: When something isn't right, you help us take it apart so it can be redone.

_____SAFETY GLASSES: You help us see ourselves clearly, yet safely.

¹Victoria Lincoln, *Teresa: A Woman* (Albany, NY: State University of New York Press, 1984), pp. 40–41.

INTRODUCTION STORY:

 The Conversion of Teresa of Avila. Teresa of Avila was a Christian mystic who lived in Spain in the sixteenth century. She wrote much on the spiritual disciplines, and her writings have inspired many. She was canonized in 1622, and in 1970 she became the first woman to be proclaimed a Doctor of the Church. But she did not come to her understandings easily. She struggled with her sexuality, and got involved in passionate, ill-advised relationships early in her life. She turned away from these to Christ after reading Augustine, whose writings had only just before been made available in her native Spanish. Her biographer Victoria Lincoln tells the story in her book, *Teresa: A Woman:*

"At that time, they gave me the *Confessions* of St. Augustine; it seems as if the Lord ordained it, for I did not try to get it for myself and had never seen a copy ... When I started reading the *Confessions* it seemed to me that I was seeing my own self right there. When I got as far as his conversion and read how he heard that voice in the garden, it was just as if the Lord gave it to me, too, to judge from the grief that filled my heart. ...

"The voice in the garden, you remember directed Augustine to pick up his Bible and read and he opened to these words of St. Paul: 'Not in rioting and drunkenness, not in whorings and lasciviousness, not in quarrelings and jealousy, but take on the nature of the Lord Jesus Christ and give no more thought to the lusts of the flesh.'

"Augustine thereafter loathed the flesh in the familiar pattern of the libertine turned puritan. Woman, he said, is a temple built over a sewer. Pious souls rarely mean anything else when they say, 'The greatest saints were the greatest sinners.'

"Teresa's conversion filled her with a love for the all-forgiving Christ that no man could rival; but she did not turn puritan. She would always take it for granted that girls needed to be guarded from temptation and make excuses for those who fell: 'They were young ... not properly watched over ... set a bad example.' ...

"Teresa's conversion was above all a release from her obsession with the sins of the flesh. Little by little it freed her to take up arms against the sins that more gravely endangered the life of the Church: hypocrisy, greed, ambition... ."[1]

1. When have you found yourself or someone you know in one of the following categories, becoming as the story says "puritanical" in campaigning for your own lifestyle change?
   - ❏ reformed smoker
   - ❏ reformed alcoholic
   - ❏ reformed healthy eater (after a health crisis)
   - ❏ reformed at expressing feelings (after counseling)
   - ❏ zealous new Christian
   - ❏ other:_____

2. What do you think is the key to following the example of Teresa of Avila in reforming her own life without becoming puritanical and judgmental toward others?

SCRIPTURE:

 A Life With Integrity. The word *integrity* means "the quality or state of being complete." And so when your life has integrity, you are able to put the "complete package" together—your words and beliefs line up with your actions. Jesus talks about that kind of life in our lectionary passage for this week. A person who thinks that just listening to Jesus' words is enough is incomplete—they lack integrity. A person who both hears Jesus' words and acts on them is complete—they have integrity. People who lack integrity, spiritual completeness, only know how to apply Jesus' words to someone else—they can speak at great lengths on what everyone else is doing wrong. Christian integrity comes when we first apply Jesus' words to ourselves, making our lives line up with what we believe. When we do that, we don't have to stand around condemning others. Our lives will serve in a much more positive way to help them see their own more clearly.

Have someone in your group read the following passage out loud. Then go around on each question and let each person share their answer. Take advantage of the Study notes following the questionnaire. Be sure to save the last 20–40 minutes for the Caring time.

39He also told them a parable: "Can a blind person guide a blind person? Will not both fall into a pit? 40A disciple is not above the teacher, but everyone who is fully qualified will be like the teacher. 41Why do you see the speck in your neighbor's eye, but do not notice the log in your own eye? 42Or how can you say to your neighbor, 'Friend, let me take out the speck in your eye,' when you yourself do not see the log in your own eye? You hypocrite, first take the log out of your own eye, and then you will see clearly to take the speck out of your neighbor's eye.

43"No good tree bears bad fruit, nor again does a bad tree bear good fruit; 44for each tree is known by its own fruit. Figs are not gathered from thorns, nor are grapes picked from a bramble bush. 45The good person out of the good treasure of the heart produces good, and the evil person out of evil treasure produces evil; for it is out of the abundance of the heart that the mouth speaks.

46"Why do you call me 'Lord, Lord,' and do not do what I tell you? 47I will show you what someone is like who comes to me, hears my words, and acts on them. 48That one is like a man building a house, who dug deeply and laid the foundation on rock; when a flood arose, the river burst against that house but could not shake it, because it had been well built. 49But the one who hears and does not act is like a man who built a house on the ground without a foundation. When the river burst against it, immediately it fell, and great was the ruin of that house."

Luke 6:39–49

QUESTIONS:

1. What was the best house you have ever lived in? What did you particularly like about it? What kind of house was it?

2. What is the rock Jesus recommends as a strong foundation?
   - ❏ belief in Jesus himself
   - ❏ acting on faith, as opposed to talking about it
   - ❏ a sound value system
   - ❏ other:_____

3. Which of the following are you most likely to be "blind" to?
   - ❏ how I look
   - ❏ my faults
   - ❏ what is going on around me
   - ❏ social convention
   - ❏ the faults of people I care about

4. Extending Jesus' analogy, how big do you think the object in your own eye is right now?
   - ❏ It's just a speck.
   - ❏ It's a full-blown tree.
   - ❏ It's a rather large speck.
   - ❏ How about a Giant Sequoia?!
   - ❏ Okay, it's a log!

5. Which of the following do you think best expresses Jesus' intent for how a person should deal with their own faults and the faults of others?
   - ❏ Once you have reformed your own life, it's fine to try to reform those around you.
   - ❏ Since you *never* fully "remove everything from your own eye," you should never try to reform someone else.
   - ❏ If you are honestly seeking to straighten out your own life, you can also give suggestions for change to someone else.
   - ❏ The more we are aware of our own faults, the more forgiving we are of the faults of others.
   - ❏ other:_____

6. How would you grade yourself on the various aspects of Christian integrity included in this passage?

NOT BEING JUDGMENTAL

1	2	3	4	5
Struggling				Doing great!

HONESTLY EVALUATING MY OWN LIFE

1	2	3	4	5
Struggling				Doing great!

8. How would you describe your relationship with God right now?
   - ❑ on top of the mountain
   - ❑ climbing the mountain
   - ❑ in the desert—bone dry
   - ❑ in the valley
   - ❑ in the swamp
   - ❑ on the rocks

9:28 *about eight days.* Why Luke has eight days instead of Mark's six days (Mark 9:2) is unclear, but it may simply represent Luke's abandonment of Mark's form of counting days that included the present one. ***the mountain to pray.*** This may be Mt. Hermon, a 9,000-foot mountain located some 12 miles from Caesarea Philippi (though early tradition says the Transfiguration occurred on Mt. Tabor, located southwest of the Sea of Galilee). In the past, God had revealed himself on other mountains, such as when he appeared to Moses on Mt. Sinai (Ex. 24) and to Elijah on Mt. Horeb (1 Kings 19). Also, when Moses went to Mt. Nebo (Deut. 34) he *saw* the future God had planned, the Promised Land; when Jesus went to the top of this mount, he *became* the future, a vision of the future God had planned.

9:29 *dazzling white.* Luke does not use the word "transfigured," but his description of the change that came over Jesus is akin to that which occurred to Moses on Mt. Sinai (Ex. 34:29–35). Similar descriptions are found in John's attempt to describe Jesus in his ascended glory in Revelation 1:13–16.

9:30 *Moses and Elijah.* Moses was the greatest figure in the OT. It was to him that God gave the Law which became the very heart of the nation. It was he who brought the religion of Israel into being. And it was Moses who prophesied that God would one day send another prophet to lead his people (Deut. 18:15). The early Christians took this to be a prophecy about Jesus. Elijah was a great prophet. The Jews expected he would return just prior to the coming of the salvation they had been promised. As Moses represented the Law, Elijah represented the prophets, and visually the message here is that the Law and the prophets both testify to Jesus as the Messiah of God.

9:31 *his departure.* Literally "his exodus." Jesus' death, resurrection and ascension are seen as a new exodus wherein he, as the new Moses, leads people to a new Promised Land.

9:33 *dwellings.* Peter might have had in mind the huts of intertwined branches which were put up at the Festival of Tabernacles to commemorate Israel's time in the wilderness. Or he might be thinking of the "tent of meeting" where God met with Moses. In making this suggestion, Peter shows his confusion about this event. Did this mean that Jesus had come into his glory without the suffering he told them about?

9:34–35 *a cloud.* In the OT when God appeared, it was often in a cloud (Ex. 16:10; 19:9; 24:15–18; 40:34–38). ***a voice.*** Once again, as he had done at the baptism of Jesus (3:22), God acclaims that Jesus is the Son. ***listen to him!*** This is an allusion to Moses' great prophecy about the coming prophet (Deut. 18:15).

9:36 *told no one.* Why didn't they tell anyone? While this is unclear in the present context, it should be noted that Jesus was often reported to have asked people to remain silent about a healing or other evidence of his messiahship (Luke 4:41; Mark 1:43–45; 3:12; 5:43; 7:36). In Mark's version of the Transfiguration it is said that Jesus ordered them to tell no one about what they had seen. The most common theory for why this secrecy was desirable is that people had too many misconceptions about what the Messiah was to be and do. The one Jesus was particularly concerned about was that the people thought the Messiah would be a military figure leading a revolt. Jesus did not want to be pressured into such a role.

 This time is for developing and expressing your caring for each other as group members. We do this by sharing our needs and praying for each other's needs, as well as by affirming the strengths we see in each other.

Think about the others in your group. What about each person has especially affected you since this group began. Perhaps it was something the person did or said. Focus on one group member at a time, and have the others share how they have been touched by that person. Make sure everyone has a chance to be affirmed. Then, remembering what people shared, close in prayer, thanking God for each other and what you are experiencing as a group.

¹Stephen Oates, *Let the Trumpet Sound: The Life of Martin Luther King, Jr.* (New York: Penguin Books, 1982), pp. 110–111.

SERENDIPITY
Small Group
HANDOUT

WEEK 10: LAST EPIPHANY
Acts of Eternal Vision
Luke 9:28–36

GATHERING 10 min.   **STUDY** 30 min.   **CARING** 20–40 min.

Leader: The agenda has three parts. In the Gathering time you'll be getting to know each other through an "ice-breaker." This will be for your total group. The Study time has two parts: (1) Story and (2) Scripture. If you are short of time, skip the Story and move to the Scripture. Begin by reading out loud the Story or the Scripture to the whole group. Then divide into groups of 4 for the Study time. Finally, regather the total group for the Caring time. Keep to this agenda: (1) Gathering—10 minutes, (2) Study—30 minutes, and (3) Caring—20–40 minutes.

My Life as a B-Grade Horror Movie. Imagine that a producer has decided to turn your life into a B-grade horror flick. Which of the following titles would it most likely have?

- ❑ *Attack of the Killer Government Report Forms*
- ❑ *Lost in Cyberspace*
- ❑ *My Mother Was an Alien*
- ❑ *The Clutter That Ate (Your Name)'s Desk*
- ❑ *Son/Daughter of Frankenstein*
- ❑ *I Was a Teenage Mutant*
- ❑ *Invasion of the Money-Sucking Relatives*
- ❑ *Attack of the Crazed Credit Card Slasher*

INTRODUCTION STORY:

 Martin Luther King, Jr.'s Vision. Martin Luther King, Jr. is known and respected throughout the world because of his campaign to bring justice and equality to African-Americans. The course was often difficult and frightening for him, but his resolve was steadied both by supportive people and the vision God gave him for what lay ahead. His biographer Stephen Oates shares King's perspective in the book, *Let the Trumpet Sound: The Life of Martin Luther King, Jr.*:

" ... On Monday night, he addressed a mass meeting, and for the first time broke down in public. Clutching the pulpit, his face contorted in pain, he invited the audience to join him in prayer—and then felt seized by an uncontrollable emotion. 'Lord,' he cried, 'I hope no one will have to die as a result of our struggle for freedom in Montgomery. Certainly I don't want to die. But if anyone has to die, let it be me.'

" 'No, no,' his people chorused.

"King could not continue his prayer. ... Finally some friends helped him to a seat.

" 'Unexpectedly,' King wrote later, 'this episode brought me great relief.' After the meeting, many people assured him that 'we were all together until the end.' But the incident was cathartic in another way too: by praying that he be killed if somebody must be, he freed himself from his guilt that *I am to blame, I have caused all this suffering*. He was ready to lead again. He felt strong again. He felt God beside him, and he did not fear to die. ...

"Before dawn on Sunday, January 27, the forces of evil struck again, as terrorizing whites bombed a Negro home and a Negro service station and cab stand. Somebody found an unexploded bomb, consisting of twelve sticks of dynamite, still smoldering on King's own porch. In the chill of the morning, King addressed a gathering crowd from his porch, 'Tell Montgomery that they can keep shooting and I'm going to stand up to them; tell Montgomery they can keep bombing and I'm going to stand up to them. If I had to die tomorrow morning I would be happy because I've been to the Mountaintop and I've seen the Promised Land, and it's going to be here in Montgomery.' "[1]

1. What do you think helped King most in getting past this time of guilt and fear?
   - ❏ getting these feelings out into the open
   - ❏ receiving the support of the people
   - ❏ getting in touch with God's "vision from the mountaintop"

2. When have you been most fearful of what the future might hold for you? What helped you get past your fear?

SCRIPTURE and QUESTIONS:

 Beyond the "Five-Year Plan." Any kind of group that wishes to survive in our changing world, whether it be a company, a community action group or a church, needs to do some form of long-range planning. Many develop something like a "five-year plan." Such a plan almost always has to be altered and adapted, but at least it is a vehicle for looking ahead and planning for the changes that might come. When Jesus stood on the Mount of Transfiguration, God was saying through him, "I have something that goes much further than a 'five-year plan'—I have a plan for eternity!" When Jesus was transfigured he became a vision of the future in himself—the glory of his triumph showed for all who were present to see. What that meant for the disciples later was that they had an even more secure source of encouragement. They knew that the Jesus who died and rose again would reign in dazzling glory like they had seen him on that mount. Knowing that, there would be nothing they could not face!

Have someone in your group read the following passage out loud. Then go around on each question and let each person share their answer. Take advantage of the Study notes following the questionnaire. Be sure to save the last 20–40 minutes for the Caring time.

> **[28]Now about eight days after these sayings Jesus took with him Peter and John and James, and went up on the mountain to pray. [29]And while he was praying, the appearance of his face changed, and his clothes became dazzling white. [30]Suddenly they saw two men, Moses and Elijah, talking to him. [31]They appeared in glory and were speaking of his departure, which he was about to accomplish at Jerusalem. [32]Now Peter and his companions were weighed down with sleep; but since they had stayed awake, they saw his glory and the two men who stood with him. [33]Just as they were leaving him, Peter said to Jesus, "Master, it is good for us to be here; let us make three dwellings, one for you, one for Moses, and one for Elijah"—not knowing what he said. [34]While he was saying this, a cloud came and overshadowed them; and they were terrified as they entered the cloud. [35]Then from the cloud came a voice that said, "This is my Son, my Chosen; listen to him!" [36]When the voice had spoken, Jesus was found alone. And they kept silent and in those days told no one any of the things they had seen.**
> *Luke 9:28–36*

1. Where have you gone in nature that, like the disciples on this mountaintop, you experienced God in a new way?

2. If you could have anyone from the past (apart from Christ himself) appear to you and talk about their spiritual journey, who would you want to appear?

QUESTIONS (cont.):

3. What do you see as the *most* significant thing about the change in Jesus' appearance?
   - ❏ The disciples were allowed to visualize Christ's spiritual purity.
   - ❏ The disciples were allowed to see the divine Christ instead of just the human Jesus.
   - ❏ The disciples were allowed to see Jesus as he would be after his resurrection and ascension.
   - ❏ other:_____

4. What do you think was wrong with what Peter said to Jesus in verse 33?
   - ❏ What would spiritual beings need with such dwellings?
   - ❏ Jesus couldn't stay on that mountain—he had a mission!
   - ❏ Peter was thinking of physical arrangements—not spiritual arrangements.
   - ❏ He didn't realize he was there to *listen*, not *say* or *do*!

5. Had *you* had the opportunity to be in Peter's place and say something to Jesus while all these things were happening, which of the following might come the closest to what you would have said?
   - ❏ duh ...
   - ❏ Do I have time to go down and get my camera?
   - ❏ So ... like, you know these guys?
   - ❏ So what does this mean ... "Dos for Dummies" version, please!
   - ❏ other:_____

6. What importance do you think this event had to the disciples later?
   - ❏ Evidently none—they were really "thick"!
   - ❏ It helped them connect Jesus to the Old Testament.
   - ❏ It helped them face death, knowing who they would meet on the other side.
   - ❏ It helped them have confidence they were following the right person.
   - ❏ other:_____

7. If you could have a vision like this of what is to come in your future, which of the following would you rather have a vision of?
   - ❏ what I will look like when I'm in heaven
   - ❏ what my legacy on earth will be after I'm gone
   - ❏ the faces of loved ones I will see in heaven
   - ❏ what the world will be like when my children are my age
   - ❏ other:_____

QUESTIONS (cont.) and BIBLE STUDY NOTES:

6. What has helped you overcome temptation when it comes?

- ☐ Scripture
- ☐ prayer
- ☐ talking to someone about it
- ☐ telling Satan to take a hike
- ☐ running away
- ☐ talking myself out of it
- ☐ other:_____

4:1 led by the Spirit. The work of the Spirit is a big concern for Luke both in his Gospel and in Acts. Jesus' struggle with Satan was not due to being apart from the Spirit, but an integral part of the Spirit's preparing him for his mission.

4:2 forty days ... tempted. Moses fasted forty days on Mount Sinai while receiving the commandments (Ex. 34:28), and Israel was in the wilderness forty years (Deut. 8:2). Matthew, in his Gospel, pictures Jesus as the new Moses, and his followers as the new Israel.

4:3 If you are the Son of God ... Satan challenges Jesus at the point of his identity. Surely it must have seemed ironic that the Son of God, a title of royalty and power, should be tired, hungry and apparently alone in such a desolate area. **bread.** Satan's suggestion is not evil in itself, but in the context of this test, it would be like Israel's complaining that God had not adequately met their needs in the desert (Ex. 16). Rather than trust God, the temptation is for Jesus to take matters into his own hands. According to *The Interpreter's Bible*, "In a country of which not more than one fifth of the land was arable under the best of conditions, and which was frequently plagued by extremes of drought and flood,

bread was a precious commodity."[2]

4:4 Jesus quotes Deuteronomy 8:3, which was originally a reflection on how God met the hunger needs of his people by providing them manna. Because of that, Moses asserts that what is ultimately important is not hunger but dependence on God.

4:5–13 Luke reverses Matthew's order for the second and third temptations. Chronology was not the main point for either author. Luke may have wanted to conclude with the scene at the temple to indicate Jesus' final victory over Satan in Jerusalem.

4:5–7 The second temptation is the appeal of ambition and glory. Probably through some form of vision, Satan enabled Jesus to see the splendor, wealth and power that is represented by the world's political authorities. For the price tag of rejecting God, Satan offers Jesus a painless, immediate way to this power and fame. The irony was that by his obedience to the Father Jesus would become the King of Kings, possessing all authority and power.

4:8 Jesus quotes Deuteronomy 6:13, again affirming his loyalty to God and his ways.

BIBLE STUDY NOTES (cont.) and CARING TIME:

4:9–12 The final temptation attempts to raise doubts about Jesus' identity, the Father's dependability, and the Scripture as a source of authority. Twice rebuked by Scripture, Satan now quotes Psalm 91:11–12 to substantiate his point. In their use of the Scripture, Jesus and Satan are not simply trading verses, but are using it in radically different ways. Satan quotes this psalm (meant to give assurance of God's presence to believers even in the midst of hard times) entirely out of its context. He does so in order to suggest that Jesus ought to do something reckless to "prove" God's faithfulness to his Word. In contrast, Jesus' quotes are summaries of major OT themes which are crystallized in the particular verses he uses.

 This time is for developing and expressing your caring for each other as group members. We do this by sharing our needs and praying for each other's needs.

Each group member should answer the question,

How can this group help you in prayer this week?

Then join together in group prayer.

[1]Frances Gies, *Joan of Arc: The Legend and the Reality* (New York: Harper & Row, 1981), pp. 88–89.
[2]S. MacLean Gilmour, "Luke," *The Interpreter's Bible*, Vol. VIII (New York: Abingdon, 1952), p. 85.

SERENDIPITY
Small Group
HANDOUT

WEEK 1: LENT 1
Temptations Along the Road
Luke 4:1–13

 GATHERING 10 min.   **STUDY** 30 min.   **CARING** 20–40 min.

Leader: The agenda has three parts. In the Gathering time you'll be getting to know each other through an "ice-breaker." This will be for your total group. The Study time has two parts: (1) Story and (2) Scripture. If you are short of time, skip the Story and move to the Scripture. Begin by reading out loud the Story or the Scripture to the whole group. Then divide into groups of 4 for the Study time. Finally, regather the total group for the Caring time. Keep to this agenda: (1) Gathering—10 minutes, (2) Study—30 minutes, and (3) Caring—20–40 minutes.

 Imports From the Past. Imagine that you are starting a new company that is very high-tech—with a push of a button you can "import" experiences from the past so people can re-experience them today. To "test market" this, what events and experiences from your own history would you want to "import" so your children or grandchildren could experience them? Import from the following categories:

1. A special place in the neighborhood where you lived the longest as a child. Describe it to the group.

2. An especially exciting community gathering. What was especially fun for children at these gatherings?

3. An intriguing person you would like your children and grandchildren to meet. Maybe they are now dead or you've lost contact or they have just changed. What was this person like then?

INTRODUCTION STORY:

Joan of Arc Prepares Her Army. Joan of Arc is one of history's great stories of female courage. She was convinced that God was speaking to her to lead the armies of France to fight for their freedom against England. But her role in history was more than a political one. She led through a spiritual vision and a courage that lifted a people who had lost heart. While many Christians today question the violent values of war, it is Joan's kind of vision we need. Joan knew that an army needed more than military preparation to go into battle—they needed spiritual preparation. Her biographer Frances Gies tells the story of how Joan prepared her army for battle at Orleans in the book, *Joan of Arc: The Legend and the Reality:*

"Joan was not pleased by the condition of the army. ... Her understanding of morale, though instinctive, was acute, and she hastily commissioned Pasquerel to have a banner made in addition to the standard and pennon which she already had. Instead of floating from a pole, this, as a religious rather than military rallying point, hung from a crosspiece, and was like the banners regularly carried in religious processions. The image was that of the crucified Christ. During the few days they were at Blois, Joan, 'Twice a day, morning and evening, caused all the priests to assemble, and, when they were met together, they sang anthems and hymns to Saint Mary, and Joan was with them and she would not allow the soldiers to mingle with the priests until they had confessed. And she exhorted all the soldiers to confess so that they might attend the assembly. ...'

"... To complete the work of purification Joan made the soldiers get rid of their camp followers (throughout her career she conducted a vendetta against the loose women who followed the armies), and she also made them leave all their baggage when they set out. The fact that she was able to impose these stringent rules on the undisciplined troops of Charles VII demonstrates the degree of ascendancy which she had already achieved. ..."[1]

1. Why do you think Joan of Arc put her army through these spiritual disciplines?
   - ❏ so they would be ready to die
   - ❏ so God would be with them in the fight
   - ❏ because people are physically strongest when they are spiritually strong
   - ❏ because it was right

2. What "battle" do you see yourself having to face in the coming weeks? What spiritual disciplines might help you prepare for it?

SCRIPTURE:

Road Tested. A staple of automobile advertising is the driver taking their particular model of car out on a winding, treacherous road, showing how the car meets every challenge. Sometimes a warning will flash on the screen saying something like, "Warning: Professional driver on a closed road—do not try this yourself!" The idea behind such road testing is to show that this car doesn't just work well in theory—it has proven itself in practice. Well, if Jesus could have hired an ad agency as he entered his ministry, they might have also used the phrase "road tested"! He could not have gone out and taught the people about how to make it on the tough roads of life, with all of the temptations along the way, if he had not been through it himself. When Christ went through his temptations in the wilderness, he was making sure that he never spoke from the safety of some ivory tower—he was talking about what he knew to work in practice.

Have someone in your group read the following passage out loud. Then go around on each question and let each person share their answer. Take advantage of the Study notes following the questionnaire. Be sure to save the last 20–40 minutes for the Caring time.

4 *Jesus, full of the Holy Spirit, returned from the Jordan and was led by the Spirit in the wilderness, ²where for forty days he was tempted by the devil. He ate nothing at all during those days, and when they were over, he was famished. ³The devil said to him, "If you are the Son of God, command this stone to become a loaf of bread." ⁴Jesus answered him, "It is written, 'One does not live by bread alone.' "*

⁵Then the devil led him up and showed him in an instant all the kingdoms of the world. ⁶And the devil said to him, "To you I will give their glory and all this authority; for it has been given over to me, and I give it to anyone I please. ⁷If you, then, will worship me, it will all be yours." ⁸Jesus answered him, "It is written,

'Worship the Lord your God,
and serve only him.' "

⁹Then the devil took him to Jerusalem, and placed him on the pinnacle of the temple, saying to him, "If you are the Son of God, throw yourself down from here, ¹⁰for it is written,

'He will command his angels concerning you,
to protect you,'

¹¹and

'On their hands they will bear you up,
so that you will not dash your foot against a stone.' "

¹²Jesus answered him, "It is said, 'Do not put the Lord your God to the test.' " ¹³When the devil had finished every test, he departed from him until an opportune time.

Luke 4:1–13

QUESTIONS:

1. When you were in the sixth grade, what were you most likely to be tempted by?
   - ❏ shoplifting my favorite candy
   - ❏ lying to my parent(s) about how the vase got broken
   - ❏ skipping school
   - ❏ an opportunity to try smoking cigarettes
   - ❏ cheating at a card or board game
   - ❏ other:_____

2. Who does the devil remind you of in this story?
   - ❏ a prostitute
   - ❏ a pushy used-car salesman
   - ❏ a drug pusher
   - ❏ the emperor in Star Wars
   - ❏ a corrupt politician
   - ❏ someone much more subtle

3. Which of the temptations Jesus faced would have been hardest for you?
   - ❏ taking an easy out—turning stones to bread
   - ❏ going after power and possession—worshiping Satan to get the kingdoms of the world
   - ❏ showing off—throwing myself off the pinnacle of the temple

4. If the devil wanted to tempt *you*, what three things would he put before you? (Choose from the following list.)
   - ❏ a chance to be more successful
   - ❏ a chance to be famous
   - ❏ a chance to be really rich
   - ❏ just a chance to be debt-free
   - ❏ a really attractive person of the opposite sex
   - ❏ a promise of complete safety for me and my family
   - ❏ other:_____

5. When do you find yourself most vulnerable to the tempter?
   - ❏ when I'm tired or under stress
   - ❏ when I'm alone or away from home
   - ❏ after a spiritual high
   - ❏ when I'm not expecting it
   - ❏ when I let my mind dwell on certain things

BIBLE STUDY NOTES:

13:31–33 Pharisees. Most often the Pharisees are mentioned as opposing Christ and his work. Based on that, some contend that these Pharisees were just trying to scare Jesus out of their territory. However, it is not necessary to think that. It is likely that some Pharisees were sympathetic to Jesus. The Pharisees were actually closer theologically to him than were their rivals the Sadducees. Jesus agreed with the Pharisees (over against the Sadducees) that the prophets were scriptural, and that there was life after death. The apostle Paul was a former Pharisee. **Herod.** Herod's dominion included Galilee and Perea, the probable location of Jesus at this point. Herod had already killed John the Baptist (see Matt. 14:1–12; Luke 9:7–9). The attitude Jesus shows here is similar to the one he showed when Pilate told him he had the power to release or crucify him, and Jesus responded that the only power Pilate had was what God had given him, and therefore all was in God's hands. It was this confidence that all was ultimately in his Father's hands that sustained Jesus.

13:32 tell that fox. Sometimes the fox was used as a symbol of a cunning person, while at other times it symbolized an insignificant person (i.e. a fox as compared to a lion). Both ideas may be in Jesus' mind. **casting out demons and performing cures.** These are representative signs of God's kingdom (7:21; 9:1; 10:9). In spite of Herod's threat, Jesus will pursue the agenda of God's kingdom until God's time for it to stop arrives.

13:33 impossible for a prophet. Prophets, like Jeremiah, did die outside of Jerusalem. The force of the saying is that just as the authorities associated with the temple in Jerusalem consistently opposed the prophets and executed some of them, so Jesus will experience the same fate.

13:34–35 Jesus, like Jeremiah (Lam. 3:49–51), was heartbroken to have to warn the city of the coming judgment due to its hardness against God (see also Matt. 23:37–39). **kills the prophets.** See 1 Kings 18:4; 19:10; Nehemiah 9:26; Jeremiah 26: 20–21. **stones those who are sent to it.** A reference to Zechariah who was stoned for confronting Israel with its sin (2 Chron. 24:20–21). **How often.** While Matthew, Mark and Luke only tell of the visit to Jerusalem which Jesus made prior to his death, John's Gospel records several confrontations with the authorities that took place during various visits Jesus made to Jerusalem. However, Jesus here may actually be speaking from a divine perspective, referring to how often God through history had wanted to gather Jerusalem to himself. The metaphor of a bird and her young to describe God's relationship to his people occurs at several places in the OT (Deut. 32:11–12; Ps. 36:7; Isa. 31:5).

13:35 your house is left to you. The house is the temple from which the presence of God will depart because of the people's rejection of the Messiah (Jer. 12:7; 22:5; Ezek. 10:18).

CARING TIME and PRAYER REQUESTS:

 This time is for developing and expressing your caring for each other as group members. We do this by sharing our needs and praying for each other's needs.

Each group member should answer the question,

> *How can this group help you in prayer this week?*

Then join together in group prayer.

¹James R. Brockman, *The Word Remains: A Life of Oscar Romero* (Maryknoll, NY: Orbis, 1982), p. 211.

SERENDIPITY
Small Group
HANDOUT

WEEK 2: LENT 2
A Road With Dangers
Luke 13:31–35

 GATHERING 10 min.   **STUDY** 30 min.   **CARING** 20–40 min.

Leader: The agenda has three parts. In the Gathering time you'll be getting to know each other through an "ice-breaker." This will be for your total group. The Study time has two parts: (1) Story and (2) Scripture. If you are short of time, skip the Story and move to the Scripture. Begin by reading out loud the Story or the Scripture to the whole group. Then divide into groups of 4 for the Study time. Finally, regather the total group for the Caring time. Keep to this agenda: (1) Gathering—10 minutes, (2) Study—30 minutes, and (3) Caring—20–40 minutes.

Roadside Service. Imagine that you are a car. If there is one thing most of us know about cars, it's that you have to repair them! What kind of "repair" do you most need as you travel on your road right now? Choose from the options listed below:

STUCK ACCELERATOR—I can't seem to slow down.

NEW WINDSHIELD WIPERS—I can't get a clear view of where I'm going.

SLUGGISH STARTER—I can't seem to get going in the morning.

NEW SHOCK ABSORBERS—I'm hitting the "bumps" of life really hard.

NEW RADIATOR—I'm "overheating" and taking my anger out on others.

NEW HEATER COIL—I'm missing warmth in my life.

JUST LIGHT MAINTENANCE—I'm "low maintenance" and am doing great!

COMPLETE ENGINE OVERHAUL—All the power is gone from my life.

INTRODUCTION STORY:

Warnings for Oscar Romero. When the need came for a new Catholic Archbishop for El Salvador in 1977, Oscar Romero was appointed as a man many saw as moderate, a compromise. Romero had spoken often against Communism and liberation theology. But powerful, moneyed interests soon found that he also spoke eloquently for the needs of the poor, and of the need for justice. And so in March of 1980 he was gunned down and joined the long line of Christian martyrs. The possibility of death, however, was a risk he had chosen to take because he believed God was leading him in the effort to help his people. The story of what happened shortly before Romero's death is found in his biography by James Brockman, *The Word Remains: A Life of Oscar Romero:*

"Not everyone thought Romero would be safer in El Salvador. The foreign minister of Nicaragua, Father Miguel D'Escoto, M.M., wrote him on February 15, offering Nicaragua as a haven. Romero replied that he could not leave his people and accepted with them 'the risks of the moment.'

"Romero's elderly confessor visited him at the retreat house. 'I dare to consider this last retreat of his as his prayer in the garden,' he later wrote. 'Archbishop Romero foresaw his very probable and imminent death. He felt terror at it, as Jesus did in the garden. But he did not for that leave his post and his duty, ready to drink the chalice that the Father might give him to drink.'

"It was a bloody week, especially in the countryside. In his homily the following Sunday, Romero commented: 'These military operations, besides being inhuman, are unconstitutional. Without any legal grounds, on the basis of rumors and without accounting for their actions, the security forces take over for three days or longer various populated areas, creating occupied zones where they abolish, as though under a state of siege, the most fundamental rights of the Salvadoran peasant. ...'[1]

1. What do you think is the most important factor in why a person like Oscar Romero is willing to face martyrdom?
   - ❏ being masochistic
   - ❏ wanting to be famous
   - ❏ denial of one's mortality
   - ❏ misguided zeal
   - ❏ a desire to be like Christ
   - ❏ a love for people
   - ❏ a commitment to following Christ

2. Rank the following in the order that you would be willing to die for them (1 = "most willing," etc.):
   - ____ my spouse
   - ____ my children
   - ____ my country
   - ____ other children
   - ____ oppressed people
   - ____ a friend in danger
   - ____ my faith
   - ____ a stranger in danger

SCRIPTURE and QUESTIONS

A World of Dangers. Many people in our country perceive the world we live in today to be a dangerous one. Certainly in many ways it is. However, the world in which Jesus lived while on earth was in most respects even more dangerous. The most common way to travel was by foot, and generally on roads where they were constantly exposed to robbers. The power of government officials had few balances, and a government official who wanted to have you killed could generally do so without fear of punishment. Jesus knew this when people came to warn him that Herod was out to kill him. He was also aware of the history of his nation where people who spoke prophetically had frequently been threatened and killed by those in power. And yet Jesus did not cower in fear. He had a sense of mission and a belief in God's presence with him that carried him through. That same presence is available to us as we seek to do God's work.

Have someone in your group read the following passage out loud. Then go around on each question and let each person share their answer. Take advantage of the Study notes following the questionnaire. Be sure to save the last 20–40 minutes for the Caring time.

> [31]**At that very hour some Pharisees came and said to him, "Get away from here, for Herod wants to kill you."** [32]**He said to them, "Go and tell that fox for me, 'Listen, I am casting out demons and performing cures today and tomorrow, and on the third day I finish my work.** [33]**Yet today, tomorrow and the next day I must be on my way, because it is impossible for a prophet to be killed outside of Jerusalem.'** [34]**Jerusalem, Jerusalem, the city that kills the prophets and stones those who are sent to it! How often have I desired to gather your children together as a hen gathers her brood under her wings, and you were not willing!** [35]**See, your house is left to you. And I tell you, you will not see me until the time comes when you say, 'Blessed is the one who comes in the name of the Lord.'"**
>
> *Luke 13:31–35*

1. What incident from your childhood is brought to mind by the phrase, "as a hen gathers her brood under her wings"? When was your mother or other caregiver especially protective of you and your siblings?

QUESTIONS (cont.)

2. Were you in the position of Jesus, what would be your attitude toward the warning of the Pharisees?
   - ❏ "You're just trying to scare me."
   - ❏ "I know! You don't have to remind me!"
   - ❏ "Thanks for the warning—I'm out of here!"
   - ❏ "Thanks—but I'm staying."

3. Why did Jesus ask the Pharisees to tell Herod what Jesus was doing?
   - ❏ to show he was acting innocently
   - ❏ to tell him that he was going to keep on doing God's work, no matter what Herod did
   - ❏ to show Herod his acts were messianic acts
   - ❏ other:_____

4. How would you describe Jesus' attitude toward Jerusalem, as he manifests that attitude here? (Check all that apply.)
   - ❏ angry
   - ❏ nostalgic
   - ❏ loving
   - ❏ sad
   - ❏ regretful
   - ❏ vengeful
   - ❏ rejected
   - ❏ apathetic

5. What message of warning would you like God to give to your children or someone else close to your heart?

6. What crisis or situation are you facing now that you need to feel God protecting and caring for you, like a mother hen guarding her brood?

7. What makes you tend to resist God's loving direction and protection?
   - ❏ my pride—I like to do things myself!
   - ❏ my history—I've always felt God as judging, not protective.
   - ❏ my values—I have some things I'm pursuing that God may not approve of.
   - ❏ nothing at all!

8. What would it mean for you to let Jesus "gather you under his wings"?

BIBLE STUDY NOTES:

13:1 the Galileans whose blood Pilate had mingled with their sacrifices. While the situation referred to here is unknown, it would not have been out of character for Pilate, who was noted for his cruel, oppressive actions. He once had Roman soldiers, disguised with cloaks to look like Jewish peasants, mingle with a crowd gathered in Jerusalem. At an appointed time these soldiers threw off their cloaks, revealing clubs and swords with which they beat and killed many people. Since there is no record of Pilate defiling the temple literally in such an obscene way, the idea of mixing their blood with that of their sacrifices is probably a figurative way of indicating the horror the Jews felt as they considered that these Galileans were murdered as they came to Jerusalem to offer sacrifice to God.

13:2–3 Some traditional Jewish teaching held that people who suffered did so because they were being punished by God for sin. While some people assumed this awful incident proved the enormity of the guilt of those killed, Jesus declares that they were no more sinful than anyone else in Galilee. **perish.** All persons die, regardless of whether they repent or not. But repentance keeps us from having to *perish*, to lose out on the eternal life God has planned. Unless people repent, they will perish spiritually as these Galileans perished physically.

13:4–5 tower of Siloam. This tower was a part of the fortifications of Jerusalem near an important spring and reservoir. Nothing is known of this incident either. **you will all perish.** Lest his audience miss the point, Jesus uses an example from Jerusalem to underscore the same lesson for those from Judea.

13:6–9 This parable shifts the focus off the guilt of particular individuals to consider that of the nation as a whole. Israel is often represented in the OT as God's vineyard (Isa. 5:1–7; 27:2–5; Jer. 8:13; Hos. 9:10). Jesus' point is that Israel as a whole is like a fig tree that consistently does not bear fruit (see 3:9). Unless it does so soon, it will be cut down. By this Jesus points out both God's patience toward his people and the reality that a day of accounting is coming.

CARING TIME and PRAYER REQUESTS:

 This time is for developing and expressing your caring for each other as group members. We do this by sharing our needs and praying for each other's needs.

Each group member should answer the question,

How can this group help you in prayer this week?

Then join together in group prayer.

SERENDIPITY
Small Group
HANDOUT

WEEK 3: LENT 3
A Road to Judgment
Luke 13:1–9

 GATHERING 10 min.   **STUDY** 30 min.   **CARING** 20–40 min.

Leader: The agenda has three parts. In the Gathering time you'll be getting to know each other through an "ice-breaker." This will be for your total group. The Study time has two parts: (1) Story and (2) Scripture. If you are short of time, skip the Story and move to the Scripture. Begin by reading out loud the Story or the Scripture to the whole group. Then divide into groups of 4 for the Study time. Finally, regather the total group for the Caring time. Keep to this agenda: (1) Gathering—10 minutes, (2) Study—30 minutes, and (3) Caring—20–40 minutes.

 On the Floor of the Stock Market. Take turns discussing question #1 and then go on to question #2.

1. If your life this past week were the stock market, how would you describe this week's activity?
   - ❑ unchanged in active trading—a lot happening; some good, some bad
   - ❑ unchanged in light trading—nothing happenning
   - ❑ closed slightly lower—no depression, but I may be going through a recession
   - ❑ closed slightly higher—Things are better, but nobody would get rich off of me.
   - ❑ a rally—Everything I'm investing in is paying dividends!
   - ❑ a crash—If I could have, I would have "suspended trading"!
   - ❑ other:_____

2. If you were a broker, advising people whether to invest in you for the coming week, would you be more "bearish" (pessimistic) or more "bullish" (optimistic)?

INTRODUCTION STORY:

Dietrich Bonhoeffer Sees Judgment for Hitler's Germany. When the Nazis rose to power in Germany, the young theologian Dietrich Bonhoeffer was one who warned against the dangers of this movement. Bonhoeffer's opposition became more active over time and he even cooperated in a plot to kill Hitler, a major struggle for a man of peace. Eventually he was imprisoned and executed just days before the end of World War II. Bonhoeffer's belief that Germany would face judgment for what was happening there are discussed in his biography by Mary Bosanquet, *The Life and Death of Dietrich Bonhoeffer.* In the following segment, Bonhoeffer is talking to church representatives from Allied countries about getting support for their German resistance movement:

"Bonhoeffer's deep grief for the sins of Germany was evident to the Bishop. It was plain that he felt them as a stain on his own soul, and was deeply moved by his country's need for the forgiveness of God and men. When Bonhoeffer heard Schonfeld's attempts to negotiate comfortable terms for Germany, his Christian conscience was not easy. 'There must be punishment by God,' so runs the Bishop's report of his conversation, 'we should not be worthy of such a solution. Our action must be such as the world will understand as an act of repentance. Christians do not wish to escape repentance, or chaos, if it is God's will to bring it upon us. We must take this judgment as Christians.'

"After his conversation with Bonhoeffer, the Bishop was entirely convinced of the accuracy of the information about the German resistance. He returned to England determined to do all he could to gain from the government, if not actual expression of support for the movement, at least some definite statement that their attitude to a reconstituted German government would be different from their attitude to one dominated by Hitler. ..."[1]

1. Do you agree with Bonhoeffer's contention that German Christians of that day should be willing to suffer punishment as an act of repentance? Why or why not?

2. What sins of our country do you feel "as a stain on your own soul"? (Remember that this is a time to share your perceptions, not debate with others!) Choose from the following or add your own:
   - ❏ our tolerance of pornography
   - ❏ racism
   - ❏ our greed and commercialism
   - ❏ abortion
   - ❏ our increasing secularism
   - ❏ domestic abuse
   - ❏ how we disregard the poor
   - ❏ other:_____
   - ❏ how we took land from Native Americans
   - ❏ how we have treated Third World nations
   - ❏ none—I see nothing but positive things in our country.

SCRIPTURE and QUESTIONS:

A World of Dangers. "Repent!—the end is near!" People have heard and seen messages like that one so many times—and lampooned it so many times—that many no longer take the idea of judgment seriously any more. The God many believe in is a kindly old George Burns who wouldn't think of judging anyone. But that is not the God of the Bible, and that is fortunate. In a world full of strong evils, we need a strong God who is willing to take a strong stand against those evils. Some today have called this "tough love." Love that is real must now allow people to wallow in a destructive, self-focused lifestyle that makes all of us less than we were created to be. Our Scripture for today makes it clear that such behavior is judged—in this life as well as in the next.

Have someone in your group read the following passage out loud. Then go around on each question and let each person share their answer. Take advantage of the Study notes following the questionnaire. Be sure to save the last 20–40 minutes for the Caring time.

13 *At that very time there were some present who told him about the Galileans whose blood Pilate had mingled with their sacrifices. ²He asked them, "Do you think that because these Galileans suffered in this way they were worse sinners than all the other Galileans? ³No, I tell you; but unless you repent, you will all perish as they did. ⁴Or those eighteen who were killed when the tower of Siloam fell on them—do you think that they were worse offenders than all the others living in Jerusalem? ⁵No, I tell you; but unless you repent, you will all perish just as they did."*

⁶Then he told this parable: "A man had a fig tree planted in his vineyard; and he came looking for fruit on it and found none. ⁷So he said to the gardener, 'See here! For three years I have come looking for fruit on this fig tree, and still I find none. Cut it down! Why should it be wasting the soil?' ⁸He replied, 'Sir, let it alone for one more year, until I dig around it and put manure on it. ⁹If it bears fruit next year, well and good; but if not, you can cut it down.' "

Luke 13:1–9

1. When you were a child or an adolescent, who was most likely to advocate for giving you "one more chance" when you messed up?
   - ❏ my mom
   - ❏ my grandpa
   - ❏ my dad
   - ❏ a favorite teacher
   - ❏ a sibling
   - ❏ nobody
   - ❏ my grandma
   - ❏ other:_____

QUESTIONS (cont.)

2. Why would the gardener in the parable plead for giving the fig tree one more chance?
   - ❏ guilt—He felt he should have cared for it better in the first place.
   - ❏ practicality—It would take a long time to grow a new tree.
   - ❏ professional pride—He wanted to show he could do it.
   - ❏ love of life—He didn't want the tree to have to die.

3. What recent tragedies can you think of that were like the two referred to in this passage? Did anyone question openly whether the victims were being judged?

4. What was Jesus trying to teach about judgment in this passage?
   - ❏ People whose lives don't produce "good fruit" die sooner.
   - ❏ Nations who don't produce "good fruit" are judged.
   - ❏ God is patient about judging people and nations.
   - ❏ Suffering in this life does not come as a judgment of God.
   - ❏ God does judge, but not always in this life.
   - ❏ other:_____

5. When has something tragic happened to you where you wondered, at least for a moment, whether God was judging you?

6. After reading this passage, what do you need to work on more?
   - ❏ remembering that suffering is part of everyone's life
   - ❏ developing a more fruitful spiritual life
   - ❏ preparing to meet God's judgment
   - ❏ working to counter some of our nation's sins
   - ❏ other:_____

7. If Christ were to say to you personally, "Unless you repent"—what would he be talking about?
   - ❏ my physical lifestyle
   - ❏ my "attitude"
   - ❏ my spiritual commitment
   - ❏ my attachment to "things"
   - ❏ my pride
   - ❏ the way I relate to others
   - ❏ other:_____

5. Which of the following has in the course of your lifetime been most likely to cause you to lose your way, as the prodigal did?

❏ a need to test limits and be irresponsible
❏ a tragedy that makes me question myself and God
❏ people teaching ways other than Christianity
❏ lack of Christian friendship and support
❏ just gradually slipping away from my faith
❏ other:_____

6. How would you describe your spiritual life right now?

❏ I am still trying to find myself
❏ I'm on my way home.
❏ I really never left home.
❏ I come home when I feel like it—and then leave.
❏ other:_____

7. What is the next step in your spiritual pilgrimage?

15:12 give me the share. Under Jewish law, the younger of two sons would receive one-third of the estate upon his father's death (Deut. 21:17). While a father might divide up his property before he died if he wished, this son's request would be considered unbelievably callous. In essence he implies that his father who still lives is getting in the way of his plans. The father was under no obligation whatsoever to grant this request, but he goes along with it. Having done so, the expectation is that while the land legally belongs to the sons, morally the sons are obliged to provide for the father while he is alive.

15:13 gathered all he had. This son's action would have been considered scandalous at a time when a person's identity and future was tied up with his family's land. By selling it off, he was separating himself from his family, reneging on his obligation to his father, and rob-

bing any children he might one day have of the security of having land.

15:15 feed the pigs. Jews considered pigs as ceremonially unclean animals (Lev. 11:7) and would not eat, raise or touch them. The fact that he was caring for pigs indicates he was working for a Gentile.

15:16 the pods. While eating the food of pigs sounds terrible even to modern readers, for the Pharisees Jesus was addressing it would have been utterly horrifying.

15:17 he came to himself. The phrase does not indicate repentance, but simply recognition that the way he has chosen is not working.

15:19 no longer worthy. This son has been brought to a point of humility where he realizes he has no right to claim even the relationship of son.

15:20 his father saw him. The implication is that the father had been looking and hoping for his son's return.

15:22 a robe—the best one. This would be reserved for distinguished guests and special occasions. **a ring.** The signet ring gives the son the authority to represent the father. **sandals.** Being shoeless was a sign of a slave. To wear shoes indicated a man was free to go where he pleased.

15:23 fatted calf. The whole village was probably invited to the feast, because such a calf would feed a hundred people.

15:25 elder son. This is the character who represents the Pharisees. Since this was told to teach them a lesson (see vv. 1–3), many would call this the parable of the elder son, rather than the parable of the prodigal son.

15:28 refused to go in. His refusal to enter the house would have been seen as a sign of grave disrespect, since the eldest son was expected to play the part of a gracious host at a family feast.

15:29 Listen! This would have been considered an extremely rude way for a son to address his father, since there is no hint of respect or affection. **never disobeyed your command.** This son apparently always viewed things in terms of a master-slave relationship, which reflected the Pharisees' reliance on law rather than love.

15:30 this son of yours. This son doesn't even acknowledge the other son as his own brother!

15:32 this brother of yours. The father reminds the elder son of the kinship he had sought to deny.

 This time is for developing and expressing your caring for each other as group members. We do this by sharing our needs and praying for each other's needs.

Each group member should answer the question,

How can this group help you in prayer this week?

Then join together in group prayer.

[1]Lush Gjergi, *Mother Teresa: Her Life, Her Works* (Hyde Park, NY: New City Press, 1991), pp. 34–35.

SERENDIPITY
Small Group
HANDOUT

WEEK 4: LENT 4
Lost on the Road
Luke 15:11–32

 GATHERING 10 min.   **STUDY** 30 min.   **CARING** 20–40 min.

Leader: The agenda has three parts. In the Gathering time you'll be getting to know each other through an "ice-breaker." This will be for your total group. The Study time has two parts: (1) Story and (2) Scripture. If you are short of time, skip the Story and move to the Scripture. Begin by reading out loud the Story or the Scripture to the whole group. Then divide into groups of 4 for the Study time. Finally, regather the total group for the Caring time. Keep to this agenda: (1) Gathering—10 minutes, (2) Study—30 minutes, and (3) Caring—20–40 minutes.

Around the House. If you could compare the way you live your life to one of the following items found around the house, which item would it be?

WELCOME MAT—I always like helping people feel at home.

FIRE EXTINGUISHER—It seems I spend a lot of my life putting out fires.

WINDOW—I like to help people get a broader view of life.

MIRROR—I like to help people see themselves more clearly.

EASY CHAIR—I like to relax and help others do so too.

GAME CLOSET—I love to play!

VACUUM CLEANER—I clean up the messes.

HOME COMPUTER—I'm a storehouse of resources and information.

INTRODUCTION STORY:

Mother Teresa Becomes a Mother. Mother Teresa is known and respected around the world for her work with the "poorest of the poor" in India and now other places around the world. For those helped by her, she is not just a social worker, nor even just a religious worker—she is a true mother for many who never knew such a parent. This role includes both showing love and teaching discipline to those who sometimes have no home to go home to. Her biographer Lush Gjergi tells the story, quoting Mother Teresa herself, in *Mother Teresa: Her Life, Her Works:*

" 'This happened a short time before I made my final vows. One day a little fellow came to me, pale and sad. He asked me if I would come back to see them, because he had heard that I was going to become "Mother." Then he started to cry and told me with tears: "Oh, don't become a Mother." I drew him close to me and asked him: "What is wrong my boy? Don't be afraid. I will come back, and I will always be your 'Ma.' " The little fellow suddenly smiled again, and dashed out into the courtyard, happy.'

"She also mentions this other occurrence.

" 'One day an English gentleman came to visit the school, and was surprised at the great number of children there. In ten large rooms we had 375 of them. It is impossible to imagine what that means. During his visit, absolute silence reigned in the school. The Englishman could not believe this, and asked me what kind of punishments we used to get such order. "For them, the severest punishment could be for me not to look at them, and to let them do whatever they want without paying attention to them; for then they would be sure that they have displeased me. Why should I strike them? They get enough blows at home!" The gentleman smiled and said: "The children must really love you, because you love them and at the same time you are working for their good." ' "[1]

1. What is the most important thing that Mother Teresa reveals about God through her style of "parenting"?
   ❏ Even those who have no parent have one in God.
   ❏ God seeks to lead us by love rather than fear.
   ❏ God in his love does not let us get by with misbehavior.
   ❏ God is always attentive to us.
   ❏ other:_____

2. Who was like a second mother to you in your childhood?

SCRIPTURE:

Disciplining the Prodigal. Each of us, at some point, lose our way on the road of life we are traveling. When it happens, how do we get back on the right road? That is one of the biggest questions of our society. It is a question for parents who lose control of their adolescent and young adult children, and find them traveling dangerous paths. It is a question for our penal system, where we wonder what the best way is to keep those who have committed crimes from offending again, and whether it is possible to turn them into productive citizens again. There are probably no easy solutions to these issues which can be applied to every circumstance. But as we wrestle with them we need to remember that God also has had to deal with his children who have turned from the right path—and that includes all of us! His solution, as shown in the parable of the prodigal son, includes both the strength to let his children face the consequences of their actions, and the love to readily forgive.

Have someone in your group read the following passage out loud. Then go around on each question and let each person share their answer. Take advantage of the Study notes following the questionnaire. Be sure to save the last 20–40 minutes for the Caring time.

[11]Then Jesus said, "There was a man who had two sons. [12]The younger of them said to his father, 'Father, give me the share of the property that will belong to me.' So he divided his property between them. [13]A few days later the younger son gathered all he had and traveled to a distant country, and there he squandered his property in dissolute living. [14]When he had spent everything, a severe famine took place throughout that country, and he began to be in need. [15]So he went and hired himself out to one of the citizens of that country, who sent him to his fields to feed the pigs. [16]He would gladly have filled himself with the pods that the pigs were eating; and no one gave him anything. [17]But when he came to himself he said, 'How many of my father's hired hands have bread enough and to spare, but here I am dying of hunger! [18]I will get up and go to my father, and I will say to him, "Father, I have sinned against heaven and before you; [19]I am no longer worthy to be called your son; treat me like one of your hired hands." ' [20]So he set off and went to his father. But while he was still far off, his father saw him and was filled with compassion; he ran and put his arms around him and kissed him. [21]Then the son said to him 'Father, I have sinned against heaven and before you; I am no longer worthy to be called your son.' [22]But the father said to his slaves, 'Quickly, bring out a robe—the best one—and put it on him; put a ring on his finger and sandals on his feet. [23]And get the fatted calf and kill it, and let us eat and celebrate; [24]for this son of mine was dead and is alive again; he was lost and is found!' And they began to celebrate.

[25]"Now his elder son was in the field; and when he came and approached the house, he heard music and dancing. [26]He called one of the slaves and asked what was going on. [27]He replied, 'Your brother has come,

SCRIPTURE (cont.) and QUESTIONS:

and your father has killed the fatted calf, because he has got him back safe and sound.' [28]Then he became angry and refused to go in. His father came out and began to plead with him. [29]But he answered his father, 'Listen! For all these years I have been working like a slave for you, and I have never disobeyed your command; yet you have never given me even a young goat so that I might celebrate with my friends. [30]But when this son of yours came back, who has devoured your property with prostitutes, you killed the fatted calf for him!' [31]Then the father said to him, 'Son, you are always with me, and all that is mine is yours. [32]But we had to celebrate and rejoice, because this brother of yours was dead and has come to life; he was lost and has been found.' "

Luke 15:11–32

1. If you had been the father in this Bible story, what would you have said to the younger son when he asked for his inheritance early in order to leave home?
   ❏ "Are you crazy?!"
   ❏ "Why you ungrateful ...!!"
   ❏ "Well, I'm disappointed, but here you are."
   ❏ "No problem, son."

2. If you had been the father and had a pretty good idea where your son had gone, would you have gone after him?
   ❏ Yes, you don't want to see your kid get in trouble.
   ❏ Maybe, if I thought I could get him to come home.
   ❏ No, you have to let people make their own mistakes.
   ❏ It all depends.

3. What in this story is *most* like your own story?
   ❏ Like the younger brother, I had my time of rebellion.
   ❏ Like the elder brother, I also felt I got the "short end of the stick" in our family.
   ❏ Like the father and younger brother, I know the joy of reconciling with a child or parent.
   ❏ Like the elder brother, I often feel "left out of the party."
   ❏ Like this story, there are ill feelings between me and a sibling.

4. What do you see in this story that you *wish* had been true in your own situation?
   ❏ I wish I would have had a time where I "sowed my wild oats."
   ❏ I wish my father would have had a fortune for me to blow!
   ❏ I wish I had a father who was as gentle and understanding as the father in the parable.
   ❏ I wish we had more celebrating in my childhood home.

QUESTIONS (cont.) and BIBLE STUDY NOTES:

7. What would need to happen for you to be willing to risk losing your own life to do what God wanted you to do?
   - ❑ I would need to hear an audible voice from God telling me to.
   - ❑ I would need for my kids to be grown first.
   - ❑ I would need to think I was the only one who could do it.
   - ❑ I would need to believe very strongly this was God's will.
   - ❑ I would need to be in a very oppressive situation, like Bonhoeffer in Hitler's Germany.
   - ❑ I could never see myself doing this.

8. What are you risking (or feeling called to risk) in following Christ right now?

12:1 Bethany. John 11:18 tells us that Bethany was about two miles from Jerusalem.

12:3 pure nard. It is uncertain whether the term "pure" means unadulterated with water, or if it is a trade name. **anointed Jesus' feet.** A parallel account says the perfume was poured on his head (Mark 14:3–9) which would be far more in accord with the custom of anointing the guest of honor at a feast. **The house was filled with the fragrance.** There was a rabbinic saying that taught that a person's good reputation would spread throughout the world just as perfume fills a house. This may be the author's way of saying the same thing Mark does when he writes that what Mary has done will be told wherever the Gospel is preached (Mark 14:9).

12:4 Judas Iscariot. Matthew records this as the complaint of all the disciples (Matt. 26:8); Mark records it was said by "some" who were there (Mark 14:4). John, written much later, may be vilifying Judas because of his later treachery and betrayal.

12:5 three hundred denarii. A denarius was the typical day's wage, so this would be what the average person would earn in a year.

12:7 She bought it ... for the day of my burial. The implication in John's version of this story is that she did not use all of it, but kept some of it for later. Mary probably did this as an act of thanks for what Jesus did in raising her brother Lazarus. Jesus uses this opportunity to once again remind his disciples that his death was coming.

12:8 You always have the poor. Jesus is not here advising the neglect of the poor, but rather he was saying that opportunities to help the poor would abound for some time, while this opportunity to minister to him previous to his death would not.

CARING TIME and PRAYER REQUESTS:

This time is for developing and expressing your caring for each other as group members. We do this by sharing our needs and praying for each other's needs.

Each group member should answer the question,

How can this group help you in prayer this week?

Then join together in group prayer.

[1] Mary Bosanquet, *The Life and Death of Dietrich Bonhoeffer* (New York: Harper & Row, 1968), pp. 180–181.
[2] James Patterson and Peter Kim, *The Day America Told the Truth* (New York: Prentice Hall Press, 1991), p. 28.

SERENDIPITY
Small Group
HANDOUT

WEEK 5: LENT 5

A Road Where Martyrs Have Led

John 12:1–8

GATHERING 10 min.	STUDY 30 min.	CARING 20–40 min.

Leader: The agenda has three parts. In the Gathering time you'll be getting to know each other through an "ice-breaker." This will be for your total group. The Study time has two parts: (1) Story and (2) Scripture. If you are short of time, skip the Story and move to the Scripture. Begin by reading out loud the Story or the Scripture to the whole group. Then divide into groups of 4 for the Study time. Finally, regather the total group for the Caring time. Keep to this agenda: (1) Gathering—10 minutes, (2) Study—30 minutes, and (3) Caring—20–40 minutes.

If I Had a Hammer ... From a perspective similar to the popular folk song from the '60s, what would you like to use a hammer (to force something from our world), a bell (to bring something to people's attention) and a song (to celebrate something) for?

I'D HAMMER OUT ...
- ❑ war   ❑ hunger   ❑ abortion   ❑ bigotry
- ❑ greed   ❑ promiscuity   ❑ abuse   ❑ ignorance

I'D RING OUT ABOUT ...
- ❑ the need to prepare for a new world
- ❑ the need to clean up the environment
- ❑ the need to respond to Christ
- ❑ the need to preserve our freedoms

I'D SING ABOUT ...
- ❑ the blessing of a loving family   ❑ friends
- ❑ how I've been forgiven   ❑ my hope for the future
- ❑ the beauty of God's world   ❑ living in this country

INTRODUCTION STORY:

Seeing the Martyr in Dietrich Bonhoeffer. When the Nazis rose to power in Germany, the young theologian Dietrich Bonhoeffer was one who warned against the dangers of this movement. Bonhoeffer's opposition became more active over time and he even cooperated in a plot to kill Hitler, a major struggle for a man of peace. Eventually he was imprisoned and executed just days before the end of World War II. Bonhoeffer also organized a seminary with a unique kind of intentional Christian community. In that community some seemed to sense Bonhoeffer's coming martyrdom. This sensing is discussed in his biography by Mary Bosanquet, *The Life and Death of Dietrich Bonhoeffer.* The author begins by quoting Bonhoeffer's friend, Wilhelm Rott:

" 'And so during these two years "Brother Dietrich"—who always had time for his brothers—used sometimes to sit down on a little staircase which led to the Inspector's room, generally after lunch and before he made his tour of the "classrooms" of the seminary. It is an unforgettable picture: the small wooden staircase, the man sitting with his legs crossed. ... Dietrich talks. Yesterday he was in Berlin. Late in the evening he had given all who were awaiting his return a vivid account of the aberrations and entanglements of that period of the Church Committees. He had talked of spiritual and temporal, of ecclesiastical and political matters, of those who stood firm, of those who wavered and those who fell. But there are still telling details which have not escaped his keen observation, and which are not suitable for sharing with the wider circle.'

"Werner Koch, one of the students later imprisoned, offers us an impression of a different order. He records the impact of his first sight of Bonhoeffer in a Berlin cafe, before he was aware of his own identity.

" 'Perhaps a Catholic Christian would have said: "I had the sense of being in the presence of a saint." Today I myself would rather say that I had a distinct impression: This is he! A man with the mark of God upon him, set apart, singled out for his future martyrdom.' "[1]

1. What do you think Werner Koch saw in Dietrich Bonhoeffer that gave him the sense that Bonhoeffer would be facing martyrdom?
   ❏ nothing—It was probably 20/20 hindsight!
   ❏ a brave man in a dangerous time
   ❏ a man of strong faith that would compel him to stand against Hitler
   ❏ something beyond the natural senses—a supernatural premonition
   ❏ other:_____

2. Are martyrs just ordinary people whom God has strengthened, or are they people to whom God has given something special the rest of us do not have? Mark your response on the continuum below:

ordinary people, _____ **special people, set**
strengthened by God   **apart by God**

SCRIPTURE and QUESTIONS:

What Would We Die For? When James Patterson and Peter Kim asked people what beliefs they were willing to die for, the answer for almost half (48%) of those who responded was "None." Fewer than one in three (30%) would be willing to die for their faith.[2] In light of that, it's important to remember that we are part of a faith that was built on martyrs—people who were willing to face death because they believed something so strongly. Certainly it all goes back to Jesus Christ himself. Jesus did not die because he failed to see the danger coming. He saw it and knew his death was necessary in order to do God's will. He was willing to face death for what was important. Early Christians did the same at the hands of the Roman Caesars. Others, some of whom we have or will read about in this lectionary series, include Joan of Arc, Sir Thomas More, Dietrich Bonhoeffer, Martin Luther King, Jr. and Oscar Romero. While we don't want to make martyrdom so glorified that people actively seek it out (as it was sometimes in the early church), it is nevertheless true that for the witness of Christ to be strong, there has to be people willing to die for him when necessary. Without that commitment the church descends into impotence and mediocrity.

Have someone in your group read the following passage out loud. Then go around on each question and let each person share their answer. Take advantage of the Study notes following the questionnaire. Be sure to save the last 20–40 minutes for the Caring time.

12 *Six days before the Passover Jesus came to Bethany, the home of Lazarus, whom he had raised from the dead. ²There they gave a dinner for him. Martha served, and Lazarus was one of those at the table with him. ³Mary took a pound of costly perfume made of pure nard, anointed Jesus' feet, and wiped them with her hair. The house was filled with the fragrance of the perfume. ⁴But Judas Iscariot, one of his disciples (the one who was about to betray him), said, ⁵"Why was this perfume not sold for three hundred denarii and the money given to the poor?" ⁶(He said this not because he cared about the poor, but because he was a thief; he kept the common purse and used to steal what was put into it.) ⁷Jesus said, "Leave her alone. She bought it so that she might keep it for the day of my burial. ⁸You always have the poor with you, but you do not always have me."*

John 12:1–8

1. How are you at giving gifts?
   ❏ I'm a tightwad.
   ❏ I'm a spendthrift.
   ❏ I'm conservative.
   ❏ I'm practical.

QUESTIONS (cont.)

2. How would you have felt about Lazarus, who had been dead for four days before being raised (John 11:1–44), being present at the dinner?
   ❏ stunned—"Has this all been a bad dream?"
   ❏ eerie—"Where's the *Twilight Zone* music?"
   ❏ grateful—"Isn't God good?!"
   ❏ celebrative—"All right! Let's party!"
   ❏ other:_____

3. Why did Mary choose this time to break out this expensive perfume and use it to anoint Jesus' feet?
   ❏ She was full of thanksgiving for her brother Lazarus being alive.
   ❏ She just acted on impulse.
   ❏ She sensed Jesus sorrow as he approached his own suffering and death.
   ❏ She just wanted to show her love in a tangible way.
   ❏ other:_____

4. If you were to take a year of your earnings (the value of Mary's perfume) to use for Christ, what would you do with it?
   ❏ give it toward a new church building or remodeling project
   ❏ use it as a fund for the homeless
   ❏ invest it in an evangelistic outreach
   ❏ use it to help suffering children
   ❏ other:_____

5. How is your answer to the previous question reflected in your budget and priorities right now?

6. What does it mean to you that Jesus was fully aware that he was facing his death soon, and yet went ahead anyway?
   ❏ It was easy for him—he was God.
   ❏ He must have loved us very much.
   ❏ He must not have loved life very much.
   ❏ other:_____

6. How would you describe the difference that Christ's death and God's forgiveness has made in the way you live your life now?

❏ a little bit
❏ a whole lot
❏ not as much as it should
❏ a lot more than it used to
❏ I'm not sure.

7. Are you closer to Christ now than you were five years ago? If yes, in what way? If no, explain why.

23:33 The Skull. In Aramaic, this is Golgotha. The name was given because it was a round, bare hill outside Jerusalem. **they crucified Jesus.** Josephus, the Jewish historian of that era, called crucifixion "the most wretched of all ways of dying." The person to be crucified was first stripped. Then his hands were tied or nailed to the crossbeam which was lifted to the upright stake already in place. At that point, the feet were nailed in place. Typically it took several hours before death occurred by asphyxiation, loss of blood and shock. **the criminals.** These were probably Zealots (perhaps associated with Barabbas), a band of fiery nationalists who were committed to the violent overthrow of Rome. The reference to being crucified alongside criminals would be seen as a fulfillment of Isaiah 53:12.

23:34 Father, forgive them. Jesus' call for mercy reflects his radical call to his disciples to forgive their enemies (6:27–28) **to divide his clothing.** The clothes of the condemned person belonged to the four soldiers who carried out the crucifixion (see John 19:23–24; Ps. 22:18).

23:35 if he is the Messiah of God. To these religious leaders, the disgraceful death Jesus was

experiencing proved beyond a shadow of a doubt that he could not possibly be the Messiah.

23:36 sour wine. The Roman soldiers sarcastically offered him the burning taste of vinegar (or soured wine) to quench his thirst (see Ps. 69:21). It would be a mockery to offer a "king" such a cheap, bitter drink.

23:38 an inscription. The crime for which the person was being crucified was specified on a whitened board fastened above the criminal. The irony was that while it was meant to be an insult to Jesus and the Jews, it was ultimately true.

23:39–43 Even while on the cross, Jesus reached out in grace to the outcast. This story serves as a reminder that it is never too late, as long as the breath of life lasts, to turn to God in faith.

23:43 today you will be with me in Paradise. Paradise derives from a Persian word meaning a garden or park. It became a type or symbol of the future bliss of God's people in Isaiah 51:3. "Today" may simply mean "very soon." This is far more than what the criminal had asked for—to be remembered in Jesus' kingdom.

23:45 curtain of the temple. The curtain in the temple separated the Holy Place (where the priests performed their daily service) and the Most Holy Place, a small dark room in which God's presence was believed to dwell in a special way. The curtain stood as a visible sign of the barrier between people and God since the high priest could pass through that curtain only once a year on the Day of Atonement. Its rending was another supernatural sign of the significance of Jesus' death: he had

opened the way for all to have immediate and direct access to God.

23:46 into your hands. Jesus' last words are words of trust in God at the time of his death.

23:47–48 When the centurion saw ... when all the crowds who had gathered ... saw. The way Jesus faced his death was a testimony to all those who saw. Mark recorded the centurion to have said, "Truly this man was God's Son!" (Mark 15:39).

 This time is for developing and expressing your caring for each other as group members. We do this by sharing our needs and praying for each other's needs, as well as by affirming the strengths we see in each other.

You have probably been richly blessed by the people in your small group. Now is the time to tell them how they have blessed you. Ask one person to sit in silence while the others go around and finish one of the sentences below about this person. Then, ask another person to remain silent while you go around again, etc.

❏ You have blessed me recently when you shared about ...
❏ What inspires me most about your character is ...
❏ The aspect of your personality I would like to adopt into my own life is ...
❏ You have a way with people that I admire very much, namely ...
❏ There is something about your faith in God that I really like, namely ...

Then remembering what people shared, close in prayer, thanking God for each other and what you are experiencing as a group.

¹James R. Brockman, *The Word Remains: A Life of Oscar Romero* (Maryknoll, NY: Orbis, 1982), pp. 219–220.

SERENDIPITY
Small Group
HANDOUT

WEEK 6: LENT 6
A Road to Death
Luke 23:33–49

 GATHERING 10 min. **STUDY** 30 min. **CARING** 20–40 min.

Leader: The agenda has three parts. In the Gathering time you'll be getting to know each other through an "ice-breaker." This will be for your total group. The Study time has two parts: (1) Story and (2) Scripture. If you are short of time, skip the Story and move to the Scripture. Begin by reading out loud the Story or the Scripture to the whole group. Then divide into groups of 4 for the Study time. Finally, regather the total group for the Caring time. Keep to this agenda: (1) Gathering—10 minutes, (2) Study—30 minutes, and (3) Caring—20–40 minutes.

 The Animal in Me. What kind of animal are you most like? With most of us it varies with the situation. For each of the characteristics below, choose which animal in each pair you are most like:

IN HOW LOVABLE I FEEL I AM ...
a cuddly bunny _____a porcupine

IN LIFE PACE ...
a turtle_____a hummingbird

IN GENTLENESS OF MOOD ...
a panda bear_____a grizzly bear

IN COORDINATION AND GRACE ...
a charging bull _____a gazelle

IN PLAYFULNESS ...
a rhinoceros _____a porpoise

INTRODUCTION STORY:

Oscar Romero Faces His Death. When the need came for a new Catholic Archbishop for El Salvador in 1977, Oscar Romero was appointed as a man many saw as moderate, a compromise. Romero had spoken often against Communism and liberation theology. But powerful, moneyed interests soon found that he also spoke eloquently for the needs of the poor, and of the need for justice. And so in March of 1980 he was gunned down and joined the long line of Christian martyrs. The possibility of death, however, was a risk he had chosen to take because he believed God was leading him in the effort to help his people. The story of what happened the day of Romero's death is found in his biography by James Brockman, *The Word Remains: A Life of Oscar Romero:*

"An announcement had been published in the newspapers for the 6 p.m. mass. Some of Romero's friends were unhappy that it had stated that the archbishop would say the mass. The threats to his life were serious. The Vatican had sent warnings months before. The papal nuncio in Costa Rica had recently urged him to tone down his preaching. ...

"The mass was for the mother of a friend, Jorge Pinto, whose weekly newspaper, *El Independiente,* had been bombed less than two weeks before. It would be a simple mass, for her family and relatives mostly. ...

"The gospel reading was from John 12:23–26: 'The hour has come for the son of man to be glorified. ... Unless the grain of wheat falls to the earth and dies, it remains only a grain. But if it dies, it bears much fruit. ...'

"The homily took only ten minutes. ... He exhorted all to follow Dona Sarita's example, each one undertaking the task in his or her own way, with hope, with faith, with love for God. 'This holy mass, this Eucharist, is an act of faith. To Christian faith at this moment the voice of diatribe appears changed for the body of the Lord, who offered himself for the redemption of the world, and in this chalice the wine is transformed into the blood that was the price of salvation ... Let us join together, then, intimately in faith and hope at this moment of prayer for Dona Sarita and ourselves.'

"At that moment a shot rang out.

"Archbishop Romero was standing behind the altar, on the left side, facing the people. He slumped to the floor behind the altar, at the foot of a large crucifix. ..."[1]

1. Had you been a friend of Oscar Romero, what would you have said to him about exposing himself to danger by saying this mass?

2. How likely are *you* to go into a situation where you might risk physical danger?

1   2   3   4   5
Not if I can help it!   I thrive on danger!

SCRIPTURE:

Of Death and Taxes. It is often said in our society that nothing is inevitable except death and taxes. And so it is that, while last week we talked about the choice of whether we would be willing to die for our faith, whether we would be willing to *die* is not a choice at all. It is something we will all do, like it or not. We can make choices of living a healthy lifestyle that will make it likely we will live longer, but death will come even to the most ardent "health nut." Redd Fox once said, "Health nuts are going to feel real stupid someday—lying in hospitals, dying of nothing." And it's true; we can do all we are supposed to do to avoid various diseases, but we will still die. The question then becomes not whether we die, but *how we die.* Those who live their life according to God's way and who stand up for what they believe right to the end, regardless of danger—believing as they do that through the grace of God this life is not the end—will be choosing a more meaningful way than those who avoid all danger only to end up dying unnoticed in the far corner of some rest home. So that is where we have some measure of choice—not whether we die, but how we face that time.

Have someone in your group read the following passage out loud. Then go around on each question and let each person share their answer. Take advantage of the Study notes following the questionnaire. Be sure to save the last 20–40 minutes for the Caring time.

33When they came to the place that is called The Skull, they crucified Jesus there with the criminals, one on his right and one on his left. 34Then Jesus said, "Father, forgive them; for they do not know what they are doing." And they cast lots to divide his clothing. 35And the people stood by, watching; but the leaders scoffed at him, saying, "He saved others; let him save himself if he is the Messiah of God, his chosen one!" 36The soldiers also mocked him, coming up and offering him sour wine, 37and saying, "If you are the King of the Jews, save yourself!" 38There was also an inscription over him, "This is the King of the Jews."

39One of the criminals who were hanged there kept deriding him and saying, "Are you not the Messiah? Save yourself and us!" 40But the other rebuked him, saying, "Do you not fear God, since you are under the same sentence of condemnation? 41And we indeed have been condemned justly, for we are getting what we deserve for our deeds, but this man has done nothing wrong." 42Then he said, "Jesus, remember me when you come into your kingdom." 43He replied, "Truly I tell you, today you will be with me in Paradise."

44It was now about noon, and darkness came over the whole land until three in the afternoon, 45while the sun's light failed; and the curtain of the temple was torn in two. 46Then Jesus, crying with a loud voice, said, "Father, into your hands I commend my spirit." Having said this, he breathed his last. 47When the centurion saw what had taken place, he

SCRIPTURE (cont.) and QUESTIONS:

praised God and said, "Certainly this man was innocent." 48And when all the crowds who had gathered there for this spectacle saw what had taken place, they returned home, beating their breasts. 49But all his acquaintances, including the women who had followed him from Galilee, stood at a distance, watching these things.

Luke 23:33–49

1. When you were a child or an adolescent, what do you remember people mocking or making fun of about you?
   - ❏ my name
   - ❏ giving wrong answers in school
   - ❏ my weight
   - ❏ my lack of ability in sports
   - ❏ things I said
   - ❏ what my dad or mom did for a living
   - ❏ my clothes
   - ❏ other:_____
   - ❏ a facial feature (a big nose, buckteeth, etc.)

2. What do you think convinced the centurion Jesus was innocent?
   - ❏ the way he forgave those who crucified him
   - ❏ the way he spoke of Paradise to the criminal
   - ❏ the supernatural signs—the sun's light failing, etc.
   - ❏ the way he committed his spirit to God in trust

3. How confident are you that you would be able to commend your spirit to God in trust at death, like Jesus did?
   - ❏ Not at all—I'm too much of a cynic!
   - ❏ Not very much—I'll probably cling to this life to the last.
   - ❏ Maybe I could say the words, but my heart might not be in it.
   - ❏ I believe I could do that, with God's help.
   - ❏ I'm very confident I could have that kind of trust.

4. In order to better prepare for the time you will face death, what do you need to do now?
   - ❏ learn more of why Christ died
   - ❏ put my faith in Jesus Christ as Lord and Savior
   - ❏ talk more about my feelings about death
   - ❏ study more about what the Bible says about death
   - ❏ hear what people of faith who are dying have to say
   - ❏ other:_____

5. How does it make you feel when you think about what God has done for you through the death of Jesus Christ on the cross?
   - ❏ guilty
   - ❏ grateful
   - ❏ interested
   - ❏ uncomfortable
   - ❏ relieved
   - ❏ loved
   - ❏ I've heard all of this before.
   - ❏ doubtful

5. What is it that you are weeping for (whether the tears are visible or not!) right now in your life?
   - ❑ a loved one who has died
   - ❑ a stupid mistake I made
   - ❑ the fearfulness of the future
   - ❑ a lost opportunity
   - ❑ some old hurts
   - ❑ other:_____

6. Were the risen Christ to come to you, what do you think he would say to you about your tears?
   - ❑ "It's okay to cry."
   - ❑ "I have wept with you."
   - ❑ "The time for tears is over—I have risen!"
   - ❑ "You will see your loved one again!"
   - ❑ other:_____

7. Has your life lately been more like the darkness of Good Friday, the joy of Easter, or somewhere in between?

20:1 while it was still dark. This probably has both literal and figurative significance. The other Gospels mention that it was very early, but this author's intent is to emphasize that spiritually it was still dark—for it seemed the darkness had overcome the light since the Resurrection was not yet known (see 1:5; 9:4). **Mary Magdalene.** Mary is mentioned in all four Gospel accounts of the Resurrection. Magdala was a village in Galilee near Capernaum. Luke 8:2 says she was one of several women who traveled with the disciples. The other Gospels mention Mary was accompanied by other women, but this author's focus is only on her. **stone.** The tomb was in a cave, the entrance of which was sealed by a large stone.

20:2 the one whom Jesus loved. This refers to John, the author of this Gospel. It is not being claimed here that John was the only disciple whom Jesus loved, only that he felt a special relationship with Jesus. **They have taken the Lord.** Mary seems to have assumed that since Jesus was laid in the tomb of a rich man (see John 19:38–41), grave robbers had plundered it, hoping to find wealth buried there as well. **we do not know.** Just as the other Gospels record, this indicates that Mary did not go to the tomb alone.

20:5–7 saw the linen wrappings. Why the "other disciple" hesitated to go in until after Peter did is unknown. The author describes the arrangement of the clothes, the sight of which inspired faith at least in the "other disciple," at some length. Grave robbers, in search of treasures entombed with the corpse, would either have taken the body still wrapped up, or scattered the strips as they tore them off. The fact that the clothes were neatly laid by was one of the evidences that led the disciples to faith.

20:12 two angels in white. The Gospels differ on whether there was one man (Mark), or an angel (Matthew), or two men (Luke) or two angels (John) present. However, angels sometimes appeared as men in Scripture (see for instance Gen. 19:1–23; 32:24–32).

20:14 she did not know that it was Jesus. Later on there is another scene when Jesus is not recognized at first (21:4; see also Luke 24:13–16). Paul speaks of the resurrected body as having a different type of splendor than the normal body (1 Cor. 15:40–42). Whether Mary was blinded by her intense grief or if there was some type of transformation in Jesus' appearance that caused Mary's lack of recognition is not known.

20:15 Supposing him to be the gardener. The tomb was located in a garden owned by Joseph. It would not be unlikely that as an aristocratic member of the Sanhedrin he would employ a gardener to care for his property.

20:16 Mary! Jesus had said that the Good Shepherd "calls his own sheep by name" and that they "will listen to my voice" (10:3,16). When Jesus speaks Mary's name, she immediately recognizes who it is that speaks to her, thus proving her discipleship.

20:17 Do not hold on to me. The verb form here indicates Mary was already holding on to Jesus. Why did Jesus not want her to hold on to him? Perhaps because she would soon have to be without him, and she, along with the other disciples, could no longer depend on his physical presence. In the same way the disciples tried to "hold on to" Jesus at the Ascension, but the angel told them they should "stop gazing up toward heaven" (Acts 1:10–11). Instead they needed to rely on the power of the Holy Spirit.

 This time is for developing and expressing your caring for each other as group members. We do this by sharing our needs and praying for each other's needs.

Each group member should answer the question,

How can this group help you in prayer this week?

Then join together in group prayer.

¹Corrie ten Boom, *The Hiding Place* (Minneapolis, MN: World Wide Publications, 1971), pp. 214–215.

SERENDIPITY
Small Group
HANDOUT

WEEK 1: EASTER 1
Courage to Look Past the Tears
John 20:1–18

GATHERING 10 min. **STUDY** 30 min. **CARING** 20–40 min.

Leader: The agenda has three parts. In the Gathering time you'll be getting to know each other through an "ice-breaker." This will be for your total group. The Study time has two parts: (1) Story and (2) Scripture. If you are short of time, skip the Story and move to the Scripture. Begin by reading out loud the Story or the Scripture to the whole group. Then divide into groups of 4 for the Study time. Finally, regather the total group for the Caring time. Keep to this agenda: (1) Gathering—10 minutes, (2) Study—30 minutes, and (3) Caring—20–40 minutes.

 How Soon Would You Notice? For each of the following mark whether, if it happened, you would be among the first or the last to notice:

THEY CLOSED THE MALL:
among the first _____ among the last

THE LOCAL COUNTRY MUSIC STATION WENT OFF THE AIR:
among the first _____ among the last

THE PASTOR'S DAUGHTER DYED HER HAIR GREEN:
among the first _____ among the last

SPACE ALIENS SHOWED UP AT A LOCAL SPORTING EVENT:
among the first _____ among the last

INTRODUCTION STORY:

The ten Booms Find God Deeper Than Their Pit. Corrie ten Boom and her family helped shelter Jews from the Nazis during World War II, and for this act of courage they were sent to the Nazi concentration camps, eventually ending up at Ravensbruck. There Corrie experienced horrid conditions and eventually had to watch her beloved sister Betsie die. But before her death, Betsie gave Corrie the vision of a message that she later proclaimed—that the God who helped her in Ravensbruck could lift people from the depth of any pit. Corrie writes of what happened when Betsie was near death in her book, *The Hiding Place:*

"When the siren blew the next morning, Maryke and I again carried Betsie from the dormitory. The Snake was standing at the street door. As we started through it with our fragile burden she stepped in front of us. 'Take her back to the bunks.'

" 'I thought all pris—' "

" 'Take her back!' "

"Wonderingly, we replaced Betsie on the bed. ... Was it possible that the atmosphere of Barracks 28 had affected even this cruel guard? As soon as roll call was dismissed I ran back to the dormitory. There, beside our bed, stood The Snake. Beside her two orderlies from the hospital were setting down a stretcher. The Snake straightened almost guiltily as I approached. 'Prisoner is ready for transfer,' she snapped.

"I looked at the woman more closely: Had she risked fleas and lice to spare Betsie the sick-call line? She did not stop me as I started after the stretcher. ... As we passed, a Polish friend dropped to her knees and made the sign of the Cross.

"Sleet stung us as we reached the outside. ... We walked past the waiting line of sick people, through the door and into a large ward. They placed the stretcher on the floor and I leaned down to make out Betsie's words.

" '... must tell people what we have learned here. We must tell them that there is no pit so deep that he is not deeper still. They will listen to us, Corrie, because we have been here.' "[1]

1. What is the most surprising thing about this story to you?
   - ❏ that a hardened Nazi concentration camp guard would help a prisoner
   - ❏ that anyone could believe in God in a concentration camp
   - ❏ that Betsie ten Boom would think of witnessing while on her death bed
   - ❏ other:_____

2. What is the "deepest pit" that God helped pull you out of?

SCRIPTURE:

A Greater Courage. When people talk of courage, they generally talk of facing physical danger—the squad leader who leads his troops in a dangerous mission, the police officer or SWAT team member who risks his or her life to free hostages, etc. But sometimes it takes greater courage to face the perils of our emotional losses. When yesterday our whole world blew apart, it takes courage to face tomorrow. It takes courage because you don't know if you can stand to let hope grow again once it has been dashed. You don't know if you can stand to invest your love in another person after you have lost someone you have loved deeply. The disciples had to muster that kind of courage when Jesus died. For three years, he had been their life. They had traveled together, eaten together, and experienced wonderful things together. Whenever they had a question or a need they went to him and he responded. Now he had been viciously and unjustly executed. What could possibly lie beyond such a tragic moment? It took courage to get past their tears, but God gave them that courage. He gave it first to a group of women who had courage enough to go tend to the body. For their reward, they were allowed to see what was beyond their tears: New life! New hope! Jesus had risen! The whole world would be changed. God gives that same courage to us, to see beyond our tears to the hope of a new tomorrow.

Have someone in your group read the following passage out loud. Then go around on each question and let each person share their answer. Take advantage of the Study notes following the questionnaire. Be sure to save the last 20–40 minutes for the Caring time.

20 *Early on the first day of the week, while it was still dark, Mary Magdalene came to the tomb and saw that the stone had been removed from the tomb. ²So she ran and went to Simon Peter and the other disciple, the one whom Jesus loved, and said to them, "They have taken the Lord out of the tomb, and we do not know where they have laid him." ³Then Peter and the other disciple set out and went toward the tomb. ⁴The two were running together, but the other disciple outran Peter and reached the tomb first. ⁵He bent down to look in and saw the linen wrappings lying there, but he did not go in. ⁶Then Simon Peter came, following him, and went into the tomb. He saw the linen wrappings lying there, ⁷and the cloth that had been on Jesus' head, not lying with the linen wrappings but rolled up in a place by itself. ⁸Then the other disciple, who reached the tomb first, also went in, and he saw and believed; ⁹for as yet they did not understand the scripture, that he must rise from the dead. ¹⁰Then the disciples returned to their homes.*

¹¹But Mary stood weeping outside the tomb. As she wept, she bent over to look into the tomb; ¹²and she saw two angels in white, sitting where the body of Jesus had been lying, one at the head and the other at the feet. ¹³They said to her, "Woman, why are you weeping?" She said to them, "They have taken away my Lord, and I do not know where

SCRIPTURE (cont.) and QUESTIONS:

they have laid him." ¹⁴When she had said this, she turned around and saw Jesus standing there, but she did not know that it was Jesus. ¹⁵Jesus said to her, "Woman, why are you weeping? Whom are you looking for?" Supposing him to be the gardener, she said to him, "Sir, if you have carried him away, tell me where you have laid him, and I will take him away." ¹⁶Jesus said to her, "Mary!" She turned and said to him in Hebrew, "Rabbouni!" (which means Teacher). ¹⁷Jesus said to her, "Do not hold on to me, because I have not yet ascended to the Father. But go to my brothers and say to them, 'I am ascending to my Father and your Father, to my God and your God.' " ¹⁸Mary Magdalene went and announced to the disciples, "I have seen the Lord"; and she told them that he had said these things to her.

John 20:1–18

1. Growing up, what was your favorite thing about Easter? What do you like the most about Easter now?

2. How do you think Mary was feeling after Jesus' death?
   - ❏ deserted by God
   - ❏ deserted by Jesus
   - ❏ angry at God
   - ❏ like her heart was crushed
   - ❏ in shock—unable to believe what had happened
   - ❏ depressed—unsure how she would make it through the day
   - ❏ other:_____

3. Imagine you were with Peter or "the other disciple" as they were running to the tomb. What would you have done?
   - ❏ waited for the other to check out the tomb first
   - ❏ hurried to see for myself whether Jesus was in the tomb or not
   - ❏ cried so much I wouldn't know what to do, like Mary
   - ❏ looked around for footprints and other evidence
   - ❏ knelt and prayed
   - ❏ other:_____

4. How has Jesus spoken your name in a time of grief or trouble? What effect did that have on you?

QUESTIONS (cont.) and BIBLE STUDY NOTES:

6. What doubts about your faith or questions about God are you struggling with right now?

7. How would you describe your spiritual life right now?
   - ❏ full of doubt
   - ❏ full of faith
   - ❏ half and half
   - ❏ increasing in doubt
   - ❏ increasing in faith

20:19 fear of the Jews. When this Gospel says "Jews" it generally means "Jewish authorities." The disciples themselves were Jews, as was Jesus. In spite of Jesus' words in John 14:27, the disciples were afraid that the authorities, who had been successful in having Jesus killed, might now turn their anti-insurrection argument against them. **Jesus came.** Nothing is said about how Jesus came to be among them, but the implication of the locked doors appears to be that Jesus simply materialized in the room (see also verse 26 and Paul's discussion of the resurrection body in 1 Cor. 15:35–49).

20:22 he breathed on them. As God originally breathed the breath of life into Adam at the first creation (Gen. 2:7), so now Jesus breathes the breath of spiritual life into his people at this, the re-creation of the people of God. **Receive the Holy Spirit.** The word for "spirit" and "breath" is the same word in Greek (pneuma) as well as in Hebrew (rhuah).

20:25 Unless I see. According to Luke 24:38, all the apostles experienced doubt. Here also it should be noted that Thomas was asking for no more evidence than what Jesus had already given the others (see v. 20). Perhaps Thomas was the one in the group who asked the questions which others were thinking. His other actions, as recorded in this Gospel, show him as a courageous skeptic who gave voice to his questions (see 11:16 and 14:5).

20:29 Blessed are those. While questioning is natural and necessary, Jesus her blesses those throughout time who would believe without having to see.

20:30–31 These words, which may have been an original ending of the Gospel, speak of the "editorial policy" with which the author chose his material, and the purpose for which he wrote.

CARING TIME and PRAYER REQUESTS:

 This time is for developing and expressing your caring for each other as group members. We do this by sharing our needs and praying for each other's needs.

Each group member should answer the question,

How can this group help you in prayer this week?

Then join together in group prayer.

[1] Stephen Oates, *Let the Trumpet Sound: The Life of Martin Luther King, Jr.* (New York: Penguin Books, 1982), pp. 12–13.
[2] Sam Keen, *Fire in the Belly* (New York: Bantam, 1991), p. 132.

WEEK 2: EASTER 2
Courage to Face Doubt
John 20:19–31

 GATHERING
10 min.

 STUDY
30 min.

CARING
20–40 min.

Leader: The agenda has three parts. In the Gathering time you'll be getting to know each other through an "ice-breaker." This will be for your total group. The Study time has two parts: (1) Story and (2) Scripture. If you are short of time, skip the Story and move to the Scripture. Begin by reading out loud the Story or the Scripture to the whole group. Then divide into groups of 4 for the Study time. Finally, regather the total group for the Caring time. Keep to this agenda: (1) Gathering—10 minutes, (2) Study—30 minutes, and (3) Caring—20–40 minutes.

 Fairy-Tale World. Which of the following characters from fairy tales would you have most identified with when you were in the sixth grade?

CINDERELLA—I felt I had to do all the work!

BASHFUL IN *SNOW WHITE*—small, shy and the good-looking girls were all bigger than I was!

SNOW WHITE—I had a special relationship with animals.

JACK IN *JACK AND THE BEAN STALK*—I felt I had to protect my mother.

HANSEL / GRETEL—I felt kids had to stick together to protect themselves from adults.

THE UGLY DUCKLING—I couldn't see the beautiful swan in me.

LITTLE RED RIDING HOOD—Grandma's was the special place I loved to go to.

PETER PAN—I had lots of adventures and didn't want to grow up.

INTRODUCTION STORY:

Martin Luther King, Jr. Struggles With Doubt as a Youth. Martin Luther King, Jr. is known as one whose faith led him in the courageous fight for human rights in the '60s. But of course he was not born with that faith; it had to develop. The death of his beloved grandmother was an important crisis in that development. Stephen Oates tells the story in his book, *Let the Trumpet Sound: The Life of Martin Luther King, Jr.*:

"One day when he was supposed to be studying, M.L. stole away from home to watch a parade in the Negro business section. It was May 18, 1941, a warm spring day with a scent of magnolias in the air. While M.L. was enjoying the parade, a messenger brought him terrible news from home. Something had happened to his grandmother. ... M.L. ran home with his heart pounding, only to find a lot of people there—his parents and people from the church. Mama [his grandmother] had suffered a heart attack and had died on the way to the hospital. God had come for her and taken her away.

"M.L. was stunned. But why? Why had God taken Mama from him? Was God punishing his family because he had sinned, because he had left the house without telling anyone, because he had run off to watch a parade? Grief-stricken, racked with guilt, the boy raced upstairs and leaped out the window after his Mama, trying to follow her from this world. He struck the ground in a painful heap. Again shouting people ran up to him. He was still alive: bruised and shaken, but still in this world. Afterward, in his bedroom, he shook with sobs, unable to bear the hurt he felt inside.

"... M.L. was tormented by doubts, and he pressed his parents about the doctrine of immortality. They tried to explain it, tried to reassure the boy that Grandmother was in Heaven. But how could they know for sure? What if she had not ascended like Jesus and was lost somewhere? What if she were just dead? Was it possible that people just died and never again saw those who loved them? He felt so miserable and alone without Mama. Who would cry for him now when Daddy had to whip him?"[1]

1. Who do you remember dying when you were a child or adolescent? How did you react? How did it affect your faith?

2. What would you have told Martin Luther King, Jr. (M.L.) if you had been there when he was struggling with this loss as a youth?

SCRIPTURE:

In Defense of Thomas. Thomas has often been overly criticized by Christians. "Doubting Thomas" we have called him, and it was implied that his faith was somehow weaker than the other disciples. However, not only did the other disciples doubt also (see the Bible Study notes), but we also need to appreciate how honestly voicing our doubts and questions is a healthy part of gaining a stronger faith. In school many of us were encouraged to ask questions because our teachers knew that was the only way we could learn. That is still true when we are adults. However, questions relating to God and our spiritual nature and destiny are so vital that it does take a kind of courage to ask them. Sam Keen compares it to the courage of knights of old, as he writes in his book on manhood, *Fire in the Belly:* "To be on a quest is nothing more than to become an asker of questions. In the Grail legend ... we are told that when the Knights of the Round Table set out on their quest, each one entered the forest at the place it was darkest and forged a path where none had been before. The inner, psychological meaning of this myth is that full manhood is to be found only when we commit ourselves to a life full of questioning."[2] While Thomas did need to be encouraged to take that step of faith that lay beyond his questions, his asking of them was a necessary step for him in his quest, as well as for the quest of those of us down through history who have also wondered.

Have someone in your group read the following passage out loud. Then go around on each question and let each person share their answer. Take advantage of the Study notes following the questionnaire. Be sure to save the last 20–40 minutes for the Caring time.

[19]When it was evening on that day, the first day of the week, and the doors of the house where the disciples had met were locked for fear of the Jews, Jesus came and stood among them and said, "Peace be with you." [20]After he said this, he showed them his hands and his side. Then the disciples rejoiced when they saw the Lord. [21]Jesus said to them again, "Peace be with you. As the Father has sent me, so I send you." [22]When he had said this, he breathed on them and said to them, "Receive the Holy Spirit. [23]If you forgive the sins of any, they are forgiven them; if you retain the sins of any, they are retained."

[24]But Thomas (who was called the Twin), one of the twelve, was not with them when Jesus came. [25]So the other disciples told him, "We have seen the Lord." But he said to them, "Unless I see the mark of the nails in his hands, and put my finger in the mark of the nails and my hand in his side, I will not believe."

[26]A week later his disciples were again in the house, and Thomas was with them. Although the doors were shut, Jesus came and stood among them and said, "Peace be with you." [27]Then he said to Thomas, "Put your finger here and see my hands. Reach out your hand and put it in my side. Do not doubt but believe." [28]Thomas answered him, "My Lord and my God!" [29]Jesus said to him, "Have you believed because

SCRIPTURE (cont.) and QUESTIONS:

you have seen me? Blessed are those who have not seen and yet have come to believe."

[30]Now Jesus did many other signs in the presence of his disciples, which are not written in this book. [31]But these are written so that you may come to believe that Jesus is the Messiah, the Son of God, and that through believing you may have life in his name.

John 20:19–31

1. When you were growing up, what might upset you enough to go to your room and lock the door?

2. "Unless I see the mark of the nails in his hands, and put my finger in the mark of the nails and my hand in his side, I will not believe." What was Thomas saying?
   - ❑ "You guys are crazy."
   - ❑ "I need proof."
   - ❑ "I want to believe, but ..."
   - ❑ "Don't break my heart again."

3. Who does Thomas remind you of in this story?
   - ❑ a science teacher   ❑ a friend of mine
   - ❑ an agnostic   ❑ myself
   - ❑ an honest person who wanted to believe

4. How do you think Jesus feels when we have doubts about our faith?
   - ❑ angry—"I can't believe you have doubts!'
   - ❑ disappointed—"How could you question me?"
   - ❑ ready—"Bring it on, I can handle your questions!"
   - ❑ glad—"I'm happy you are dealing with this."
   - ❑ other:_____

5. When you have struggles and doubts in your faith, what have you found helpful?
   - ❑ going to the Bible
   - ❑ talking openly about them with other believers
   - ❑ being encouraged by the faith of others in the midst of their struggles
   - ❑ spending time alone with God
   - ❑ falling back on what my church teaches
   - ❑ going ahead "on faith"
   - ❑ other:_____

4. What is the closest you have come to "throwing in the towel" and going back on your promise to follow Jesus? How did God bring you back?

5. If Jesus said to you, "Tend my sheep"—what would he mean?
   ❑ Pick yourself up and get going.
   ❑ I want you to carry on my work.
   ❑ Get your eyes off of yourself.
   ❑ I'm still counting on you.
   ❑ Do something about other people's needs.
   ❑ Use your gifts.

6. What evidence is there in your life that you truly love Jesus?
   ❑ I want to spend time with him.
   ❑ Scripture has come alive to me.
   ❑ It's easier to show love to others.
   ❑ I want to go to church, small group, etc.
   ❑ His joy has been my strength.
   ❑ My concern for others has grown.
   ❑ I want to share my faith.

7. If Jesus showed up today and asked you to go out to eat with him, what would he want to talk to you about?

21:3–6 This is very similar to the story told in Luke 5:1–11, when Jesus called the first disciples (four fishermen) and told them, "From now on you will be catching people." Here, however, the nets do not break, symbolic of the fact that these fishermen would bring in many followers, but none would be lost (John 17:12).

21:7 That disciple whom Jesus loved. Jesus loved all of his followers, but most authorities would say that this is John's way of referring to himself, one who felt the love of Jesus in a special way. **It is the Lord!** It was Jesus' voice who revealed his identity to Mary (20:16), but for John it was his

miraculous actions. Perhaps this is because women have traditionally focused more on relationships, while men have focused more on accomplishments. **he put on some clothes.** He would have taken off his outer garment (leaving a loin cloth) to do the hard work of fishing. Peter's typically impetuous action shows his eagerness to make things right with his Lord.

21:9 a charcoal fire. The same word was used in John 18:18 to describe the fire around which Peter denied knowing Jesus. As such, it serves to indicate a connection between that scene and the one that follows.

21:11 fish, a hundred fifty-three. Jerome, referring to a Cicilian poet named Opian, said there were 153 species of fish in the ancient world. Some have seen this to represent people of every race and nation. *The Interpreter's Bible* notes, "If that was a common belief in the ancient world, it would be possible to infer that the evangelist is thinking of the universal mission of the apostles, and that by the unbroken net he was thinking of the power given to the church to hold together men of every race."[2]

21:14 the third time. The other two times are recorded in 20:19–23 and 26–29, but the chronology is difficult.

21:15 do you love me more than these? This question is ambiguous, but Jesus is probably asking Peter if indeed he loves him more than the others do. In asking this question, Jesus allows Peter the opportunity three times to pledge his love for him, to counter his threefold denial. **Feed my lambs.** After each query about his love, Jesus calls Peter to demonstrate that love by being a "good shepherd" to his sheep.

21:18–19 stretch out your hands. This may be an allusion to Peter's being crucified. Since Peter is believed to have been killed during Nero's persecution of Christians in the early '60s, the manner and reality of his death would have been known by this Gospel's first readers.

 This time is for developing and expressing your caring for each other as group members. We do this by sharing our needs and praying for each other's needs.

Each group member should answer the question,

How can this group help you in prayer this week?

Then join together in group prayer.

[1] James R. Brockman, *The Word Remains: A Life of Oscar Romero* (Maryknoll, NY: Orbis, 1982), p.223.
[2] Wilbert F. Howard, "John," *The Interpreter's Bible* (New York: Abingdon Press, 1952), p. 805.

SERENDIPITY
Small Group
HANDOUT

WEEK 3: EASTER 3
Courage to Serve
John 21:1–19

 GATHERING
10 min.

 STUDY
30 min.

 CARING
20–40 min.

Leader: The agenda has three parts. In the Gathering time you'll be getting to know each other through an "ice-breaker." This will be for your total group. The Study time has two parts: (1) Story and (2) Scripture. If you are short of time, skip the Story and move to the Scripture. Begin by reading out loud the Story or the Scripture to the whole group. Then divide into groups of 4 for the Study time. Finally, regather the total group for the Caring time. Keep to this agenda: (1) Gathering—10 minutes, (2) Study—30 minutes, and (3) Caring—20–40 minutes.

 Me as a World Landmark. If you were a world landmark, which of the following would you most likely be?

STATUE OF LIBERTY—Standing firm with my torch held high!

GOLDEN GATE BRIDGE—I spread out my arms to welcome all.

BIG BEN—Tradition is very important to me.

PYRAMIDS—I long for the eternal.

GREAT WALL OF CHINA—I protect those I care about from the dangers beyond.

LEANING TOWER OF PISA—I've always been a little "off-center."

STATUES OF EASTER ISLAND—I'm full of mystery.

ROCK OF GIBRALTAR—I stand firm against the tides.

INTRODUCTION STORY:

Archbishop Oscar Romero Vows to Serve. When the need came for a new Catholic Archbishop for El Salvador in 1977, Oscar Romero was appointed as a man many saw as moderate, a compromise. Romero had spoken often against Communism and liberation theology. But powerful, moneyed interests soon found that he also spoke eloquently for the needs of the poor, and of the need for justice. And so in March of 1980 he was gunned down and joined the long line of Christian martyrs. The possibility of death, however, was a risk he had chosen to take because he believed God was leading him in the effort to serve his people. His thoughts about the possibility of his own death are shared in his biography by James Brockman, *The Word Remains: A Life of Oscar Romero:*

"Jose Calderon Salazar, Guatemala correspondent of the Mexican newspaper *Excelsior,* reported the following words spoken to him over the telephone by Archbishop Oscar Romero about two weeks before his death:

" 'I have often been threatened with death. Nevertheless, as a Christian, I do not believe in death without resurrection. If they kill me, I shall arise in the Salvadoran people. I say so without meaning to boast, with the greatest humility.

'As Pastor, I am obliged by divine mandate to give my life for those I love—for all Salvadorans, even for those who may be going to kill me. If the threats come to be fulfilled, from this moment I offer my blood to God for the redemption and for the resurrection of El Salvador.

'Martyrdom is a grace of God that I do not believe I deserve. But if God accepts the sacrifice of my life, let my blood be a seed of freedom and the sign that hope will soon be reality. Let my death, if it is accepted by God, be for the liberation of my people and as a witness of hope in the future.

'You may say, if they succeed in killing me, that I pardon and bless those who do it. Would that thus they might be convinced that they will waste their time. A bishop will die, but the church of God, which is the people, will never perish.' "[1]

1. How would you describe the attitude shown by Archbishop Romero in this segment of his story? (Check as many as apply.)
   - ❏ naive
   - ❏ faithful
   - ❏ arrogant
   - ❏ foolish
   - ❏ courageous
   - ❏ masochistic
   - ❏ humble
   - ❏ committed

2. Finish this sentence: "If all Christians had the confidence of Oscar Romero that death was not the final victor ..."

SCRIPTURE:

Failure and Responsibility. The first reaction of most of us when someone fails us is to make sure they are not in the position to fail us again. We take away any responsibility we have given them. We take the car keys away from the teen who has acted irresponsibly. We demote or fire the person who has failed on the job. We decide not to put that relief pitcher who has blown the last two save attempts into the game. This is only good sense. But it's interesting to note that Jesus took the opposite approach when Peter committed one of the biggest failures in human history. Peter was not there when Jesus needed him at his crucifixion. He denied Jesus three times. But after the resurrection, rather than taking Peter off of his leadership team, he "promoted" him! He gave him the special responsibility of "feeding his sheep." And when we take a second look this is not unprecedented in secular settings. Oftentimes a coach will *intentionally* put that reliever who failed into the next game, just to give him that boost of confidence that can make all the difference in performance. That is what Jesus did with Peter. Jesus knew Peter had the capability; all he needed was a vote of confidence from his "coach." Jesus does that with us too. Just because we fail doesn't mean he gives up on us. Rather he puts us back into the game, and let's us know he believes in us. That's just one more reason why he is the coach of the team that will win in the end.

Have someone in your group read the following passage out loud. Then go around on each question and let each person share their answer. Take advantage of the Study notes following the questionnaire. Be sure to save the last 20–40 minutes for the Caring time.

21 *After these things Jesus showed himself again to the disciples by the Sea of Tiberias; and he showed himself in this way.* [2]*Gathered there together were Simon Peter, Thomas called the Twin, Nathanael of Cana in Galilee, the sons of Zebedee, and two others of his disciples.* [3]*Simon Peter said to them, "I am going fishing." They said to him, "We will go with you." They went out and got into the boat, but that night they caught nothing.*

[4]*Just after daybreak, Jesus stood on the beach; but the disciples did not know that it was Jesus.* [5]*Jesus said to them, "Children, you have no fish, have you?" They answered him, "No." [6]He said to them, "Cast the net to the right side of the boat, and you will find some." So they cast it, and now they were not able to haul it in because there were so many fish.* [7]*That disciple whom Jesus loved said to Peter, "It is the Lord!" When Simon Peter heard that it was the Lord, he put on some clothes, for he was naked, and jumped into the sea.* [8]*But the other disciples came in the boat, dragging the net full of fish, for they were not far from the land, only about a hundred yards off.*

[9]*When they had gone ashore, they saw a charcoal fire there, with fish on it, and bread.* [10]*Jesus said to them, "Bring some of the fish that you have just caught." [11]So Simon Peter went aboard and hauled the*

SCRIPTURE (cont.) and QUESTIONS:

net ashore, full of large fish, a hundred fifty-three of them; and though there were so many, the net was not torn. [12]*Jesus said to them, "Come and have breakfast." Now none of the disciples dared to ask him, "Who are you?" because they knew it was the Lord.* [13]*Jesus came and took the bread and gave it to them, and did the same with the fish.* [14]*This was now the third time that Jesus appeared to the disciples after he was raised from the dead.*

[15]*When they had finished breakfast, Jesus said to Simon Peter, "Simon son of John, do you love me more than these?" He said to him, "Yes, Lord; you know that I love you." Jesus said to him, "Feed my lambs." [16]A second time he said to him, "Simon son of John, do you love me?" He said to him, "Yes, Lord; you know that I love you." Jesus said to him, "Tend my sheep." [17]He said to him the third time, "Simon son of John, do you love me?" Peter felt hurt because he said to him the third time, "Do you love me?" And he said to him, "Lord, you know everything; you know that I love you." Jesus said to him, "Feed my sheep." [18]Very truly, I tell you, when you were younger, you used to fasten your own belt and to go wherever you wished. But when you grow old, you will stretch out your hands, and someone else will fasten a belt around you and take you where you do not wish to go." [19](He said this to indicate the kind of death by which he would glorify God.) After this he said to him, "Follow me."*

John 21:1–19

1. What do you do when you want to get away for awhile to get something off of your mind?
   - ❏ like Peter—go fishing!
   - ❏ go for a walk or drive
   - ❏ read some good escapist fiction
   - ❏ go shopping
   - ❏ play computer games
   - ❏ other:_____

2. If you had been Peter and knew you had blown it by recently denying Jesus, how would you feel when he appeared?
   - ❏ terrible—I can't face him.
   - ❏ panicky—He's going to chew me out.
   - ❏ defeated—I'm no good.
   - ❏ hopeful—Maybe there is still hope for me.
   - ❏ reenergized—Jesus is alive and I'm going for it.
   - ❏ other:_____

3. How would you have felt after Jesus asked you three times if you loved him?
   - ❏ angry
   - ❏ hurt
   - ❏ guilty
   - ❏ humiliated
   - ❏ healed
   - ❏ frustrated

BIBLE STUDY NOTES:

10:22 *the festival of the Dedication.* This festival commemorated Judas Maccabeus' deliverance of Jerusalem—and the temple—from the grasp of the Syrian King, Antiochus Epiphanes in 165 B.C. For the three years prior to that time, this ruler had profaned the temple by placing a statue of the Greek god Zeus in the Most Holy Place. Given the background of this festival, national pride ran high at this time. The Roman officials would therefore be particularly hard on any incipient rebellious movement. In light of this, the purpose of the Pharisees, as they try to get Jesus to proclaim himself as the Messiah (v. 24), is revealed as an attempt to bring the displeasure of Rome upon him.

10:23 *the portico of Solomon.* This was a large covered porch on the east side of the temple. The porch was constructed upon a foundation that was believed to have been part of King Solomon's original temple.

10:24 *the Jews.* Generally, John means the Jewish leadership who opposed Jesus. *How long will you keep us in suspense?* The idiomatic expression literally reads, "How long will you take away our life?" reflecting the author's fondness for irony. Although Jesus has come to give life to those who follow him (10:10), those who refuse him will indeed die in their sins (8:24). *tell us plainly.* Is this a question indicating openmindedness to the answer, or a question to trap Jesus into alienating the Romans (see note on 10:22)?

10:25 *The works that I do ... testify to me.* While in the synoptics Jesus says that an "evil and adulterous generation" seeks a sign, but no sign will be given (Matt. 12:38–39; 16:1–4; Mark 8:11–12; Luke 11:29), in John's Gospel Jesus uses signs to demonstrate who he is (John 2:18–19; 6:14; 10:41–42).

10:27 *My sheep hear my voice.* Shepherds had names and calls for their sheep as a means of aiding them in separating their flocks from mixed herds, such as would be found in a typical sheep pen.

10:28 *No one will snatch them out of my hand.* This is not a promise that no follower of Jesus will die or come to injury, as the years of persecution of Christians demonstrated. It is a promise of eternal security that death cannot conquer.

10:29 *What my father has given me is greater.* This is an obscure text with variant readings. The essence is that God's power is greater than the opposition and will eventually win out.

10:30 *The Father and I are one.* Having avoided a direct answer to their question regarding whether he was the Messiah or not, Jesus heightens the controversy by this statement. In this context, the oneness asserted is oneness in their care and protection of the flock. Jesus has previously claimed oneness in power, judgment and honor (5:21–23), in mission (8:29), and in divine qualities and the divine name (8:58).

CARING TIME and PRAYER REQUESTS:

 This time is for developing and expressing your caring for each other as group members. We do this by sharing our needs and praying for each other's needs.

Each group member should answer the question,

How can this group help you in prayer this week?

Then join together in group prayer.

¹Shirley DuBoulay, *Tutu: Voice of the Voiceless* (London: Hodder & Stoughton, 1988), pp. 94–95.

WEEK 4: EASTER 4
Courage to Trust God
John 10:22–30

 GATHERING 10 min.   **STUDY** 30 min.   **CARING** 20–40 min.

Leader: The agenda has three parts. In the Gathering time you'll be getting to know each other through an "ice-breaker." This will be for your total group. The Study time has two parts: (1) Story and (2) Scripture. If you are short of time, skip the Story and move to the Scripture. Begin by reading out loud the Story or the Scripture to the whole group. Then divide into groups of 4 for the Study time. Finally, regather the total group for the Caring time. Keep to this agenda: (1) Gathering—10 minutes, (2) Study—30 minutes, and (3) Caring—20–40 minutes.

Acting Out My Life Story. If they were going to make a movie of your life story, which of the following persons would be cast to play you? Tell why you chose that person.

Men:
- ❏ Robin Williams
- ❏ Tom Cruise
- ❏ Bill Cosby
- ❏ Dennis Franz
- ❏ Nicholas Cage
- ❏ Denzel Washington
- ❏ Harrison Ford
- ❏ other:_____

Women:
- ❏ Sandra Bullock
- ❏ Helen Hunt
- ❏ Meg Ryan
- ❏ Rosie O'Donnell
- ❏ Meryl Streep
- ❏ Whoopi Goldberg
- ❏ Bette Midler
- ❏ other:_____

INTRODUCTION STORY:

Desmond Tutu Braves a Return to South Africa. Desmond Tutu is known and respected throughout the world for having led the people of South Africa in the fight against apartheid. Interestingly, there was a time when the Tutu family had left South Africa and lived in England. They found life there to be good, with little of the oppression they had found in their native country. So when Tutu was asked to become the Dean of Johannesburg, it brought great stress to the Tutu family. The story is told in Shirley DuBoulay's book, *Tutu: Voice of the Voiceless:*

"The Tutu family were thrown into turmoil. Leah quite simply did not want to go; she was very happy in England, where they had their own house, their own friends. The three girls were living at home and going to grad schools. Trevor had just started a degree course in Zoology at Imperial College, London, and came home frequently. Returning to South Africa, once again to be enslaved under apartheid, would change all this.

"For Tutu, it was more complex. While from the personal and domestic point of view he was in total agreement with his wife—after all, he had said he found life in England 'a paradisial existence'—he needed to discover God's will for him, then to find the courage to do it. ...

[He went on retreat at a place called Woking to work through his decision, and sought the advice of friends.]

"However much Tutu values advice from his friends, it is, in the end, the voice of God to which he listens. Few of the retreatants realized that during those few days in Woking he was himself at a watershed, agonizing, though twelve years later they all remember noticing a special quality of inspiration and dynamism about him during those few days. Frankie Brownrigg, though she did not at the time appreciate the personal implications, was deeply moved at the way he talked about the courage needed to take a leap in the dark—'the capacity to jump with confidence into the everlasting arms in the darkness of God.' "[1]

1. When, either in the family in which you grew up or your present family, have you had to make a decision about leaving a comfortable, familiar place to go to a riskier place?

2. What do you think most helped Desmond Tutu to eventually "jump with confidence into the everlasting arms in the darkness of God"?
   - ❏ his own ambitions
   - ❏ his foresight
   - ❏ the power of God
   - ❏ his love for his country and people

SCRIPTURE and QUESTIONS:

In His Hands. The much-loved spiritual says, "He's got the little bitty babies in his hands." Perhaps this spiritual is loved so much because of the spirit of trust it engenders, especially when we remember it was first sung by slaves in the American South. These slaves had every right to feel that God had abandoned them, and there was no one to whom they could entrust themselves. Jesus, in our Gospel lectionary reading for this week, reinforces the message of the song: "My sheep hear my voice. ... No one will snatch them out of my hand." But do we have the courage to truly believe that message? Maybe it would be safer to invest our trust (and money) in elaborate security systems for our homes, or in buying guns to keep beside our bed at night, or mace for our purse, or maybe we should just stay home behind locked doors to avoid all dangers. These approaches basically make us prisoners in our own homes, and even then we cannot be totally secure. Courage is believing God's promise that he will care for us, and then going out into an uncertain and sometimes dangerous world to live and love in his name. Such courage is the key to living freely.

Have someone in your group read the following passage out loud. Then go around on each question and let each person share their answer. Take advantage of the Study notes following the questionnaire. Be sure to save the last 20–40 minutes for the Caring time.

> [22]*At that time the festival of the Dedication took place in Jerusalem. It was winter,* [23]*and Jesus was walking in the temple, in the portico of Solomon.* [24]*So the Jews gathered around him and said to him, "How long will you keep us in suspense? If you are the Messiah, tell us plainly."* [25]*Jesus answered, "I have told you, and you do not believe. The works that I do in my Father's name testify to me;* [26]*but you do not believe, because you do not belong to my sheep.* [27]*My sheep hear my voice. I know them, and they follow me.* [28]*I give them eternal life, and they will never perish. No one will snatch them out of my hand.* [29]*What my Father has given me is greater than all else, and no one can snatch it out of the Father's hand.* [30]*The Father and I are one."*
>
> *John 10:22–30*

1. The Jews of Jesus time went to Jerusalem for their special holidays. Where did you go as a child for special holidays like Christmas and Thanksgiving? What do you especially remember about the place you went?

QUESTIONS (cont.):

2. What was the "plain" answer Jesus was giving to these particular Jews about his messiahship?
   - ❏ Their mind wasn't truly open to knowing.
   - ❏ If they didn't hear who he was through his actions, they wouldn't hear through his words.
   - ❏ Since he and the Father were one, the answer should be obvious.
   - ❏ other:_____

3. What would you like Jesus to "tell you plainly"?
   - ❏ what he wants me to do with my life
   - ❏ when he is coming again
   - ❏ what is right and wrong in relation to_____
   - ❏ why I don't see my prayers answered
   - ❏ other:_____

4. What did Jesus mean when he said, "My sheep hear my voice. I know them, and they follow me. I give them eternal life, and they will never perish. No one will snatch them out of my hand"?
   - ❏ Christians don't die.
   - ❏ Christians cannot lose their faith.
   - ❏ Christians are under the eternal protection of God.
   - ❏ other:_____

5. Jesus said that what he did showed who he was (v. 25). What do your actions say about you?
   - ❏ I'm angry.
   - ❏ I care.
   - ❏ I don't want to get involved.
   - ❏ I'm trying to change.
   - ❏ I trust God.
   - ❏ other:_____

6. If you really trusted Christ to keep you in the safety of his hand, what difference would it make in the way you acted?
   - ❏ I would take more risks.
   - ❏ I would worry less.
   - ❏ I would chase after worldly power and privilege less.
   - ❏ I would love Christ more.
   - ❏ I trust Christ this way now.
   - ❏ other:_____

BIBLE STUDY NOTES:

13:31 Son of Man. In the synoptic Gospels this is the favorite description of Jesus for himself, but it is used much less frequently in John. Perhaps that is because the title "Son of Man" suggests Jesus' human side, while John emphasizes more the divine aspect of Jesus. **has been glorified.** To glorify Jesus or God is to reveal their divine essence and make it plain for all to see. Jesus would thus be glorified by his coming death and resurrection, which was now a step closer since Judas had just left to go betray him.

13:33 Little children. Rabbis used this term to address their disciples. In the letters of John he characteristically uses this term also for his readers (1 John 2:1; 2:18; 2:28; 3:18; 4:4; 5:21). **to the Jews.** Nearly all the people Jesus addressed were Jews, as was Jesus himself. John uses this term to refer to the Jewish religious leadership. **Where I am going you cannot come.** Jesus was leaving this world, but here he makes it clear that his followers must continue to live in this world for the time being. There is no room here for those who wish to escape to heaven—we must stay here and do the hard work of loving weak, hard-to-love mortals.

13:34–35 a new commandment. While the command to love is found in the OT (Lev. 19:18), the new covenant raises it up as a first principle that is to characterize the Christian community. **love one another.** Repeated three times in these verses, this sums up the essence of the Christian lifestyle. Love not only creates harmony in their community, but also is a sign to the world that they really are Jesus' followers. According to *The Revell Bible Dictionary*, "The key word for love in the NT is *agape*. A little-used term in classical Greek, *agape* is transformed in the NT into the most powerful word imaginable for love. This transformation was accomplished when the Christian community used this word to portray the love of God in Christ. ... In him, we discern God's love, which is sacrificial, redeeming, unmerited, an expression of the character of the lover rather than dependent on qualities in the beloved."[2] Whenever we show this kind of love as Christians, we point the way to Christ, the one who introduced that kind of love to the world.

CARING TIME and PRAYER REQUESTS:

 This time is for developing and expressing your caring for each other as group members. We do this by sharing our needs and praying for each other's needs.

Each group member should answer the question,

How can this group help you in prayer this week?

Then join together in group prayer.

[1]Mary Bosanquet, *The Life and Death of Dietrich Bonhoeffer* (New York: Harper & Row, 1968), p. 153.
[2]"Love," *The Revell Bible Dictionary* (Old Tappan, NJ: Fleming H. Revell Co., 1990), p. 651.

SERENDIPITY
Small Group
HANDOUT

WEEK 5: EASTER 5
Courage to Love
John 13:31–35

| GATHERING 10 min. | STUDY 30 min. | CARING 20–40 min. |

Leader: The agenda has three parts. In the Gathering time you'll be getting to know each other through an "ice-breaker." This will be for your total group. The Study time has two parts: (1) Story and (2) Scripture. If you are short of time, skip the Story and move to the Scripture. Begin by reading out loud the Story or the Scripture to the whole group. Then divide into groups of 4 for the Study time. Finally, regather the total group for the Caring time. Keep to this agenda: (1) Gathering—10 minutes, (2) Study—30 minutes, and (3) Caring—20–40 minutes.

Paying Relational Bills. At least every month most of us have to sit down to do one of our least favorite activities—paying the bills! We divide up what we owe for things like our car, the food we eat and our home. But what if we had to pay for the relational blessings we receive? Imagine that you have $1,000 to pay for the following relational blessings. Who would you pay, and how much to each one?

For listening to me when I've needed it, $_____ to _____.

For bringing humor into my life, $_____ to _____.

For helping me feel accepted as I am, $_____ to _____.

For sharing time with me in my favorite sport or hobby, $_____ to _____.

For pitching in and helping me with my work, $_____ to _____.

For helping me find spiritual direction, $_____ to_____.

INTRODUCTION STORY:

Dietrich Bonhoeffer Establishes a Community of Love. When the Nazis rose to power in Germany, the young theologian Dietrich Bonhoeffer was one who warned against the dangers of this movement. Bonhoeffer's opposition became more active over time and he even cooperated in a plot to kill Hitler, a major struggle for a man of peace. Eventually he was imprisoned and executed just days before the end of World War II. Bonhoeffer also organized a seminary with a unique kind of intentional Christian community, the love in which contrasted sharply with the hate and suspicion growing so ominously in their country. This community is discussed in his biography by Mary Bosanquet, *The Life and Death of Dietrich Bonhoeffer:*

"This sense of intense and vital significance also gave point and power to the courses in theology. Through them all ran three strands of enquiry: Who is Christ? What is the nature of the Church? What is discipleship? The answers to these questions were sought not only in study and discussion, but above all in life, in endeavoring to make Finkenwalde a living cell of the Church, where Christ might be truly encountered 'existing as community.' For this to begin to be true, the brothers must learn to live together in love, not simply in a mild tolerance but truly in that charity which is the gift of God's grace, and which must be understood as different in kind from human love. Bonhoeffer has defined his sense of this fundamental difference:

" '... Human love is directed to the other person for his own sake, spiritual love loves him for Christ's sake. Therefore human love seeks direct contact with the other person; it loves him not as a free person, but as one whom it binds to itself. ... Because Christ stands between me and others, I dare not direct fellowship with them. As only Christ can speak to me in such a way that I can be saved, so others too can be saved only by Christ himself. This means that I must release the other person from every attempt of mine to coerce and dominate him with my love.'

" ... None of these words represented idle theorizing. At Finkenwalde their truth was wrought out daily in struggle and sacrifice and daily experienced in victory and joy."[1]

1. Dietrich Bonhoeffer felt that an essential quality of divine love was that it did not coerce and dominate. What is the most essential quality of love to you?
   - ❏ lets a person be themself
   - ❏ sacrifices own good for others
   - ❏ commits to the relationship
   - ❏ can both give and receive
   - ❏ affirms a person and believes in them
   - ❏ same as Bonhoeffer—does not coerce and dominate
   - ❏ forgives
   - ❏ trusts and is trustworthy
   - ❏ listens
   - ❏ other:_____

2. When, if ever, have you been in a community like Bonhoeffer sought to build at Finkenwalde?

SCRIPTURE and QUESTIONS:

The Sign of the Church. In front of most of our church buildings is a sign that identifies the building to the community. Most churches try to make sure this sign is attractive to those passing by. But this sign, no matter how attractive we make it, is not the true sign of the church. The true sign of the church is love. A modern Christian hymn declares, "They will know we are Christians by our love," and that is what this week's Gospel reading also declares—"By this everyone will know that you are my disciples, if you have love for one another." No matter how attractive the physical sign in front of our building, unless the love of the people point to Jesus and his true church, people will never find it. They may find the building, but they will never find the church.

Have someone in your group read the following passage out loud. Then go around on each question and let each person share their answer. Take advantage of the Study notes following the questionnaire. Be sure to save the last 20–40 minutes for the Caring time.

[31]When he had gone out, Jesus said, "Now the Son of Man has been glorified, and God has been glorified in him. [32]If God has been glorified in him, God will also glorify him in himself and will glorify him at once. [33]Little children, I am with you only a little longer. You will look for me; and as I said to the Jews so now I say to you, 'Where I am going, you cannot come.' [34]I give you a new commandment, that you love one another. Just as I have loved you, you also should love one another. [35]By this everyone will know that you are my disciples, if you have love for one another."

John 13:31–35

1. Who do you remember in your life who was with you for only a little while, and who you wish you could have had around longer? What was this person like?

2. What is the most important reason why Jesus tells his disciples that he would only be with them a little while longer?
   - ❏ to give them a "preview of coming attractions"
   - ❏ to emotionally prepare them for the change
   - ❏ to get them to start depending on themselves a little more
   - ❏ to get them to pay more attention to what he still had to teach them
   - ❏ other:_____

QUESTIONS (cont.):

3. Why does Jesus choose this time to talk to his disciples about love?
   - ❏ so they would appreciate how the sacrifice he would be making was an act of love
   - ❏ because they would be going through hard times, and they would need love
   - ❏ if they didn't learn to love, his influence would not survive his leaving
   - ❏ other:_____

4. If you were to ask people on the street how they would know someone was Jesus' disciple, what would they most likely say?
   - ❏ by the sour expression on their face
   - ❏ by how judgmental they are
   - ❏ by the Scriptures they quote
   - ❏ by their naivete
   - ❏ by their love

5. What acts of love do you see being done by your church that help people know they are followers of Jesus Christ?

6. How well do you feel *you* are doing at letting people know you are Jesus' disciple through your acts of love?

1	2	3	4	5	6	7	8	9	10
Totally wiping out!									**Doing great!**

7. What do you need to do to better show your Christian discipleship through love?
   - ❏ think more of how Jesus has loved me
   - ❏ start by slowing down to better love my family
   - ❏ get in better control of my time management
   - ❏ investigate some caring ministry opportunities to find one that fits me
   - ❏ learn to start taking risks
   - ❏ pray about it more
   - ❏ other:_____

8. What one thing will you do at home, school, work or church this week to follow Jesus' commandment to love?

7. What do you need to do to find more peace in your life?
- ❐ open my life more to the Holy Spirit
- ❐ get away from my hectic schedule more often
- ❐ believe what Jesus taught—that there is something beyond this life
- ❐ turn the things I am worried about over to God
- ❐ learn from the example of people like Bonhoeffer
- ❐ other:_____

14:23 *will keep my word.* Here we have the connection between love and action that is emphasized throughout the NT (see Luke 6:46; James 2:8–17; 1 John 3:18). In an age when love is sometimes identified with an often fickle feeling, this emphasis on the obedience of action is essential. ***make our home with them.*** Where does God live? People of various faiths sometimes get the idea that God lives in "sacred buildings"—for many Jews of Jesus' time this was the temple, and for many Christians today this is the church's building, which we call "God's house." But here it is made clear that God lives in the hearts of those who do his will (see also Acts 17:24; 1 Cor. 3:16).

14:24 *not mine.* Jesus repeatedly emphasizes throughout this Gospel that the words he says are not on his own authority alone, but are simply the message that God had entrusted to him (see John 5:19,30,37–38; 8:16–18,26–28; 10:38; 14:8–11).

14:26 *the Advocate.* This is a translation of the difficult to define word *paraclete*. Other translations render this word "Counselor" (NIV), "Comforter" (KJV), or "Helper" (GNB and NASB). The literal Greek of the word means "one who is called alongside." In any case, Jesus is assuring his disciples that he would not leave them without resources. The Holy Spirit would remind the disciples of his teachings, so that those teachings could reassure and direct them.

14:27 *Peace I leave.* Normally when someone leaves this life in death those left have anything but peace, but Jesus wanted his followers to have this spirit. This peace would be a reliable peace that was different than the peace "the world gives" because it would go through difficult times as well as good times. According to *The Interpreter's Bible,* "In those days the ordinary salutation at parting from a casual meeting ... was 'Peace be with you.' But as the meaningful ancient prayer which we still use, 'May God be with you,' has been shortened to the curt 'Goodbye,' which nowadays often means little more than 'Well, I must be going,' so in the world of men the peace they flung to one another had little substance or significance."[2]

14:28 *If you loved me, you would rejoice.* Most of the time

we act like loving someone means we cling to them at all cost, especially if they are facing death. But there are times where, as a popular modern saying goes, "If you love someone, you let them go." When a loved one has been suffering a long time, the loving thing is often to give them "permission" to die, to leave this life with our blessing. In Jesus' case, he was saying that his disciples should rejoice at his leaving this life to be with his Father.

 This time is for developing and expressing your caring for each other as group members. We do this by sharing our needs and praying for each other's needs.

Each group member should answer the question,

How can this group help you in prayer this week?

Then join together in group prayer.

[1]Mary Bosanquet, *The Life and Death of Dietrich Bonhoeffer* (New York: Harper & Row, 1968), pp. 270–271.
[2]Arthur John Gossip, "John," (Exposition) *The Interpreter's Bible* (New York: Abingdon Press, 1952), p. 713.

SERENDIPITY

Small Group
HANDOUT

WEEK 6: EASTER 6
The Peace Courage Brings
John 14:23–29

 GATHERING 10 min.   **STUDY** 30 min.   **CARING** 20–40 min.

Leader: The agenda has three parts. In the Gathering time you'll be getting to know each other through an "ice-breaker." This will be for your total group. The Study time has two parts: (1) Story and (2) Scripture. If you are short of time, skip the Story and move to the Scripture. Begin by reading out loud the Story or the Scripture to the whole group. Then divide into groups of 4 for the Study time. Finally, regather the total group for the Caring time. Keep to this agenda: (1) Gathering—10 minutes, (2) Study—30 minutes, and (3) Caring—20–40 minutes.

 That Little Light of Yours. Your group may soon be saying good-bye, as next week ends this Easter series. In a spirit of affirmation, select one kind of light that best describes each group member. Then focus on one person at a time and share what light you chose for them.

FLASHLIGHT: You showed insight that brought light into an area that had been dark for me.

SUNLIGHT: You brought warmth and happiness to my day.

WARNING LIGHT: You gave some needed cautions, without which I or the group may have gotten into trouble.

CANDLELIGHT: You brought us a relaxed, gentle mood.

LIGHTHOUSE BEAM: You showed us the way to go when we got "lost in the fog."

NEON LIGHT: You brought color and personality to the group.

PORCH LIGHT: You were the light that said, "You are welcome here!"

MOONLIGHT: You reflect well the light of the Son.

INTRODUCTION STORY:

The Peace of Dietrich Bonhoeffer's Last Days. When the Nazis rose to power in Germany, the young theologian Dietrich Bonhoeffer was one who warned against the dangers of this movement. Bonhoeffer's opposition became more active over time and he even cooperated in a plot to kill Hitler. Eventually he was imprisoned and executed just days before the end of World War II. In his biography by Mary Bosanquet, *The Life and Death of Dietrich Bonhoeffer*, she discusses his mindset in his last days at Buchenwald concentration camp:

"And now happened one of those curious coincidences which the tangled skein of the war sometimes provided. Captain Payne Best, one of the two British officers taken prisoner on the borders of Holland in 1940 by means of a German hoax ... was transferred to Buchenwald two weeks after Bonhoeffer's arrival and shared in his adventures during the last weeks of his life. ... This detached and ironical spectator, highly trained in the arts of critical observation, and without any knowledge of Bonhoeffer's previous history, appreciated without reserve the spiritual nature to which he had now attained. 'Bonhoeffer,' he wrote, 'was different; just quite calm and normal, seemingly perfected at his ease ... his soul really shone in the dark desperation of our prison.'

"Bonhoeffer was passing the last landmarks in his spiritual journey. The struggles of the Tegel days had ended in victory, and he seems to have attained that peace which is the gift of God and not as the world giveth. The struggle to abandon to God his rich and treasured past, the struggle with the last vestiges of his pride, the struggle to suffer, in full measure and yet in gratitude, his human longings and to remain open to others in the midst of his own pain; all this had led him to that experience of the Cross, in which at last, through a grasp of reality so intense that it fused all the elements of his being into a single shining whole, he learnt what life can be when 'we throw ourselves completely into the arms of God, taking seriously not our own sufferings, but the sufferings of the world.' Out of this death to the last vestiges of self Bonhoeffer seems to have been raised up quietly, unspectacularly, into the last stage of his life, in which he was made whole, made single, fully integrated into Christ."[1]

1. Payne Best said of Bonhoeffer, "his soul really shone in the dark desperation of our prison." Who have you met whose soul, at least for one moment in time, really seemed to shine?

2. When, if ever, have you found yourself "thrown completely into the arms of God"? How has that experience changed you?

SCRIPTURE and QUESTIONS:

What the World Cannot Give. The advertising all around us is very good at letting us know all that the world can give—not only food for our table (prepared for us any way we like), but also every kind of luxury, including expensive cars, boats and home computers, and other items not even thought about when Jesus walked this earth two thousand years ago. But nonetheless what Jesus said years ago still holds true—the world still cannot give us peace like Jesus can. It can give us Prozac and other drugs that take the edge off our distress. It can send us counselors and psychologists who can help us understand the reasons *why* we are in distress. But the world cannot give us peace. Peace comes from knowing who we are and *Whose* we are. It comes from knowing we have a purpose in a drama with eternal implications. It comes from knowing that the Creator of all that is knows and loves us. This peace cannot be purchased from a department store—it must come from surrendering to a relationship. The advertising of that reality will not come across our TV screens—it must come across from the way Christians live their lives. Are we advertising this peace?

Have someone in your group read the following passage out loud. Then go around on each question and let each person share their answer. Take advantage of the Study notes following the questionnaire. Be sure to save the last 20–40 minutes for the Caring time.

[23]*Jesus answered him, "Those who love me will keep my word, and my Father will love them, and we will come to them and make our home with them. [24]Whoever does not love me does not keep my words; and the word that you hear is not mine, but is from the Father who sent me.*

[25]*"I have said these things to you while I am still with you. [26]But the Advocate, the Holy Spirit, whom the Father will send in my name, will teach you everything, and will remind you of all that I have said to you. [27]Peace I leave with you; my peace I give to you. I do not give to you as the world gives. Do not let your hearts be troubled, and do not let them be afraid. [28]You heard me say to you, 'I am going away, and I am coming to you.' If you loved me, you would rejoice that I am going to the Father, because the Father is greater than I. [29]And now I have told you this before it occurs, so that when it does occur, you may believe."*

John 14:23–29

1. What do you wish someone had warned you about before it occurred?
   - ❏ puberty
   - ❏ the trials of the early years of marriage
   - ❏ the trials of being a parent
   - ❏ how tough the work world is compared to school
   - ❏ the stress of retirement
   - ❏ How about coming out of the womb in the first place?!
   - ❏ other:_____

QUESTIONS (cont.):

2. How do you generally react when you are warned ahead of time about something?
   - ❏ I ignore the warning.
   - ❏ I do what I'm warned against.
   - ❏ I proceed, but with more caution.
   - ❏ I consider the reasons behind the warning carefully.
   - ❏ I avoid what I'm warned about—I'm very cautious!

3. If you had been one of Jesus' disciples and were told ahead of time about his "leaving" and going to be with his Father in heaven, how do you think you would have reacted?
   - ❏ panic city!
   - ❏ with nostalgia
   - ❏ with confidence—I would know I could handle it.
   - ❏ with hope—If he knew ahead of time, he must also know everything would be okay.
   - ❏ with rejoicing—I would be glad for Jesus and know it would bring *me* closer to heaven.
   - ❏ other:_____

4. What do you see the Holy Spirit promised by Jesus as being most like in modern terms?
   - ❏ a substitute teacher
   - ❏ a cheerleader
   - ❏ a lawyer for the defense
   - ❏ a coach
   - ❏ "Power-Aide" or similar sports drink
   - ❏ other:_____

5. Which aspect of the Holy Spirit do you most need in your life right now?
   - ❏ Advocate—someone to take my side before God
   - ❏ Counselor—someone to show me the way
   - ❏ Helper—someone to strengthen me for the challenges I face
   - ❏ Comforter—someone to ease the pain of my life

6. How much peace do you feel you have in your life right now? Answer on the scale below.

1	2	3	4	5
like being stuck in traffic with all the horns blaring				like relaxing beside a quiet mountain stream

BIBLE STUDY NOTES:

17:20–23 Here in John 17:1–26 we have recorded Jesus' longest prayer. In verses 20–23, Jesus' prayer now focuses on believers in the future. By including this, the author reinforces the idea that believers after the time of Jesus are not at a disadvantage to those who lived with him (14:16,20; 20:29). This is probably important since John's writing was written latest in the history of the canonical Gospels (near the close of the first century), and at a time when many if not most of his readers would not have been alive during Christ's life on earth. ***that they may all be one.*** While Acts presents a vision of a unified church (see Acts 2:43–47; 4:32–37), Paul alludes to divisions according to personality at Corinth (1 Cor. 1:10–17), and divisions based on differing views of the Judaic Law in many other places (see especially Gal. 2:11–14). These rifts apparently grew over time, and were a major concern at the time John wrote.

17:24 *I desire ... may be with me where I am.* This final request captures Jesus' desire for union and fellowship with his people. In

14:1–3 he spoke of the disciples being with him in the Father's house. He looks forward to that reality with joy. ***before the foundation of the world.*** John, more than any other of the Gospel writers, emphasizes that the drama of redemption—and Christ's role in that drama—started even before the Creation (see also 1:1–5).

17:26 *I made your name known to them.* The name of God, was really made known back in Exodus, when Moses asked God his name and he said, "I AM WHO I AM" (Ex. 3:1–15). However, what Jesus was talking about was revealing what God is truly like. John is bold to assert that while we cannot know God directly, we *can* know him by knowing what Jesus Christ is like (John 1:18). It is through knowing Jesus Christ that we know that "God is love" (1 John 4:8), and to truly be God's children we must also love (1 John 4:7–21). And so John in this passage says that when Jesus truly makes God's name, God's identity, known to us, the love with which the Father loved Jesus comes to be in us.

CARING TIME and PRAYER REQUESTS:

 This time is for developing and expressing your caring for each other as group members. We do this by sharing our needs and praying for each other's needs, as well as by affirming each other.

At special times in life we give people we care about gifts. Since this group has sought to become a close, caring gathering, let's think of gifts to give each other—not physical gifts, but spiritual gifts. Have each person in the group, one at a time, sit in the center of the group. Then have the others select one of the following gifts that they would like to give that person. Everyone needs to take a turn in the center of the group. Here are the gifts:

❏ self-worth—that you may see yourself as the jewel you truly are
❏ joy—that you may receive the joy which you give so much to others
❏ reassurance—that you may have a new confidence of your status with God
❏ peace—that you may find healing from your anxieties
❏ forgiveness—that you might put behind the mistakes of your past
❏ comfort—that your sorrows might be healed
❏ security—that you might know you are safe in the hands of God

After the group shares the gifts they would give each member, close with a prayer of thanks for what you have experienced.

¹Stephen Oates, *Let the Trumpet Sound: The Life of Martin Luther King, Jr.* (New York: Penguin Books, 1982), pp. 138–139.

WEEK 7: EASTER 7
A Courageous Community
John 17:20–26

 **GATHERING**
10 min.

 STUDY
30 min.

 CARING
20–40 min.

Leader: The agenda has three parts. In the Gathering time you'll be getting to know each other through an "ice-breaker." This will be for your total group. The Study time has two parts: (1) Story and (2) Scripture. If you are short of time, skip the Story and move to the Scripture. Begin by reading out loud the Story or the Scripture to the whole group. Then divide into groups of 4 for the Study time. Finally, regather the total group for the Caring time. Keep to this agenda: (1) Gathering—10 minutes, (2) Study—30 minutes, and (3) Caring—20–40 minutes.

On My Summer Vacation. When many of us were kids, our first assignment when we got back to school in the fall was to write about "What I did on my summer vacation." Today we're going to do the same—only opposite! We are going to talk about our summer plans in advance. But we're looking here for some specific plans—how are you going to tend to your spirit this summer? Choose which of the following would be most appropriate for you:

❏ "Exploring some mountaintops"—reaching for higher spiritual goals

❏ "Settling in some green valleys"—finding needed peace and relaxation

❏ "Doing some off-season training"—utilizing the time to develop my spiritual disciplines

❏ "Exploring new places"—not in a car, but learning about new interests through books and media

❏ "Seeing family"—not just far-off family members, but really seeing those in my own household

❏ "Doing projects"—not on the house, but for the family of God

INTRODUCTION STORY:

Martin Luther King, Jr. Finds Broad Community Support. Martin Luther King, Jr. is known as an African-American hero, because he made it possible for African-Americans to rise up out of oppression. But his base of community support was much broader than that, as he learned one day after being assaulted. A crazed black woman stabbed him in the chest with a razor-sharp Japanese letter opener, penetrating perilously close to his heart. His biographer Stephen Oates tells the story in *Let the Trumpet Sound: The Life of Martin Luther King, Jr.*:

"An ambulance bore him to Harlem Hospital, where orderlies wheeled him to an operating table in an emergency room. ... a black physician came in, introduced himself as Aubre D. Maynard, and examined the blade in King's chest. Assisted by an interracial surgical team, Dr. Maynard had to remove one of King's ribs and part of his breastbone to get the knife free. In a burst of inspiration, he made the incision over King's heart in the shape of a cross. ...

"Four days after the operation, King was out of bed and moving about the room and the corridors in a wheelchair. He read through the messages of sympathy—telegrams from Eisenhower and Nixon, cards and letters from people all over the world. But one letter in particular caught his eye. He would never forget what it said,

Dear Dr. King,

I am a ninth grade student at the White Plains High School. While it shouldn't matter, I would like to mention that I'm a white girl. I read in the paper of your misfortune and of your suffering. And I read that if you had sneezed you would have died. I'm simply writing to you to say that I'm so happy that you didn't sneeze.

"That letter brought tears to his eyes. He told Coretta he was glad he hadn't sneezed too. 'What makes you think you are the "exclusive property" of the Negro race only?' a white woman wrote him. 'You belong to us too, because we love you. Your voice is the only true voice of love today & we hear, we hear. ... Please don't lose faith in us "whites," there are so many of us who are good & pray for your triumph.' "[1]

1. What do you see as the most significant aspect of this story?
   ❏ King kept on going after such a close call.
   ❏ Not all blacks supported King; not all whites opposed him.
   ❏ King benefited from what he had worked for—an interracial surgical team saved his life.
   ❏ Whites were part of the community that supported and prayed for King.

2. When have you received an expression of sympathy or support from an unexpected source? How did you react?

SCRIPTURE and QUESTIONS:

Heroes and Heroic Communities. Over the course of these lectionary studies we have heard about the lives of some great people of faith—Martin Luther King, Jr., Mother Teresa, Dietrich Bonhoeffer and Corrie ten Boom, to name a few. We commend and honor their faith. But we don't want to make the mistake of thinking that these were people standing courageously alone. Their courage and faith cannot be isolated from the courage and faith of the communities of which they were a part—Martin Luther King, Jr. was part of the black church in the American South that rallied by his side; Dietrich Bonhoeffer was part of his seminary community at Finkenwalde, as well as the courageous German underground resistance; Corrie ten Boom also profited from the underground community in Haarlem, as well as from the support of the women who met for Bible study in Ravensbruck; and even Mother Teresa could not have gotten far without the sisters who have rallied in support of her work. What this means is that at the same time we honor the individual heroism, we need also honor and learn from how communities came together in support during hard times. That is how God works! As we search for the courage faith gives, we also must search in the context of caring Christian community.

Have someone in your group read the following passage out loud. Then go around on each question and let each person share their answer. Take advantage of the Study notes following the questionnaire. Be sure to save the last 20–40 minutes for the Caring time..

[20] "I ask not only on behalf of these, but also on behalf of those who will believe in me through their word, [21]that they may all be one. As you, Father, are in me and I am in you, may they also be in us, so that the world may believe that you have sent me. [22]The glory that you have given me I have given them, so that they may be one, as we are one, [23]I in them and you in me, that they may become completely one, so that the world may know that you have sent me and have loved them even as you have loved me. [24]Father, I desire that those also, whom you have given me, may be with me where I am, to see my glory, which you have given me because you loved me before the foundation of the world.

[25]"Righteous Father, the world does not know you, but I know you; and these know that you have sent me. [26]I made your name known to them, and I will make it known, so that the love with which you have loved me may be in them, and I in them."

John 17:20–26

1. Who, more than any other person, has helped you know God by the way they lived, or by the way they treated you?
   ❏ my dad   ❏ a coworker
   ❏ my mom   ❏ a pastor
   ❏ a grandparent   ❏ a teacher
   ❏ a friend   ❏ other:_____

QUESTIONS (cont.):

2. What was the most important thing that Jesus did to make God's name and nature known to his followers?
   ❏ taught them how to love
   ❏ showed them God's forgiveness
   ❏ died for them
   ❏ other:_____

3. What is the greatest threat you see to the kind of oneness Jesus prayed for in relation to his followers?
   ❏ self-righteousness and dogmatism
   ❏ false teaching
   ❏ people following cultural norms instead of Christ's teachings of love
   ❏ church denominational structures
   ❏ other:_____

4. What is the most important thing that helps you feel a sense of oneness with the others around you?
   ❏ a unifying faith
   ❏ seeing our common hurts, needs, joys
   ❏ working for a common cause
   ❏ having a good time together
   ❏ other:_____

5. To what degree do you feel you have achieved a feeling of oneness with the others in this group over the course of the time you have been meeting?

1	2	3	4	5
not at all				more than I ever thought possible

6. What do you feel you need to do in the future to be more a part of a caring community?
   ❏ stay connected to a group like this
   ❏ learn more of what I have in common with those I used to think of as different
   ❏ learn more of what the Bible says on the matter
   ❏ pray more for this oneness
   ❏ open myself more to others
   ❏ other:_____

6. What does it mean to "carry the cross" and follow Christ?
   - ❑ never thinking of yourself
   - ❑ being a martyr
   - ❑ sacrificing for the good of others
   - ❑ following Christ, whatever it takes, wherever it takes you
   - ❑ other:_____

7. What has following Jesus cost you?

8. If you are going to get serious about carrying your cross for Christ in the next week, where do you need to start?
   - ❑ be more sensitive to people at work
   - ❑ share my faith more
   - ❑ be more caring toward the people in my family
   - ❑ respond more humanely toward the people in need around me
   - ❑ stop focusing on myself and my problems
   - ❑ be more regular in my devotional life in order to see Christ's leading
   - ❑ other:_____

14:26 does not hate. This is a hyperbolic way of saying that one's love and loyalty to Jesus must exceed that which one naturally has toward one's family. Poetic overstatement was a typical way of teaching by the rabbis, and this should not in any way be interpreted literally as a command to hate family. Jesus himself looked after the well-being of his mother, even while hanging on the cross (see John 19:26–27).

14:28–30 The tower in view might be a vineyard tower used as a lookout to watch for thieves. It would be humiliating to have to stop construction because one planned so poorly that money ran out after only the foundation was completed. In the same way, one must consider the implications of

following Jesus. To do so is a commitment of one's entire life and resources. If we are not willing to give that, then we should stop before we even get started.

14:31–32 going out to wage war. Jesus is not here commending the idea of going to war, any more than he commends the dishonesty of the shrewd manager in his parable in Luke 16:1–9. He is simply making the point again that a person has to count the cost before acting, and this is particularly true in relation to committing ourself to following Christ. It costs everything, and the person making this choice must be willing to pay the cost.

14:33 give up all your posses-sions. We may not have to literal-

ly give up all we possess, but what we have to give up is the *idea* of possession. We have been sold the idea in our culture that we *own* things. The reality is that God owns all, and we must turn all that we have over to God when we decide to serve him. We may keep some things under our care, but we remember that we are stewards of them on behalf of God.

This means that when God calls us to literally give them up, by sharing our money with the poor or needy, or by investing in the work of the church, we do so willingly because we realize these things were not "ours" in the first place. This then is one more example of what it means to give God top priority.

 This time is for developing and expressing your caring for each other as group members. We do this by sharing our needs and praying for each other's needs.

Each group member should answer the question,

How can this group help you in prayer this week?

Then join together in group prayer.

¹Stephen B. Oates, *Let the Trumpet Sound: The Life of Martin Luther King, Jr.* (New York: Penguin Books, 1982), pp. 149–150.
²Dietrich Bonhoeffer, *The Cost of Discipleship* (New York: Macmillan Co., 1959), p. 37.

 SERENDIPITY

Small Group
HANDOUT

WEEK 1: PENTECOST 16
Choosing Our Priority
Luke 14:25–33

 GATHERING
10 min.

 STUDY
30 min.

CARING
20–40 min.

Leader: The agenda has three parts. In the Gathering time you'll be getting to know each other through an "ice-breaker." This will be for your total group. The Study time has two parts: (1) Story and (2) Scripture. If you are short of time, skip the Story and move to the Scripture. Begin by reading out loud the Story or the Scripture to the whole group. Then divide into groups of 4 for the Study time. Finally, regather the total group for the Caring time. Keep to this agenda: (1) Gathering—10 minutes, (2) Study—30 minutes, and (3) Caring—20–40 minutes.

 Childhood Wishes. Have everyone in the group answer the first question. Then go around again on question #2.

1. Give your name and tell where you spent the largest part of your childhood.

2. If you could have made a wish when you were in the sixth grade, which of the following TV situations, animals or items, would you have wished for?
   - ❑ the dolphin on *Flipper* as a playmate
   - ❑ Injun Joe's cave (*Tom Sawyer*) to explore
   - ❑ to be able to talk to animals like Dr. Doolittle
   - ❑ living in the tree house on *Swiss Family Robinson*.
   - ❑ our own maid or butler, like on *The Brady Bunch* or *Family Affair*
   - ❑ Batman's "Batmobile"
   - ❑ the horse on *National Velvet*
   - ❑ Sky King's airplane

INTRODUCTION STORY:

Martin Luther King, Jr. Shuns Materialism. Martin Luther King, Jr. led the United States toward the dream of a world no longer divided by skin color. In working toward this goal he was led by God, and not by a desire to enrich himself. In fact, he gained very little materially from his work. We read about his attitude toward material things in Stephen Oates' book, *Let the Trumpet Sound: The Life of Martin Luther King, Jr.:*

"... King still professed indifference to material things and still tried to be like Gandhi. He drove a dusty three-year-old Chevrolet, and his personal income was scarcely commensurate with his labors and prestige. He accepted only $1 a year as SCLC [Southern Christian Leadership Conference] president, received an annual salary of $4000 from Ebenezer [Baptist Church] and another $2000 for 'pastoral care,' and kept only $5000 from his sizable royalties and honorariums (up to $230,000 in a good year, nearly all of which he donated to SCLC). Still, King was ambivalent about bourgeois values. He liked to stay in posh hotels and was always immaculately dressed in gray and black suits, white shirt, and tie. His work, of course, required that he be neat in appearance. Nobody, certainly no whites, would have attended his addresses or contributed to movement treasuries had he shown up in a Gandhian loincloth. ...

"Because of his prominence, rumors flew about black Atlanta that King was rich. 'The first thing some people ask me,' King said in bewilderment, 'is, "All right, Reverend, now where's the Cadillac?" ' Many Negroes found it inconceivable that King had no flashy car, no personal fortune stashed away, no opulent mansion in a plush Negro neighborhood."[1]

1. If you could drive any car you wanted, what would *you* drive?

2. How do you react to Martin Luther King, Jr.'s attitude toward material things?
   - ❏ He must have been stashing away some money on the sly!
   - ❏ Somebody should have shown him how to enjoy the good life.
   - ❏ To each his own!
   - ❏ He knew what was truly important.
   - ❏ Certain TV preachers could have learned a lot from him!
   - ❏ other:_____

SCRIPTURE:

What Is It Worth to You? One of the great modern Christian classics is Dietrich Bonhoeffer's *The Cost of Discipleship.* The central idea of the book is that the church has seemingly sought to sell people a Christian faith that costs them nothing. "Just believe in Jesus Christ, and you've got it made. You don't have to give up anything. You don't have to change the way you live. Just believe, and God will forgive all of those things you are doing." Bonhoeffer called this "cheap grace." He countered this by saying, "What cost God much cannot be cheap for us."[2] Bonhoeffer's ideas certainly are well-supported by our Scripture for this week. Christ wants us to know from the beginning that following him will cost us everything. Yes, we are forgiven when we fall short. But that does not mean we can go whichever way we want and do whatever we want. Our way must be the way of the Cross—giving up self in order to show the love of God. That is a dear price. But like many people have learned in this world, "You get what you pay for!" Those who want a cheap faith will find a worthless faith. Those who know the cost of a faith that costs their life, and are nevertheless willing to pay that cost, will find a faith that is worth everything.

Have someone in your group read the following passage out loud. Then go around on each question and let each person share their answer. Take advantage of the Study notes following the questionnaire. Be sure to save the last 20–40 minutes for the Caring time.

25 Now large crowds were traveling with him; and he turned and said to them, 26 "Whoever comes to me and does not hate father and mother, wife and children, brothers and sisters, yes, and even life itself, cannot be my disciple. 27 Whoever does not carry the cross and follow me cannot be my disciple. 28 For which of you, intending to build a tower, does not first sit down and estimate the cost, to see whether he has enough to complete it? 29 Otherwise, when he has laid a foundation and is not able to finish, all who see it will begin to ridicule him, 30 saying, 'This fellow began to build and was not able to finish.' 31 Or what king, going out to wage war against another king, will not sit down first and consider whether he is able with ten thousand to oppose the one who comes against him with twenty thousand? 32 If he cannot, then, while the other is still far away, he sends a delegation and asks for the terms of peace. 33 So therefore, none of you can become my disciple if you do not give up all your possessions."

Luke 14:25–33

QUESTIONS:

1. When you were a teenager, which of the following would you have been most likely to save up for?
   - ❏ my own car
   - ❏ a special trip
   - ❏ college
   - ❏ a stereo
   - ❏ a big date with a special someone
   - ❏ Save?—I didn't know the meaning of the word!
   - ❏ other:_____

2. Again, as a teenager, if you came up short for what you were saving for, what strategy would you most likely employ?
   - ❏ give up on it, and just spend the money on something else
   - ❏ sweet-talk my parents or grandparents to get the rest
   - ❏ work a little harder and a little longer until I got it
   - ❏ modify my plans—buy a cheaper car, go on a less expensive date, etc.

3. What do you see as the "bottom line" lesson Jesus is teaching in the two parables he tells here?
   - ❏ Don't try anything that will make you look foolish if you fail.
   - ❏ Plan ahead.
   - ❏ Before you commit yourself to something as big as discipleship, count the cost.
   - ❏ Following Christ is expensive—it costs everything.

4. In light of what Jesus says about family here, what do you think ought to be the relationship between our duties to family and our duties to Christ?
   - ❏ Regardless of what this says, family comes first!
   - ❏ If we put Christ first, it will ultimately be best for our family.
   - ❏ If family pulls us away from God, then our family should be sacrificed.
   - ❏ If you think you have to neglect family to serve God, you need to rethink what it means to serve God.
   - ❏ Sometimes families can be self-serving—Christ never is!
   - ❏ other:_____

5. Which of the following do you have the hardest time giving Christ priority over?
   - ❏ my family   ❏ my material possessions
   - ❏ my future   ❏ my friendships

6. What is God saying to you through this study?
- ❏ God loves me greatly—enough to seek me out.
- ❏ God loves everyone—even those I have a hard time loving.
- ❏ God wants me to help him reach out to "sinners."
- ❏ other:_____

7. What hurting person do you know who might appreciate spending time with you this week?

15:1 *tax collectors.* Considered as vile as robbers or murderers, these were Jews who were seen as traitors because they collaborated with the Roman power in order to become wealthy. Since only the tax collectors knew the tax rate required by Rome, they were free to charge whatever the market would bear. Once they paid what they owed Rome, the rest was theirs to keep.

15:2 *eats with them.* As much as possible, strict Pharisees avoided religious, social or business relations with other Jews who did not attempt to adhere to their religious traditions. The Pharisees had a proverb that went, "There will be joy in heaven over one sinner who is obliterated before God." Jesus' relationship with such sinners scandalized the religious sensibilities of these leaders.

15:4 A hundred sheep would have constituted a large flock in Jesus' day, but even with so large a flock the individual sheep was valued. A lone sheep in the wilderness was in great danger from wild animals or from falling over the cliffs.

15:5–6 The successful search culminates in a party. Although the Old Testament often pictured God as a shepherd (Ps. 23; Isa. 40:11; Ezek. 34:12,23), the Pharisees missed this aspect of God's love for sinners. One of the unique elements of Chrsitianity is that it emphasizes God's search for people more than people's search for God.

15:7 *who need no repentance.* Jesus probably said this with a degree of sarcasm. What he meant was "who perceive themselves as needing no repentance." He was calling into question the self-righteous assumption of the Pharisees that they were not also sinners in need of repentance. Jesus is saying that if they insist on holding to that perspective, there will be no rejoicing in heaven for them.

15:8 *ten silver coins.* This might represent her dowry. One of these coins was equal to about a day's wage for a laborer and therefore represented a substantial loss for a person who lived a hand-to-mouth existence. ***light a lamp.*** Peasant homes were poorly illuminated because of a lack of windows. Note that while the first parable would have more relevance to men, this parable was more relevant to Jesus' followers who were women. Jesus was in this way inclusive in the kind of illustrations he used.

 This time is for developing and expressing your caring for each other as group members. We do this by sharing our needs and praying for each other's needs.

Each group member should answer the question,

> *How can this group help you in prayer this week?*

Then join together in group prayer.

¹Shirley DuBoulay, *Tutu: Voice of the Voiceless* (London: Hodder & Stoughton, 1988), p.153.

SERENDIPITY

Small Group
H A N D O U T

WEEK 2: PENTECOST 17
A Choice for Hurting People
Luke 15:1–10

 GATHERING 10 min.   **STUDY** 30 min.   **CARING** 20–40 min.

Leader: The agenda has three parts. In the Gathering time you'll be getting to know each other through an "ice-breaker." This will be for your total group. The Study time has two parts: (1) Story and (2) Scripture. If you are short of time, skip the Story and move to the Scripture. Begin by reading out loud the Story or the Scripture to the whole group. Then divide into groups of 4 for the Study time. Finally, regather the total group for the Caring time. Keep to this agenda: (1) Gathering—10 minutes, (2) Study—30 minutes, and (3) Caring—20–40 minutes.

A Different Kind of Medical History. Anything you get involved in today seems to require you to fill out a sheet on your medical history. So it seems we have been remiss! Look over the "highly scientific," but not-so-rare diseases listed below, and share the ones you have experienced.

INTERNET-ITIS—staring at a monitor for hours while typing messages to people you've never met

MONOTONE-EOSIS—having people move away from you like you have the plague when you sing "The Star Spangled Banner"

CHOCO-HOLISM—snarling when people suggest you share your "chocolate decadence" dessert

CHARGECARD-ITIS—a strong compulsion to hand plastic to anyone standing behind a store counter

ESPN DEFICIENCY SYNDROME—going into convulsions when you haven't heard the sports scores in too long a time

CHANNELSURF-EOSIS—cramps in your index finger from pushing the remote control buttons so much—often makes you bed or couch-ridden

INTRODUCTION STORY:

Desmond Tutu Takes a Stand for the Oppressed. Desmond Tutu has become known throughout the world for leading his people in freeing South Africa from the curse of apartheid. Such notoriety has come because he has been willing to take a stand for the poor, hurting people of his country. Thus it was that when the South African government decided to relocate many poor black people to poorer lands, Tutu took a stand. Shirley DuBoulay, in her book, *Tutu: Voice of the Voiceless,* tells the story:

"Tutu was so deeply shocked by the obscenity of forced removals that he was determined to show solidarity personally. In 1983 the people of Mogopa, a small village in the western Transvaal, were told they were to be moved from land they had tilled for generations and sent to the independent 'homeland' of Bophuthatswana. (Mogopa was on good land and the envy of white eyes, so it had been designated a 'black spot'—an area in which Africans own land, but which the apartheid regime has decided belongs to another group, usually white.) The lovingly built stone houses were demolished, bulldozers tore through the churches and schools, water pumps were taken away and the buses stopped. In the face of this brutal show of State strength the people refused to move: they simply began to rebuild their houses. Tutu telephoned other Church leaders and arranged an all-night vigil to protest against the removals. Dr. Allan Boesak and Tutu were among those able to be present and it is easy to imagine what their presence meant to the villagers, whose community and way of life were threatened with destruction; equally, it is no surprise that their peaceful protest made not the smallest dent in the government's resolve."[1]

1. When have you had to move when you really didn't want to? How did you react?

2. When has someone taken your side when the odds seemed against you? What was the effect of their intervention?

SCRIPTURE:

Where Is God When You're Hurting? One of the questions people ask most of God is: Where is God when you are hurting? Various religions answer that question in one of three different ways. One is that God is there, doing the hurting. Generally the idea here is that all pain and misfortune is a punishment from God for something you have done, either in this life or some "previous life." Hinduism says that even the suffering of seemingly innocent children is becuse of wrongdoing in a previous life. That all pain is a punishment was also the view of many in Old Testament times. But the book of Job was bold to proclaim that Job suffered even though he was righteous, and the author of Ecclesiastes observed that righteous people sometimes die young, while wicked people sometimes live long and prosper (Eccl. 7:15). A second way religions deal with the question is to say that God is distant and uncaring. God is too big to worry himself about human affairs. The Deists, many of whom were among the founders of our country, taught that God set the universe in motion, and then simply let it run on its own. Many Greek philosophers taught that God simply does not care, because feeling is weakness—a weakness which God does not share. The final way that religions deal with this question is what the New Testament and most of the Old Testament teaches—that God is involved in life, and is involved on behalf of those people who hurt the most. God demands of his people that they care for the most vulnerable of the society—the widow, the orphan, the stranger (see Deut. 24:14; 27:19). Jesus Christ, God's Son, proclaimed his mission to be "to bring good news to the poor ... to proclaim release to the captives and recovery of sight to the blind, to let the oppressed go free ..." (Luke 4:18). Maybe that's why, in the midst of all the other teaching about hostile or impassive gods, they called Jesus' teaching "good news"!

Have someone in your group read the following passage out loud. Then go around on each question and let each person share their answer. Take advantage of the Study notes following the questionnaire. Be sure to save the last 20–40 minutes for the Caring time.

15 Now all the tax collectors and sinners were coming near to listen to him. ²And the Pharisees and the scribes were grumbling and saying, "This fellow welcomes sinners and eats with them."

³So he told them this parable: ⁴"Which one of you, having a hundred sheep and losing one of them, does not leave the ninety-nine in the wilderness and go after the one that is lost until he finds it? ⁵When he has found it, he lays it on his shoulders and rejoices. ⁶And when he comes home, he calls together his friends and neighbors, saying to them, 'Rejoice with me, for I have found my sheep that was lost.' ⁷Just so, I tell you, there will be more joy in heaven over one sinner who repents than over ninety-nine righteous persons who need no repentance.

SCRIPTURE (cont.) and QUESTIONS:

⁸"Or what woman having ten silver coins, if she loses one of them, does not light a lamp, sweep the house, and search carefully until she finds it? ⁹When she has found it, she calls together her friends and neighbors, saying, 'Rejoice with me, for I have found the coin that I had lost.' ¹⁰Just so, I tell you, there is joy in the presence of the angels of God over one sinner who repents."

Luke 15:1–10

1. When you were a child or adolescent, what do you remember losing that caused you anguish?
   - ❏ a pet
   - ❏ a bicycle
   - ❏ some money I had saved up
   - ❏ a special piece of jewelry
   - ❏ a gift from someone special
   - ❏ other:_____

2. What do you remember doing to search for that object, and how did things turn out?

3. What was Jesus saying through his parables about the tax collectors and sinners he was spending time with?
   - ❏ They were too precious to give up on.
   - ❏ Everyone should rejoice that such people were finding God.
   - ❏ God valued them as much as the Pharisees.
   - ❏ God valued them even more than the Pharisees.

4. What does this passage reveal about the attitude Jesus had toward "sinners"?
   - ❏ They weren't really sinners—people just thought of them that way.
   - ❏ We are all sinners—some are just seen more as such by their society.
   - ❏ No sin can keep God from loving us.
   - ❏ People should be defined by their successes, rather than by their failures.
   - ❏ other:_____

5. If Jesus were to minister on earth today like he did in New Testament times, who would he eat with and spend time with?
   - ❏ drug addicts and prostitutes
   - ❏ people like those who go to our church
   - ❏ homeless street people
   - ❏ people in the bars and pubs
   - ❏ the crowd that goes golfing on Sunday morning
   - ❏ people who are recovering in support groups
   - ❏ business people who could fund his ministry

6. How do you feel about Jesus' words: "You cannot serve God and wealth"? What practical changes can you make in your life to make you less of a servant or slave to money?

7. If God were to call you into account for your use of money right now, what do you think he would say?

16:1–2 Landowners commonly hired someone to manage the day to day affairs of their estates. The debtors (v. 5) were tenant farmers who would give an annual amount of produce to the landowner as rent. The master, hearing rumors of mismanagement by his chief steward, fires him, and insists that he turn in the books on his accounts.

16:3 dig. Manual labor was considered below the dignity of a man of business like the steward. However, his main concern is that he is not physically able to do that type of work. **beg.** Since he is unable to do physically demanding work and he would be considered unsuitable for another position as a steward, begging appears to be his only other alternative. However, the social stigma associated with that is more than he can bear.

16:6–7 The reduction of 100 jugs (400 gallons) of olive oil and 100 containers (200 bushels) of wheat both amount to the same in cash value, about 500 denarii. The common reduction also hints at the speed with which the manager was doing business, lopping off about the same amount for all the master's tenants. The large amounts of rent due the master

indicate that these tenants were wealthy people in their own right and would be able to afford to help out this steward later on when he was unemployed. Since a denarii was considered a fair daily wage for a laborer, these large reductions would greatly impress the tenants regarding the graciousness of the landowner, whom they would have assumed had authorized the reductions.

16:8 his master commended. What exactly is being commended here? The steward who at first was guilty of squandering property has now seemingly falsified accounts! Certainly what is being commended is not dishonesty. The point or lesson of this parable is somewhat obscure, probably because we do not know what the original situation was that was being spoken to. What is evident is that the rich master became aware of the action and commended it. Perhaps the steward and the master were both aware that these two debtors would never be able to repay all of the original debt, and that what the steward did was exact the largest amount the debtors could manage, in a manner like financial re-structuring is done today.

16:9 dishonest wealth. This is sometimes translated "mammon," which is a transliteration of an Aramaic word which means "money," but whose derivation is a matter of dispute. The use of the word here does not necessarily mean wealth obtained by dishonest activities, but rather probably refers to the fact that Luke (and other early Christians) saw all worldly wealth (as opposed to heavenly treasure) as at least a little tainted. **may welcome you into the eternal homes.** What the steward did for himself was to secure his future by making these debtors indebted to him. By winning this reduction in debt for them, they would be more likely to welcome him into their homes (v. 4). Jesus was seemingly calling disciples to show the same shrewdness in preparing

for their future spiritually, so that God would welcome them into eternal homes.

16:12 what belongs to another. All material goods are ultimately to be seen as belonging to God to whom their possessor is accountable as steward.

16:13 No slave can serve two masters. The illustration here is the impossibility of a slave trying to serve two masters who claim ultimate authority over his or her services. You either serve God or the world's system of wealth—you cannot be committed to both. While we can (and should—v. 9) use wealth in the service of God, we cannot attempt to use God in the service of wealth.

 This time is for developing and expressing your caring for each other as group members. We do this by sharing our needs and praying for each other's needs.

Each group member should answer the question,

How can this group help you in prayer this week?

Then join together in group prayer.

¹Julien Green, *God's Fool: The Life and Times of Francis of Assisi* (San Francisco: Harper & Row, 1983), pp. 74–75.

WEEK 3: PENTECOST 18
A Practical Choice
Luke 16:1–13

 GATHERING 10 min.　 **STUDY** 30 min.　**CARING** 20–40 min.

Leader: The agenda has three parts. In the Gathering time you'll be getting to know each other through an "ice-breaker." This will be for your total group. The Study time has two parts: (1) Story and (2) Scripture. If you are short of time, skip the Story and move to the Scripture. Begin by reading out loud the Story or the Scripture to the whole group. Then divide into groups of 4 for the Study time. Finally, regather the total group for the Caring time. Keep to this agenda: (1) Gathering—10 minutes, (2) Study—30 minutes, and (3) Caring—20–40 minutes.

 My Money History. Go around on question #1 and let everyone share. Then go around again on question #2.

1. When you were in junior high, what did you do to get money (allowance, odd jobs, babysitting, etc.), and how did you normally spend it?

2. Which of the following phrases best describes what your parents taught you about money?
- ❏ You can't take it with you.
- ❏ If I can't take it with me, I'm not going!
- ❏ A fool and his money are soon parted.
- ❏ Money can't buy happiness.
- ❏ The love of money is the root of all evil.
- ❏ Money isn't everything—but it's way ahead of whatever is in second place!
- ❏ The best things in life are free.
- ❏ other:_____

INTRODUCTION STORY:

St. Francis Seeks a Good Use for "Dishonest Wealth." The man known as Francis of Assisi was not always a "saint." For much of his early life he was a wealthy partier known more for irresponsibility than humility and love. But when he turned his life over to God, he knew right away that this had implications for how he used his time and resources. In the following segment of his story, as told by Julien Green, he sought the proper way to get the resources he needed to repair a dilapidated church building he felt God had called him to repair. He hit upon the idea of taking some cloth from his father's store:

"Here begins the great adventure. The contemplative turns to action. Money—he needed money, and a lot of it, to repair the church. Francis ran to the store where, luckily, he found his father absent—a detail of some significance. ... Francis grabbed several bales of carefully chosen scarlet material, then mounted his horse and galloped back to Foligno. There he sold both the fabric and the horse and set off on foot without delay.

"At San Damiano the priest in charge, a poor old man, was in the church when he saw the door open and Francis appear. The priest knew him well: a good lad who sometimes gave him alms very graciously, but an incorrigible roisterer, living in sin. ... Francis bowed, then went up to the priest and kissed his hand. His respect for the clergy was as well-known as his riotous behavior. This time the priest could not help feeling that he looked bizarre. Dressed very simply—where was his usual elegance?—he seemed a bit overexcited and abruptly plunged into an explanation of his visit: He wanted to repair San Damiano. He had all the money needed for that, here, in his purse. Would the lord priest accept it? This hastily delivered speech left the priest flabbergasted. Caught off guard by this sudden invasion of charity, he flatly refused, given the sum involved, which struck him as suspiciously large.

"Changing his tactic, Francis revealed to the priest that he had undergone a conversion, that his life had become completely different, and that his plan should be trusted. Here too the priest was recalcitrant and remained skeptical about these sensational but short-lived conversions. Then came pleas and supplications: At least he should let Francis take refuge for a while in the church that he wished to repair. He begged until the priest, out of weariness, agreed; but the priest didn't want any money."[1]

1. Why do you think Francis thought it was all right to take something from his father's store and sell it for this project?
   ❑ He figured the end justifies the means.
   ❑ He figured what was his father's was his.
   ❑ He thought he could put it to better use than his father would.
   ❑ He was a naive new Christian

2. How would you describe Francis' attitude toward money in this story: Irresponsible? Practical? Impulsive? Spiritual?

SCRIPTURE:

"No Earthly Good"? It is said of some Christians that they are "so heavenly minded, they're no earthly good." What is meant is that they focus so much on the spiritual and the next life, that they provide nothing of value in this life. The indictment certainly holds for some Christians. Jesus commends us in the following parable to use practical, down-to-earth reasoning in going about our lives as his followers. But in Christ we also must remember the most "practical" decision we can make is not to let temporary comforts deprive us of an eternal reward—to do so would simply not make sense! So the Christian is called to steer a life course using both down-to-earth practicality and an awareness of the eternal reward for which we must prepare. Keeping both in mind is required for shrewd choices.

Have someone in your group read the following passage out loud. Then go around on each question and let each person share their answer. Take advantage of the Study notes following the questionnaire. Be sure to save the last 20–40 minutes for the Caring time.

16 *Then Jesus said to the disciples, "There was a rich man who had a manager, and charges were brought to him that this man was squandering his property. ²So he summoned him and said to him, 'What is this that I hear about you? Give me an accounting of your management, because you cannot be my manager any longer.' ³Then the manager said to himself, 'What will I do, now that my master is taking the position away from me? I am not strong enough to dig, and I am ashamed to beg. ⁴I have decided what to do so that, when I am dismissed as manager, people may welcome me into their homes.' ⁵So, summoning his master's debtors one by one, he asked the first, 'How much do you owe my master?' ⁶He answered, 'A hundred jugs of olive oil.' He said to him, 'Take your bill, sit down quickly, and make it fifty.' ⁷Then he asked another, 'And how much do you owe?' He replied, 'A hundred containers of wheat.' He said to him, 'Take your bill and make it eighty.' ⁸And his master commended the dishonest manager because he had acted shrewdly; for the children of this age are more shrewd in dealing with their own generation than are the children of light. ⁹And I tell you, make friends for yourselves by means of dishonest wealth so that when it is gone, they may welcome you into the eternal homes.*

¹⁰"Whoever is faithful in a very little is faithful also in much; and whoever is dishonest in a very little is dishonest also in much. ¹¹If then you have not been faithful with the dishonest wealth, who will entrust to you the true riches? ¹²And if you have not been faithful with what belongs to another, who will give you what is your own? ¹³No slave can serve two masters; for a slave will either hate the one and love the other, or be devoted to the one and despise the other. You cannot serve God and wealth."

Luke 16:1–13

QUESTIONS:

1. When do you remember getting called "on the carpet" like this manager was?
   ❑ when I was at college and asked my parents for more money
   ❑ when my spouse saw the credit card bill
   ❑ when our department or business lost money
   ❑ when the boss questioned my expense account
   ❑ when my tax return was audited
   ❑ This has never happened to me.
   ❑ other:_____

2. What do you think the point of this parable is?
   ❑ That's a good question!
   ❑ Sometimes it's better to be practical than honest.
   ❑ Money should be used to prepare for our eternal future, by helping others.
   ❑ If we misuse money, we will be called into account.
   ❑ other:_____

3. When it comes to handling money now, where do you fall on the following continuums?

1	2	3	4	5
Saver				Spender

1	2	3	4	5
Conservative investor				Daring speculator

1	2	3	4	5
Cash only				Charge!!

4. How do you view your money?
   ❑ It's mine—keep your hands off!
   ❑ It's my creditors.
   ❑ It's God's—I just manage it.

5. What do you think is the best way to use your money to invest in your spiritual future?
   ❑ giving to the church
   ❑ taking care of my family
   ❑ giving to the poor and oppressed
   ❑ giving to evangelistic causes
   ❑ other:_____

BIBLE STUDY NOTES:

16:19 *rich man.* This man is often called "Dives," the word with which the Latin Vulgate translated the adjective "rich." Another version called him "Nineve," and the name "Phinees" also was popular in the third century A.D. *purple and fine linen.* Only the rich could afford woolen clothes dyed with the reddish-purple dye extracted from a type of shellfish, and the fine linen cloth probably manufactured in Egypt.

16:20 *Lazarus.* This name means "he who God helps," indicating the poor man's piety before God. If this is a parable, as most assume, then this is the only parable of Jesus in which a character is given a name. This man was diseased and apparently crippled in that he needed to be brought to the gate of the rich man's house to beg.

16:21 *longed to satisfy his hunger.* Since there were no eating utensils at this time, people ate with their hands. After the meal, wealthy people would clean their hands by wiping them on pieces of bread which would then be discarded. It is this dirty, greasy bread that Lazarus hopes to be given. *even the dogs.* Dogs were considered to be unclean animals, and their attention would have been unwelcome, even though a homeless person today might relish such a companion.

16:22 *to be with Abraham.* Abraham was the Father of the Jews. To be at his side means to be in a position of honor at the heavenly banquet. *buried.* There is no mention that Lazarus was buried. How a person was treated after death was one of the big differences between rich and poor in this society. Jesus was buried in a rich man's tomb, only because of the intervention of Joseph of Arimathea. Many poor were simply left to the dogs, especially if they had committed a crime.

16:23 *In Hades.* Whether this means the abode of the dead prior to the final judgment (a place in which the rabbis taught there would be some measure of torment) or the final place of punishment for those opposed to God is not clear.

16:24 *Father Abraham.* As a descendant of Abraham, the rich man undoubtedly assumed he has special privileges that should be his. *send Lazarus.* The rich man continues to think of Lazarus as one who exists to serve him.

16:25–26 The uncrossable gap between them indicates the finality of God's judgment on the matter.

16:30–31 The rich man betrays the attitude of his own heart: His brothers, like him, will not listen to the Scripture. However, he asserts that a miracle would convince them. In a clear allusion to Jesus' own resurrection and the stubborn unbelief of the religious authorities even in the face of that event, the story concludes with the point that no miracle will penetrate the heart of a person closed to God and his Word.

CARING TIME and PRAYER REQUESTS:

 This time is for developing and expressing your caring for each other as group members. We do this by sharing our needs and praying for each other's needs.

Each group member should answer the question,

How can this group help you in prayer this week?

Then join together in group prayer.

[1] John Pollock, *To All the Nations: The Billy Graham Story* (San Francisco: Harper & Row, 1985), p.134.
[2] Reported by Casey Kasem on "Casey's Top 40," on December 3, 1996.

SERENDIPITY
Small Group
HANDOUT

WEEK 4: PENTECOST 19
Choosing to Care
Luke 16:19–31

 GATHERING 10 min.   **STUDY** 30 min.   **CARING** 20–40 min.

Leader: The agenda has three parts. In the Gathering time you'll be getting to know each other through an "ice-breaker." This will be for your total group. The Study time has two parts: (1) Story and (2) Scripture. If you are short of time, skip the Story and move to the Scripture. Begin by reading out loud the Story or the Scripture to the whole group. Then divide into groups of 4 for the Study time. Finally, regather the total group for the Caring time. Keep to this agenda: (1) Gathering—10 minutes, (2) Study—30 minutes, and (3) Caring—20–40 minutes.

Emotional "Nutrients." Go around on question 1 and let everyone share their answer. Then go around again on question #2.

1. If you were to choose the equivalents of a well-balanced "diet" to nourish your emotional well-being ("religious" activities not included) what would they be?

   ❐ getting hugs from friends
   ❐ attention from the opposite sex
   ❐ shopping
   ❐ watching old movies
   ❐ playing with my grandchildren
   ❐ camping in the mountains
   ❐ listening to music
   ❐ having time alone
   ❐ jogging
   ❐ taking a walk
   ❐ watching my "soaps"
   ❐ professional success
   ❐ watching sports on TV
   ❐ reading romance novels
   ❐ traveling
   ❐ fishing
   ❐ laying on the beach
   ❐ talking on the phone
   ❐ other:_____

2. Which of the above do you feel most "hungry" for right now?

INTRODUCTION STORY:

Billy Graham Responds to Need in India. Billy Graham is best known for his preaching, and for getting people to respond to God's offer of personal salvation. But it is also true that Billy Graham and his organization have responded with Christian compassion to human physical need. In no situation was this more true than when Billy responded to a cyclone and tidal wave in India. His biographer John Pollock tells the story in *To All the Nations: The Billy Graham Story:*

"As Billy landed he could see funeral pyres, and as he walked in the washed out fields and villages, where relief workers helped feed orphans and put up shelter, more bodies were recovered and he prayed over them. Survivors took his hand in theirs: 'Kill us or build us houses,' pleaded one, in a harrowing scene which was afterwards seen on film by millions.

"Billy was escorted by the state minister of education, a devout Hindu who had been at his home in the immediate area on the night of the disaster. He had taken charge of relief. It was he who suggested that Billy Graham build in his own name an entire new village. The minister pointed out that Indians always pronounce the name as *Billy Gram*, and that the word for 'village' in Telegu, the local language, is *gram*. Billy agreed at once.

"Other organizations were sending relief quickly but Billy's coming in person, and his grief and love, touched all India. Indians called him 'Angel of Mercy.'

"On return to America he immediately raised money. The film of the festivals and of the cyclone disaster, shown on television, brought in $100,000. Meanwhile the Team set up the Andhra Pradesh Christian Relief and Rehabilitation committee, headed by the two co-chairmen of the festival: the Roman Catholic Archbishop of Hyderabad and a leading Baptist, Ch. Devananda Rao, who was minister of tourism in the state cabinet, and had come with Billy to the scene of the disaster. Plans for the new model township were drawn quickly. The state government gave nearly a quarter of the cost of the houses; the Billy Graham Association raised more than three quarters, and the cost of the church and the water tower. On April 21, 1978, only six months after the tidal wave, Archbishop Arulappa dedicated the foundation stone of Billy Graham Naga."[1]

1. How would you describe the relationship between sharing the Gospel and responding to physical needs in a concrete way?
   ❏ If a person has Jesus, physical needs don't matter.
   ❏ We aren't called to be "social workers"—but to convert people!
   ❏ Physical needs are less important than sharing the Gospel.
   ❏ We should help with physical needs so people will listen when we share the Gospel.
   ❏ If we know Jesus, we will be concerned with the whole person—physical and spiritual.
   ❏ The best way to share God's love is to help people in need.

2. When have you seen poverty that truly touched your heart?

SCRIPTURE:

Another Day in Paradise. Popular singer Phil Collins wrote and sang a song not too long ago entitled, "Just Another Day in Paradise." The song was inspired by his own reaction to meeting homeless people. He found that they made him uncomfortable, and he didn't know how to react. Oftentimes he would just walk on, pretending not to notice them.[2] How do people who live in a relative paradise relate to the hurting people along the way? Is our discomfort due to the realization that with a few breaks going the other way, we could be where they are? Is it due to guilt, feeling we haven't done enough? Or is it simply due to not knowing exactly how to help, especially when many homeless people suffer from emotional difficulties? Whatever our discomfort comes from, Jesus calls us *not* to simply walk on, pretending not to notice. Scripture is consistent in saying that how we treat our brother or sister in need in this life has a lot to say about how God relates to us in the next.

Have someone in your group read the following passage out loud. Then go around on each question and let each person share their answer. Take advantage of the Study notes following the questionnaire. Be sure to save the last 20–40 minutes for the Caring time.

[19]*"There was a rich man who was dressed in purple and fine linen and who feasted sumptuously every day.* [20]*And at his gate lay a poor man named Lazarus, covered with sores,* [21]*who longed to satisfy his hunger with what fell from the rich man's table; even the dogs would come and lick his sores.* [22]*The poor man died and was carried away by the angels to be with Abraham. The rich man also died and was buried.* [23]*In Hades, where he was being tormented, he looked up and saw Abraham far away with Lazarus by his side.* [24]*He called out, 'Father Abraham, have mercy on me, and send Lazarus to dip the tip of his finger in water and cool my tongue; for I am in agony in these flames.'* [25]*But Abraham said, 'Child, remember that during your lifetime you received your good things, and Lazarus in like manner evil things; but now he is comforted here, and you are in agony.* [26]*Besides all this, between you and us a great chasm has been fixed, so that those who might want to pass from here to you cannot do so, and no one can cross from there to us.'* [27]*He said, 'Then, father, I beg you to send him to my father's house—* [28]*for I have five brothers—that he may warn them, so that they will not also come into this place of torment.'* [29]*Abraham replied, 'They have Moses and the prophets; they should listen to them.'* [30]*He said, 'No, father Abraham; but if someone goes to them from the dead, they will repent.'* [31]*He said to him, 'If they do not listen to Moses and the prophets, neither will they be convinced even if someone rises from the dead.'"*

Luke 16:19–31

QUESTIONS:

1. The rich man dressed in purple. What are your favorite colors in which to dress?

2. If the rich man had been given a second chance to go back and do things differently, what do you think he would have done?
   ❏ forgotten his lesson, and did the exact same things
   ❏ made sure Lazarus got his best table scraps
   ❏ fixed a turkey dinner for Lazarus, and said "God bless us, every one!"
   ❏ established a family foundation for street beggars
   ❏ given away all his possessions and became a beggar himself

3. In all honesty, if you had met Lazarus on the street what would you have done?
   ❏ looked past him
   ❏ given him some change, and then went on
   ❏ talked to him to understand his story
   ❏ referred him to community or church resources
   ❏ prayed with him
   ❏ bought him a meal
   ❏ other:_____

4. Which of the following would you say is your biggest problem in knowing how to relate to homeless street people?
   ❏ separating guilt feelings from my true responsibility
   ❏ knowing how to help someone who may have addictions
   ❏ helping without endangering myself or my family
   ❏ not being taken advantage of by those who don't want to help themselves
   ❏ knowing where to refer them for the help they really need
   ❏ pausing long enough in my busy schedule to really care
   ❏ just having the love and courage it takes to care

5. If Jesus came to you today to talk to you about how you have treated the "Lazaruses" in your world, what do you think he would say?

6. If you died tonight, what could be said about you? Fill in your name in the blanks and finish the following sentences:
   _____ will always be remembered for ...
   _____ always had time for ...
   _____ felt possessions were ...
   _____ treated people ...

QUESTIONS (cont.) and BIBLE STUDY NOTES:

7. What is keeping you right now from doing what you shared in the last question?

17:5–6 This may represent a request for help in obeying the command of verses 3–4. **mustard seed.** This was traditionally assumed to be the tiniest of all seeds. This is not an invitation for believers to become conjurers or magicians, but it is simply saying that faith can accomplish far more than we, in our limited perspectives, can understand.

17:7 your slave. While Christianity was grasped most quickly by the poor and oppressed, Jesus did also have followers who were rich and who were probably slave holders.

17:8–9 The point is not that the master is demanding or ungrateful, but simply that the servant's job involves these tasks. The performance of them is a normal, expected part of the role. Since we don't live today in a slave economy, we don't understand this as

well as Jesus' original hearers did. But Jesus' use of this analogy does not mean that God does not appreciate and reward our obedience. It just means that he does so as an act of grace and love, not because he is obligated to do so.

17:10 We are worthless slaves. Jesus is not here counseling self-depreciating behavior. He is rather counseling against self-righteous behavior. The Pharisees and other religious leaders of the time felt they had earned honor and a place before God by their actions. Jesus was just telling them, "That doesn't earn you *anything*. It's just what ought to be minimally expected!"

CARING TIME and PRAYER REQUESTS:

 This time is for developing and expressing your caring for each other as group members. We do this by sharing our needs and praying for each other's needs.

Each group member should answer the question,

How can this group help you in prayer this week?

Then join together in group prayer.

†Thomas Merton, *The Seven Storey Mountain* (New York: Harcourt, Brace, Jovanovich, 1976), pp.282–283.

WEEK 5: PENTECOST 20
Choosing Obedience
Luke 17:5–10

 GATHERING
10 min.

 STUDY
30 min.

 CARING
20–40 min.

Leader: The agenda has three parts. In the Gathering time you'll be getting to know each other through an "ice-breaker." This will be for your total group. The Study time has two parts: (1) Story and (2) Scripture. If you are short of time, skip the Story and move to the Scripture. Begin by reading out loud the Story or the Scripture to the whole group. Then divide into groups of 4 for the Study time. Finally, regather the total group for the Caring time. Keep to this agenda: (1) Gathering—10 minutes, (2) Study—30 minutes, and (3) Caring—20–40 minutes.

 Assessing the Future. Go around and let each person answer one of the questions below, or both.

1. Which phrase would best describe your philosophy about facing the future?
- ❏ "I don't want to grow up!"
- ❏ "Back to the future!"
- ❏ "You can't go home again."
- ❏ "One day at a time, sweet Jesus."
- ❏ "He who isn't busy being born is busy dying."
- ❏ "The future belongs to those who plan for it."
- ❏ "I don't know what the future holds, but I know who holds the future."
- ❏ "Every day in every way, things are getting better."
- ❏ "The future's so bright, I've got to wear shades!"

2. Finish this sentence: "One thing that I expect to have in the future which I do not have now is ..."

INTRODUCTION STORY:

Thomas Merton Responds in Obedience. Thomas Merton was raised in a nominally Protestant family, but without any really strong religious upbringing. As an adult he began to struggle with faith questions, and ended up becoming part of the Catholic church. It was a struggle for him to submit to that decision, but he went through even more of a struggle when he felt the call to the priesthood. In his autobiography, *The Seven Storey Mountain*, he tells of how he surrendered in obedience to that call:

" 'You know, I think I ought to go and enter a monastery and become a priest.'

"Gibney had heard that before, and thought I was fooling. The statement aroused no argument or comment, and anyway, it was not one to which Gibney was essentially unsympathetic. As far as he was concerned, any life made sense except that of a businessman.

"As we went out the door of the house I was thinking:

" 'I am going to be a priest.'

"When we were on the Chicken Dock, my mind was full of the same idea. Around three or four in the afternoon Gibney left and went home to Port Washington. Peggy and I sat looking at the dirty river for a while longer. Then I walked with her to the subway. In the shadows under the elevated drive over Tenth Avenue I said:

" 'Peggy, I mean it, I am going to enter a monastery and be a priest.'

"She didn't know me very well and anyway, she had no special ideas about being a priest. There wasn't much she could say. Anyway, what did I expect her to say?

"... Now that I was alone, the idea assumed a different and more cogent form. Very well: I had accepted the possibility of the priesthood as real and fitting for me. It remained for me to make it, in some sense, more decisive.

"I must have been a long time over ... these thoughts. When I came out into the street again, it was dusk. The side streets, in fact, were already quite dark. I suppose it was around seven o'clock. ... [He describes finding and entering a worship where mass was being celebrated.]

"I fixed my eyes on the monstrance, on the white Host.

"And then it suddenly became clear to me that my whole life was at a crisis. Far more than I could imagine or understand or conceive was now hanging upon a word—a decision of mine.

"I had not shaped my life to this situation: I had not been building up to this. Nothing had been further from my mind. There was, therefore, an added solemnity in the fact that I had been called in here abruptly to answer a question that had been preparing, not in my mind, but in the infinite depths of an eternal Providence."[1]

1. What do you think Thomas Merton was looking for in telling his friends about his decision to become a priest?

STORY (cont.) and SCRIPTURE:

2. When you experience a crisis in life direction, which of the things that Thomas Merton did are you most likely to do?
   - ❒ find some friends to talk it over with
   - ❒ get some books and read up on the issues I face
   - ❒ get away alone where I can think
   - ❒ go to church for some spiritual guidance

You've Got to Serve Somebody. Singer Bob Dylan, during a period of his life when he was exploring Christian faith for himself, wrote a song called, "You've Gotta Serve Somebody." The song rightly said that "it may be the devil or it may be the Lord," but you have to serve somebody. Some of us may deny that. We may say we only live for ourselves, and we are in service to no one. But the truth is that when we don't serve God and what is good, we serve evil and the spirits that represent that evil. The question then becomes, who would we rather serve? Scripture strongly affirms that when we serve God, it works out the best for us, as well as for others. If we believe that to be true, then we must choose obedience to God. Such obedience often means doing what we believe God calls us to do, even when it doesn't look like a good idea to us. It may entail sacrifice. It may entail doing what doesn't seem natural to us. But the servant of a good master must trust the direction of that master! That doesn't mean we stop thinking. It just means that sometimes we have to step beyond our thoughts in trust. It doesn't mean we need to show no care for our own needs. It just means we trust those needs to one whose knowledge is beyond ours, and in whose hands we ultimately are.

Have someone in your group read the following passage out loud. Then go around on each question and let each person share their answer. Take advantage of the Study notes following the questionnaire. Be sure to save the last 20–40 minutes for the Caring time.

[5]The apostles said to the Lord, "Increase our faith!" [6]The Lord replied, "If you had faith the size of a mustard seed, you could say to this mulberry tree, 'Be uprooted and planted in the sea,' and it would obey you.

[7]"Who among you would say to your slave who has just come in from plowing or tending sheep in the field, 'Come here at once and take your place at the table'? [8]Would you not rather say to him, 'Prepare supper for me, put on your apron and serve me while I eat and drink; later you may eat and drink'? [9]Do you thank the slave for doing what was commanded? [10]So you also, when you have done all that you were ordered to do, say, 'We are worthless slaves; we have done only what we ought to have done!' "

Luke 17:5–10

QUESTIONS:

1. What is the closest you have come in your life to feeling like a slave?
   - ❒ when I lived with my parents
   - ❒ at work ("They can't fire us: slaves have to be sold!")
   - ❒ at home—My kids treat me like that all of the time!
   - ❒ in the armed forces
   - ❒ I've never had that experience.
   - ❒ other:_____

2. If you could have a servant for a day to do anything you wanted them to do, what would be the first thing you would have them do?

3. What was Jesus saying with the parable of the mustard seed?
   - ❒ People of faith should all be doing great miracles.
   - ❒ We don't need more faith; we need to use the faith we have.
   - ❒ Nothing is impossible if we only believe.
   - ❒ The miracles of nature show what God can do through us if we let him.
   - ❒ other:_____

4. What part of this passage bothers you the most?
   - ❒ the part about the mustard seed—I must have no faith at all!
   - ❒ Jesus' seeming acceptance of human slavery
   - ❒ the idea we should think of ourselves as worthless slaves
   - ❒ the idea that whatever we do, it can gain us no merit
   - ❒ None of this bothers me.

5. What is the main implication of Jesus' slave analogy?
   - ❒ We are all worthless nothings.
   - ❒ God doesn't need to affirm or thank us just for doing our duty.
   - ❒ We shouldn't feel that obedient acts earn us merit—we are affirmed as an act of love and grace.
   - ❒ I don't know—this is confusing!
   - ❒ other:_____

6. If you had "faith the size of a mustard seed," what would you do?
   - ❒ go after my dreams
   - ❒ take on a major world problem, like hunger
   - ❒ "uproot" some evil influences in our society
   - ❒ get on the outreach committee—and get our church moving!
   - ❒ overcome my own compulsions
   - ❒ go into professional ministry
   - ❒ other:_____

QUESTIONS (cont.) and BIBLE STUDY NOTES:

6. When it comes to expressing gratitude to God, are you more like the one who returned or the nine who didn't?

7. What has God done for you recently that you need to "go back" and thank him for?

17:12 *lepers.* Although this term was used to cover those with a wide range of skin diseases besides the true leprosy of Hanson's Disease, no diagnosis was dreaded more than leprosy since it brought not only slow death and physical disfigurement, but also social banishment. ***keeping their distance.*** Lepers were forbidden to approach uninfected people under penalty of stoning (Lev. 13:45–46).

17:14. In response to their cry, Jesus sends the lepers away to the priests. Old Testament law required people with skin diseases feared to be leprosy to be examined by a priest who would determine if the infection was clearing up or progressing (Lev. 14:1–7). Only upon the priest's declaration of healing could the leper reenter society.

17:15–16 Saving the punch line for the end, Luke reveals that the one man who came back to give thanks to Jesus was someone his Jewish hearers would least expect to do so—a Samaritan. Samaritans were looked down upon by Jews as heretics and "half-breeds," as they had intermarried with Gentiles. That this Samaritan was traveling with Jewish lepers, however, is a testimony to how people with a common hurt often let these cultural barriers fall.

17:17 *Were not ten made clean?* In one respect, the answer to this question is "no." Nine persons simply exchanged diseases—the disease of leprosy for the equally dangerous disease of ingratitude.

CARING TIME and PRAYER REQUESTS:

 This time is for developing and expressing your caring for each other as group members. We do this by sharing our needs and praying for each other's needs.

Each group member should answer the question,

How can this group help you in prayer this week?

Then join together in group prayer.

¹Corrie ten Boom, *The Hiding Place* (Minneapolis, MN: World Wide Publications, 1971), pp.198–199, 207–208

SERENDIPITY

Small Group
HANDOUT

WEEK 6: PENTECOST 21
A Choice of Gratitude
Luke 17:11–19

 GATHERING 10 min.   **STUDY** 30 min.   **CARING** 20–40 min.

Leader: The agenda has three parts. In the Gathering time you'll be getting to know each other through an "ice-breaker." This will be for your total group. The Study time has two parts: (1) Story and (2) Scripture. If you are short of time, skip the Story and move to the Scripture. Begin by reading out loud the Story or the Scripture to the whole group. Then divide into groups of 4 for the Study time. Finally, regather the total group for the Caring time. Keep to this agenda: (1) Gathering—10 minutes, (2) Study—30 minutes, and (3) Caring—20–40 minutes.

My Favorite Things. In *The Sound of Music*, Maria says that when sad or painful events happen to her she "simply remembers my favorite things and then I don't feel so bad." Take some time now to think about and share those favorite things.

1. When you were between 6 and 10 years old, which of the following would you have included as part of "your favorite things"?
   - ❏ a day off from school
   - ❏ my pet
   - ❏ sports
   - ❏ Christmas
   - ❏ having a sleep-over with friends
   - ❏ stuffed animals
   - ❏ watching television
   - ❏ reading
   - ❏ going to my grandparents' house
   - ❏ other:_____

2. What do you count as "your favorite things" now?
   - ❏ gardening
   - ❏ relaxing with friends
   - ❏ sports (still!)
   - ❏ Christmas (still!)
   - ❏ hiking and camping
   - ❏ exercising
   - ❏ reading
   - ❏ having time to myself
   - ❏ listening to music
   - ❏ traveling
   - ❏ spending time with my family
   - ❏ other:_____

INTRODUCTION STORY:

 Corrie ten Boom Learns Gratitude in Tough Times. Corrie ten Boom and other members of her family were sent to prison camps for sheltering Jews from the Nazis during World War II. There they experienced very hard times. But Corrie's sister Betsie counseled her to find even there things to be thankful for. She tells of the lesson she learned in her autobiographical book, *The Hiding Place.* They were looking at a previously read Bible verse, seeking the answer to how to deal emotionally with all the fleas in their barracks:

" 'Rejoice always, pray constantly, give thanks in all circumstances; for this is the will of God in Christ Jesus—'

" 'That's it, Corrie! That's His answer. "Give thanks in all circumstances!" That's what we can do. We can start right now to thank God for every single thing about this new barracks!'

"I stared at her, then around me at the dark, foul-aired room.

" 'Such as?' I said.

" 'Such as being assigned here together.'

"I bit my lip. 'Oh yes, Lord Jesus!'

" 'Such as what you're holding in your hands.'

"I looked down at the Bible. 'Yes! Thank You, dear Lord, that there was no inspection when we entered here! Thank you for all the women, here in this room, who will meet You in these pages.'

" 'Yes,' said Betsie. 'Thank You for the very crowding here. Since we're packed so close, that many more will hear!' She looked at me expectantly. 'Corrie!' she prodded.

" 'Oh, all right. Thank you for the jammed, crammed, stuffed, packed, suffocating crowds.'

" 'Thank you,' Betsie went on serenely, 'for the fleas and for—'

"The fleas! This was too much. 'Betsie, there's no way even God can make me grateful for a flea. ...'

[At first neither can find a reason to be thankful for fleas, but much later an insight comes:]

"One evening I got back to the barracks late from a wood-gathering foray outside the walls. ... Betsie was waiting for me, as always, so that we could wait through the food line together. Her eyes were twinkling.

" 'You're looking extraordinarily pleased with yourself,' I told her.

" 'You know we've never understood why we had so much freedom in the big room,' she said. 'Well—I've found out.'

"That afternoon, she said, there'd been confusion in her knitting group about sock sizes and they'd asked the supervisor to come and settle it.

" 'But she wouldn't. She wouldn't step through the door and neither would the guards. And you know why?'

"Betsie could not keep the triumph from her voice: 'Because of the fleas! That's what she said, "That place is crawling with fleas!" '

"My mind rushed back to our first hour in this place. I remembered Betsie's bowed head, remembered her thanks to God for creatures I could see no use for."[1]

STORY (cont.) and SCRIPTURE:

1. What do you think about Betsie's approach to thanking God "in all circumstances"?
   - ❏ She was being too literalistic.
   - ❏ The tough circumstances had affected her mind.
   - ❏ She may have taken a good approach too far.
   - ❏ She had hit on the best way to survive those circumstances.
   - ❏ She was truly living out the scriptural teaching.

2. Corrie had the hardest time thanking God for fleas. What would you have the hardest time thanking God for in your life right now?

 Left With a Long Putt. The story is told of a golfer who hit a long drive, only to see that drive slice into the woods. The ball bounced off a tree and then ricocheted off a rock, only to roll onto the green, about 15 feet from the hole. The golfer just shook his head and said, "Can you beat that!—left myself with a long putt!" This golfer's attitude reflects the attitudes of many people in America. We have been given many breaks, but all we can think of is what has *not* gone right. Most people in our country have a good home, at least two cars, so many toys for our children that our closets bulge, more than enough food to eat, and many entertainment products to boot. But still most of us find plenty of room to complain about what we don't have. This kind of negative focus really hurts us in the long run, for if we focus on what we don't have, we make ourselves miserable. Only when we focus on the blessings we have received do we truly enjoy them.

Have someone in your group read the following passage out loud. Then go around on each question and let each person share their answer. Take advantage of the Study notes following the questionnaire. Be sure to save the last 20–40 minutes for the Caring time.

*[11]**On the way to Jerusalem Jesus was going through the region between Samaria and Galilee. [12]As he entered a village, ten lepers approached him. Keeping their distance, [13]they called out, saying, "Jesus, Master, have mercy on us!" [14]When he saw them, he said to them, "Go and show yourselves to the priests." And as they went, they were made clean. [15]Then one of them, when he saw that he was healed, turned back, praising God with a loud voice. [16]He prostrated himself at Jesus' feet and thanked him. And he was a Samaritan. [17]Then Jesus asked, "Were not ten made clean? But the other nine, where are they? [18]Was none of them found to return and give praise to God except this foreigner?" [19]Then he said to him, "Get up and go on your way; your faith has made you well."*

Luke 17:11–19

QUESTIONS:

1. If you could go back to someone to thank them for what they did for you when you were a child or adolescent, who would it be?
   - ❏ my father
   - ❏ my mother
   - ❏ a grandparent
   - ❏ a teacher
   - ❏ a coach or mentor
   - ❏ a pastor or youth leader
   - ❏ a sibling
   - ❏ a childhood friend
   - ❏ other:_____

2. Why did all but one of the lepers fail to come back and thank Jesus?
   - ❏ They couldn't find him.
   - ❏ They weren't grateful enough to make the effort.
   - ❏ They had what they wanted.
   - ❏ They thought it was time something good happened to them.
   - ❏ They were too busy telling others their good news.
   - ❏ They were too busy getting reunited with their families and friends.
   - ❏ They were only interested in the miracle, not the one providing it.

3. What was significant about the man who did return to thank Jesus?
   - ❏ As a Samaritan, being looked down on made him more grateful.
   - ❏ The others received physical healing, but only he received salvation.
   - ❏ His being a foreigner shows that Jesus came for *all* people.
   - ❏ He provides an example for our attitude toward Jesus.

4. Which aspects of this story can you relate to personally?
   - ❏ being an outcast
   - ❏ the pain of a physical condition
   - ❏ finding how a common pain breaks down cultural barriers
   - ❏ neglecting to express thanks for my own blessings
   - ❏ having others neglect to thank me
   - ❏ being more interested in what God can do for me than in God himself
   - ❏ other:_____

5. When someone does something special for you, what do you usually do in return?
   - ❏ say "thank-you"
   - ❏ send a thank-you note
   - ❏ give them a gift
   - ❏ do something for them
   - ❏ forget to do anything
   - ❏ other:_____

QUESTIONS (cont.) and BIBLE STUDY NOTES:

7. When it comes to prayer, what are you most likely to do?
- ❏ cry out to God day and night
- ❏ worry constantly, rather than pray
- ❏ hang tough
- ❏ give up

8. As a result of this study, what do you now feel you need to do?
- ❏ keep on praying
- ❏ *start* praying
- ❏ trust more in what God will do
- ❏ do more for myself
- ❏ submit more fully to what God wants
- ❏ other:_____

18:2 *a judge.* In small towns, local people of prominence were appointed to act in this capacity. Although Jewish judges were to be impartial (2 Chron. 19:4–7), and were, in fact, to give special precedence to cases involving widows and orphans, far too often in actuality judges required bribes to settle a case. Widows, who were most often poor, had no such influence. ***neither feared God.*** If he feared God he would have acted in accordance with the demands of Scripture to care for widows (Ex. 22:22–23; Deut. 24:17; 27:19). ***nor had a respect for people.*** The Syriac and Arabic translations here speak of the judge's inability to be shamed. While the needs of a poor widow ought to have at least shamed the judge into doing something for her, his conscience was such that he was unmoved by the common public opinion regarding what was the right and decent thing to do.

18:3 *my opponent.* The nature of the case is not explained, but widows, who at this time had little or no influence with which to resist oppression, would be prime targets for unscrupulous people. It could have been that a bribe from this opponent had even led the judge to ignore her case.

18:5 *wear me out.* Literally, this is "give me a black eye"! While physical assault was not probably feared, this phrase has the same metaphorical use that it does in English. The judge was concerned about the damage to his reputation that she could inflict as she continually complained about his disregard for her case. Arabic translations treat this even more figuratively to be "give me a headache"! Whether to avoid more negative reports about himself or simply to rid himself of an annoyance, he finally renders a judgment. His concern is not for justice; he simply wants to be rid of this persistent woman.

CARING TIME and PRAYER REQUESTS:

18:7 Like the parable of the unjust steward (16:1–8) or the parable of the friend at midnight (11:5–8), this parable makes its point by use of a "how much more" argument. If even such an unjust judge would finally render justice due to the persistent plea of an aggrieved person, *how much more* will God intervene to bring deliverance and justice to his followers who call out to him?

18:8 *will he find faith on earth?* While the disciples are assured that God will answer their prayers for redemption, a passage of time will occur during which some of them will give up hope. This is a challenge to those who are wavering in faith, to keep on praying "Your kingdom come," retaining confidence in God's character even when there is no visible evidence of deliverance.

 This time is for developing and expressing your caring for each other as group members. We do this by sharing our needs and praying for each other's needs.

Each group member should answer the question,

How can this group help you in prayer this week?

Then join together in group prayer.

¹Lush Gjergji, *Mother Teresa: Her Life, Her Work* (Hyde Park, NY: New City Press, 1991), pp. 46–47.

SERENDIPITY
Small Group
HANDOUT

WEEK 7: PENTECOST 22
Choosing to Pray
Luke 18:1–8

 GATHERING 10 min.   **STUDY** 30 min.   **CARING** 20–40 min.

Leader: The agenda has three parts. In the Gathering time you'll be getting to know each other through an "ice-breaker." This will be for your total group. The Study time has two parts: (1) Story and (2) Scripture. If you are short of time, skip the Story and move to the Scripture. Begin by reading out loud the Story or the Scripture to the whole group. Then divide into groups of 4 for the Study time. Finally, regather the total group for the Caring time. Keep to this agenda: (1) Gathering—10 minutes, (2) Study—30 minutes, and (3) Caring—20–40 minutes.

 The Light We Shine. Over the past few weeks, we have gotten to know each other better. Knowing what you know now, what kind of light best describes each of the members in your group? For each of the lights below, choose a group member who best fits that category. Share these with each other in a spirit of affirmation.

CAMPFIRE LIGHT: You give warmth and light to the cold night.

FLASHLIGHT: You direct light to the especially dark areas where it is needed most.

100-WATT BULB: Your personality lights up the room!

MOONLIGHT: You reflect well the light of the Son.

FIREPLACE LIGHT: You bring people together around your crackling warmth.

SUNLIGHT: You are a natural light that gives life to those around you.

NEON LIGHT: Your light brings personality, flash and color to the group.

LIGHTHOUSE BEAM: You showed us the way when we got "lost in the fog."

INTRODUCTION STORY:

Mother Teresa Gets What She Petitions For. Mother Teresa is known and respected throughout the world for her work with "the poorest of the poor" in Calcutta, India, and in other parts of the world. Her work necessitates not only dedication by her and the other sisters involved in the work, but also help from business people. Her biographer Lush Gjergji tells of how she appealed for such help in one case:

"Mr. Gomes remembered his first meeting with her.

" 'It was February. Mother Teresa came with a lady who worked as a servant at St. Mary's school; she was a widow named Charur. But before long Mother Teresa went off again to the suburbs, where her poor people lived. Not only that, but she took my daughter along with her. She needed a lot of medicines. That was how I too began to beg. Once we went into a large pharmacy with a long list. The druggist was very busy. Mother Teresa showed him the list and asked him to give us these medicines gratis. "Madam," he told her, "you came to the wrong door. Let me finish my work." So both of us sat down, and she began saying her rosary. When the druggist got through he told her: "Here are three packages of medicine that you need; please consider them as a gift from the company."

'Besides medicines other things too were in short supply: food, clothes, and so on. It was difficult, but she always appeared calm and sure of herself, intent on doing the work of divine providence. ... ' "[1]

1. Why do you think the druggist changed his mind?
   ❑ He was ashamed after seeing her piety.
   ❑ He figured it was bad for business having her stick around.
   ❑ God moved upon his heart, in accordance with her prayers.
   ❑ He figured she was so persistent, he might as well give in sooner than later.
   ❑ other: _____

2. What do you think made Mother Teresa so calm and sure of herself?
   ❑ her natural self-confidence
   ❑ her belief in her mission
   ❑ her confidence in God's provision
   ❑ her belief in the goodness of people—that they always "come around"
   ❑ other: _____

SCRIPTURE:

Prayer or Demands? The story is told of a young boy who wanted a bicycle very badly, and so decided to pray for it. He knelt beside his bed and asked God to get him a bicycle. He promised Jesus that if he did, he would clean his room every day for a week, without being told. Then he went to bed. As he lay there he thought of how much work it was to clean his room, and so he began to have regrets. He got up and knelt beside his bed again. He told Jesus to cancel the previous agreement, but told him that if God would just make it so he could have a bicycle, he would be nice to his sister all week. Once again he got up and lay in his bed, but once again he began to have regrets. He thought of what a pain his sister could be and how hard it would be to be nice to her for a whole week. Suddenly he got an idea. He went to his dresser, took down a statue of the Virgin Mary, wrapped it up tightly in a towel, and tossed it in his closet and shut the door. Then he went to his desk and wrote, "Dear Jesus: I'm holding your mother! If you ever want to see her again ..." While we are not usually so blatant, sometimes we use prayer like this little boy did. Prayer should be submission to God's will, but we use it like it were a set of demands. If they aren't filled right away we'll use what leverage we have—let God know we don't believe in him anymore, stop attending church, etc. Our parable for today lets us know that God will respond to our prayers without these pressures that are required in the world. But we must have patience and we must submit to God, believing God is a good Parent who will do what is best for us.

Have someone in your group read the following passage out loud. Then go around on each question and let each person share their answer. Take advantage of the Study notes following the questionnaire. Be sure to save the last 20–40 minutes for the Caring time.

18 *Then Jesus told them a parable about their need to pray always and not to lose heart. [2]He said, "In a certain city there was a judge who neither feared God nor had respect for people. [3]In that city there was a widow who kept coming to him and saying, 'Grant me justice against my opponent.' [4]For a while he refused; but later he said to himself, 'Though I have no fear of God and no respect for anyone, [5]yet because this widow keeps bothering me, I will grant her justice, so that she may not wear me out by continually coming.' " [6]And the Lord said, "Listen to what the unjust judge says. [7]And will not God grant justice to his chosen ones who cry to him day and night? Will he delay long in helping them? [8]I tell you, he will quickly grant justice to them. And yet, when the Son of Man comes, will he find faith on earth?"*

Luke 18:1–8

QUESTIONS:

1. When you were in junior high, who were you most likely to have a dispute with?
   ❑ a brother or sister
   ❑ a parent
   ❑ a kid in the neighborhood or in my school
   ❑ the law!
   ❑ other:_____

2. Which of the following two songs best describes how you felt about the kind of justice you received at that age?

   "Nobody likes me, everybody hates me,
   I'm going to eat some worms!"   "It's a Wonderful
   _____World"

3. What would you have done if you were the widow in this story?
   ❑ figured out a way to bribe the judge
   ❑ figured it was useless, so why try
   ❑ figured I didn't deserve justice
   ❑ made myself a "pain in the neck," just like she did
   ❑ hit the judge and gotten myself thrown in jail
   ❑ other:_____

4. What would you say is the main point Jesus was making in this parable?
   ❑ "The squeaky wheel gets the grease."
   ❑ God wants to see how persistent we are willing to be.
   ❑ If even an unjust judge will respond to persistence, certainly God will.
   ❑ We need to endure faithfully until Jesus returns.
   ❑ We should never give up on God or get tired of praying.
   ❑ If you really have faith, God will answer all your prayers.
   ❑ other:_____

5. To what prayer concern of yours have you felt God was being slow to respond?

6. What do you think is the most likely reason God has been seemingly slow in regard to the need you listed in question #6?
   ❑ God has a backlog of requests.
   ❑ God really doesn't care about little things like my concern.
   ❑ Maybe my request would not be for the best.
   ❑ Maybe God wants me to do more for myself.
   ❑ Maybe these things just take more time.
   ❑ Maybe God wants to see how badly I want this.
   ❑ other: _____

7. What do you most need to start doing if you are to take this week's lesson seriously?

- ❏ ask for God's forgiveness and mercy
- ❏ stop looking down on others
- ❏ admit my own faults
- ❏ stop trying to overdo the humble bit by putting myself down
- ❏ share my real feelings with others
- ❏ other:_____

18:9 to some who trusted in themselves. The Pharisees were undoubtedly in Luke's mind as the specific audience in view. **regarded others with contempt.** The Pharisees considered themselves superior to other Jews who were unable or unwilling to conform with their detailed interpretation of the Law of Moses.

18:10 went up to the temple to pray. Twice daily, the priests at the temple offered a lamb as a sacrifice of atonement for the sins of the people. At these services, people would gather to join in the liturgy and pray. The Pharisee and tax collector represent polar opposites in the Jewish society of the time. **Pharisee.** The Pharisees were a small, powerful religious sect whose prime concern was keeping the Law in all its detail. While modern readers of the New Testament tend to assume the Pharisees are "the bad guys" in the story, the original listeners of this parable respected them as especially devout, godly people. **tax collector.** Jesus' listeners would have considered a tax collector as vile as a robber or murderer. Tax collectors were Jews who were considered by other Jews to be traitors because they collaborated with the Roman power in order to

become wealthy. Since only the tax collector knew the tax rate required by Rome, he was free to charge whatever the market would bear. Once he paid what he owed Rome, the rest was his to keep.

18:11 standing by himself. Standing was the typical posture for prayer. He was probably by himself because he didn't think anyone else was good enough to stand with him. As a Pharisee, he would not want to risk becoming ritually unclean by brushing up against someone in the crowd who was somehow ceremonially defiled. The listeners would not think this unusual for a holy man. **I thank you that.** One well-known rabbinic prayer that dates to a time not too long after the time of Jesus reads, "Praise be to the Lord that he did not make me a heathen, for all heathen are as nothing before Him; praised be He that He did not make me a woman, for woman is not under obligation to fulfill the law; praised be He that He did not make me ... an uneducated man, for the uneducated man is not cautious to avoid sins." The Pharisee may have felt it his duty to offer such a prayer aloud as a way of instructing "sinners" in the crowd about the way of righteousness.

18:12 I fast twice a week. While Jews were only required to fast on the Day of Atonement, Pharisees fasted every Monday and Thursday in an attempt to gain merit with God. **I give a tenth.** Although all Jews were expected to tithe their produce, Pharisees carefully tithed even things that were not required.

18:13 standing far off. The tax collector likewise stands apart from the crowd, but not because of any sense of moral superiority. Instead, he is too ashamed to join them. **would not even look up.** While praying with head bowed is traditional for us, Jews prayed with head and arms lifted toward heaven. **was beating his breast.** This was done only on occasions of great anguish. **be merciful.** Literally, this is "make an atone-

ment." In light of the ceremony under way at the temple, the tax collector pleads that the atoning sacrifice might apply to him. He realizes this is his only hope before God.

18:14 I tell you this man went down to his home justified. Here is where the listeners would have been surprised. How could it be that the Pharisee, the model of righteousness, is not right before God, whereas the tax collector is forgiven, acquitted by God? The surprising twist in the parable is that righteousness is a matter of humble self-recognition of sin and dependence upon the atonement God provides as a gift (rather than a matter of impressing God with one's performance).

 This time is for developing and expressing your caring for each other as group members. We do this by sharing our needs and praying for each other's needs.

Each group member should answer the question,

How can this group help you in prayer this week?

Then join together in group prayer.

¹Julien Green, *God's Fool: The Life and Times of Francis of Assisi* (San Francisco: Harper & Row, 1983), pp.104–105.

SERENDIPITY

Small Group
HANDOUT

WEEK 8: PENTECOST 23
Choosing Humility
Luke 18:9–14

 GATHERING
10 min.

 STUDY
30 min.

 CARING
20–40 min.

Leader: The agenda has three parts. In the Gathering time you'll be getting to know each other through an "ice-breaker." This will be for your total group. The Study time has two parts: (1) Story and (2) Scripture. If you are short of time, skip the Story and move to the Scripture. Begin by reading out loud the Story or the Scripture to the whole group. Then divide into groups of 4 for the Study time. Finally, regather the total group for the Caring time. Keep to this agenda: (1) Gathering—10 minutes, (2) Study—30 minutes, and (3) Caring—20–40 minutes.

 Life Is a Beach! A popular bumper sticker says, "Life is a beach!"—Is it?! What has life been for you? Choose from one of the following or make up your own:

"LIFE IS A BEACH!"

"LIFE WAS A BEACH"—until the tidal wave hit!

"LIFE IS A MOUNTAIN"—full of challenging ascents and beautiful vistas

"LIFE IS A WINDING RIVER"—continually changing, with a new view around every corner

"LIFE IS A DESERT"—an empty, hostile place where you fight for what you get

"LIFE IS A DESERT MIRAGE"—You never know what is real.

"LIFE IS A FARMER'S FIELD"—What you get depends on what you put into it.

"LIFE IS A TOXIC-WASTE DUMP"—We're killing each other!

other:_____

INTRODUCTION STORY:

St. Francis' Humble Band of Followers. Francis of Assisi was born to a wealthy family, and spent his early life partying and squandering his father's wealth. But then he learned another way was more powerful and more satisfying—the way of poverty and humility, the way of Christ. He traded his wealth for rags and a life of service, and soon others, disillusioned with a society and even a church that knew only the values of wealth and privilege, followed in Francis' footsteps. Francis' biographer Julien Green tells how it was in his book, *God's Fool: The Life and Times of Francis of Assisi:*

"What mysterious force drew men to that little group they saw passing by, singing in the streets of the hill towns of Umbria or wandering through the fields and woods? Barefoot, dressed like paupers with a robe resembling a sack and a cord for a belt, but joyful like children, they seemed to have come from another world where sadness didn't exist. Could one own nothing and live happily on this earth? Had the Golden Age returned? Assisi watched with a vague admiration, but a bit uneasily, the ragged fellows who were upsetting convention—in the name of the Lord.

"... In the streets of Assisi these vagabonds were greeted with sarcasm and, occasionally, some rather pointed questions: 'Yesterday you had plenty to live on, and now that you've sold everything, you come to ask us for bread. Aren't you crazy?' They answered meekly, invoking the love of God and wishing peace and happiness to everyone. In the end they carried away, along [with] the jibes, a few crusts of bread and some indescribable leftovers—unwanted garbage from the kitchen—but they considered themselves fortunate because the joy that swept over Francis's soul lived in theirs as well.

"Moreover, Francis never stopped encouraging them, because when they faced the world's hostility, some of them couldn't help trembling a little. They were taken for hopeless boors, and the blasphemers sneered when they spoke of God. But as for that, said Francis, they must reply serenely by preaching repentance and never forget that the Lord himself was speaking through them to the proud and the wicked. Gradually the consensus grew that they weren't ordinary beggars. If they met people still poorer than themselves out on the road, they would rip a sleeve off of their wretched habits, a broad swatch of coarse cloth, and give it away in the name of Christ."[1]

1. What made the followers of Francis so joyful?
- ❏ delirium from lack of food
- ❏ freedom from slavery to material possession
- ❏ their intense fellowship in Christ
- ❏ lack of responsibility

2. Who are you more like right now, Francis and his followers or the townspeople who made fun of them?

Francis_____Townspeople

SCRIPTURE and QUESTIONS:

Humble Heroes? In our age there are few humble heroes. Football players who score touchdowns strut and point proudly at their chests. Rap singers, when they're not reciting profanity, are singing their own praises. Sports stars try to get the highest contract, as much for their vanity as for the money. Television and movie stars compete for top billing. In a sense, that was true in Bible times also. The only difference is that it was religiosity that they tried to be the best at. Knowing the Scriptures and following all the laws was the sport of the day, and some were quite good at it. But Jesus tried to point his age, as he would try to point ours, to a different way to be a hero—a way where you can feel good about what you have accomplished without trying to make others feel bad about their failures; a way where we can see that even our most momentous achievements are but small stones in the massive structure of what God has built. To be this kind of hero, we need not ignore our accomplishments, or put ourselves down for our failures—we need only to see ourselves clearly and accurately as loved, but imperfect persons—working together with other loved, but imperfect persons, to build something that will last beyond human applause.

Have someone in your group read the following passage out loud. Then go around on each question and let each person share their answer. Take advantage of the Study notes following the questionnaire. Be sure to save the last 20–40 minutes for the Caring time.

[9]*He also told this parable to some who trusted in themselves that they were righteous and regarded others with contempt:* [10]*"Two men went up to the temple to pray, one a Pharisee and the other a tax collector.* [11]*The Pharisee, standing by himself, was praying thus, 'God, I thank you that I am not like other people: thieves, rogues, adulterers, or even like this tax collector.* [12]*I fast twice a week; I give a tenth of all my income.'* [13]*But the tax collector, standing far off, would not even look up to heaven, but was beating his breast and saying, 'God, be merciful to me, a sinner!'* [14]*I tell you, this man went down to his home justified rather than the other; for all who exalt themselves will be humbled, but all who humble themselves will be exalted."*

Luke 18:9–14

1. When you were an adolescent, who do you remember "regarding you with contempt"?
- ❏ the "jocks"
- ❏ the "popular" kids
- ❏ the teachers
- ❏ my parents
- ❏ adults in general
- ❏ the "goodie-two-shoe" types
- ❏ the hoods and druggies
- ❏ mostly myself
- ❏ other:_____

QUESTIONS (cont.):

2. Why do you think the Pharisee went to the temple to pray?
- ❏ to let others see how righteous he was
- ❏ to do what he thought was right
- ❏ to put down others
- ❏ to reassure himself that he was one of the "good guys"
- ❏ to talk to God
- ❏ other:_____

3. Why do you think the tax collector went to the temple to pray?
- ❏ to salve his conscience
- ❏ to feel sorry for himself
- ❏ to find forgiveness
- ❏ to talk to God
- ❏ to do what he thought was right
- ❏ to get a new life direction
- ❏ other:_____

4. What does Jesus mean when he says, "... all who exalt themselves will be humbled, but all who humble themselves will be exalted"?
- ❏ We should never brag.
- ❏ We should never think of ourselves as better than others.
- ❏ We all need to be humble enough to see our faults.
- ❏ Only the humble go to heaven.
- ❏ other:_____

5. With whom do you "humble yourself" and share your problems?
- ❏ God
- ❏ my spouse
- ❏ my parent(s)
- ❏ another family member
- ❏ a close friend
- ❏ my pastor or small group leader
- ❏ this group
- ❏ no one
- ❏ other:_____

6. How do you feel about sharing personal matters in your life with this group?
- ❏ uncomfortable—I don't talk about these things.
- ❏ scared—I don't know if I want to talk about these things.
- ❏ okay—I can handle it.
- ❏ thrilled—I love this stuff.
- ❏ I'm not sure.

QUESTIONS (cont.) and BIBLE STUDY NOTES:

6. What is God calling you to do in your spiritual life right now?
- ❑ stop "watching" Jesus from a distance
- ❑ accept Jesus' invitation to get to know him better
- ❑ lay claim to God's gift of salvation
- ❑ celebrate God's acceptance
- ❑ repent and make amends for my wrongs
- ❑ other:_____

7. To whom do you need to make amends? How are you planning to do so?

19:2 Zacchaeus. This name means "pure" or "righteous"—Is there an intentional irony here? **chief tax collector.** Tax collectors were among the most hated people in Jewish society because they collaborated with the Romans and overcharged the people besides. The title of chief tax collector is one that would have been suitable for an official at such an important frontier post as Jericho, but one that has not been confirmed by other literature.

19:3 short in stature. Short men were not always afforded respect. A hated tax collector who was short was probably especially subject to ridicule.

19:4 climbed a sycamore tree. Then, as today, this would have been considered very undignified for an adult, especially one who was an important official! The sycamore tree referred to was a type of wild fig tree known as the fig mulberry. Its short trunk and spreading branches would have made it easy to climb.

19:5–7 Jesus' invitation of himself to Zacchaeus' home doubtlessly shocked everyone. Not only would the self-righteous Pharisees disapprove, but Zacchaeus' ill-gotten wealth made association with him difficult to accept even for the people in general.

19:8 half of my possessions. Zacchaeus' quick and enthusiastic response shows that he had been hungering for this kind of acceptance, and realized Jesus was someone special because he showed it. As a sign of the reality of his repentance and faith, Zacchaeus immediately forsakes money as his main priority, instead seeking to show love and generosity to others. **I will pay back four times as much.** Giving half of his wealth to the poor did not mean he would keep the other half for himself. Instead, the remaining wealth would be used to recompense those whom he had defrauded. The Old Testament demanded fourfold restitution only in the case of theft of a livestock animal (Ex. 22:1); in other cases of fraud or theft, the guilty party was to repay

BIBLE STUDY NOTES (cont.) and CARING TIME:

the value of what was stolen plus 20 percent (Lev. 6:1–5). Zacchaeus is so eager to be restored to God and his community that he pledges to go far beyond what the Law requires.

19:9 son of Abraham. This is referring to a *spiritual* child of Abraham. All Jews would consider themselves physical children of Abraham, and some thought that was enough to gain God's favor. But those who are spiritual children of Abraham are those who act with the same faith with which he acted (see Luke 3:8; John 8:39–42; Rom. 4:1–25).

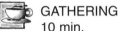 *This time is for developing and expressing your caring for each other as group members. We do this by sharing our needs and praying for each other's needs.*

Each group member should answer the question,

How can this group help you in prayer this week?

Then join together in group prayer.

¹Julien Green, *God's Fool: The Life and Times of Francis of Assisi* (San Francisco: Harper & Row, 1983), pp.124-125.
²Karl Menninger, *Whatever Became of Sin?* (New York: Bantam Books, 1973), pp. 1–2.

SERENDIPITY
Small Group
HANDOUT

WEEK 9: PENTECOST 24
Choosing Repentance
Luke 19:1–10

 GATHERING 10 min.

STUDY 30 min.

 CARING 20–40 min.

Leader: The agenda has three parts. In the Gathering time you'll be getting to know each other through an "ice-breaker." This will be for your total group. The Study time has two parts: (1) Story and (2) Scripture. If you are short of time, skip the Story and move to the Scripture. Begin by reading out loud the Story or the Scripture to the whole group. Then divide into groups of 4 for the Study time. Finally, regather the total group for the Caring time. Keep to this agenda: (1) Gathering—10 minutes, (2) Study—30 minutes, and (3) Caring—20–40 minutes.

 My Family. What was your family of origin like? Pick a fairy tale and a comic strip which best describes your family. Tell your group what you chose and then explain your selections.

IF MY FAMILY OF ORIGIN WERE A FAIRY TALE, IT WOULD'VE BEEN:
- ❑ Hansel and Gretel
- ❑ The Emperor's New Clothes
- ❑ Sleeping Beauty
- ❑ Cinderella
- ❑ Jack and the Beanstalk
- ❑ Beauty and the Beast
- ❑ The Pied Piper

IF MY FAMILY OF ORIGIN WERE A COMIC STRIP, IT WOULD'VE BEEN:
- ❑ Blondie
- ❑ Dennis the Menace
- ❑ Family Circus
- ❑ The Far Side
- ❑ Andy Capp
- ❑ Little Orphan Annie
- ❑ Calvin and Hobbes
- ❑ For Better or Worse
- ❑ Peanuts
- ❑ Hagar the Horrible
- ❑ Adam
- ❑ Outland

INTRODUCTION STORY:

 St. Francis Calls a Country to Repentance. Francis of Assisi was born to a wealthy family, and spent his early life partying and squandering his father's wealth. But then he learned another way was more powerful and more satisfying—the way of poverty and humility, the way of Christ. He traded his wealth for rags and a life of service, and this life of service included preaching to those still enslaved to materialism. Francis' biographer Julien Green tells how it was in his book, *God's Fool: The Life and Times of Francis of Assisi:*

"We have a hard time imagining the enthusiasm Francis stirred up in a country as spiritually weakened as Italy was in those days. Sensibility was paralyzing the flow of grace. People were often misled by a purely formal, ostentatious piety. The period also felt—thereby resembling our own era—a void that pleasure couldn't fill, a hunger for something different, a restlessness of the heart. The Church had forgotten how to speak to the soul, because it was bogged down in the material world.

"Then in the piazza or at a turn in the road, there appeared a man with bare feet, dressed like a beggar and crying in a joyful voice. ...

"... It was incredible: He was in love with God—and that wasn't all, because he went much too far, this madman with the lilting voice. He said that God was in love with us all; he would suddenly weep, weep for love, and some people would begin to weep too, the women first, with the talent they have for that, then the men, starting with the young ones. ...

"They felt terror from the secret sins their lives were full of, without Francis's having to tell them. But he told them anyhow, not with the trumpetings of righteous indignation, as the clergy did, or with their threats of fire and torment, but with an unconsolable sorrow and burst of searing tenderness, as if he were about to lose his beloved children. And, no longer able to find the words, he began to gesture, his face streaming tears. What eloquence could match those hands stretched out to them?"[1]

1. What impression do you get of Francis of Assisi from this story?
   ❒ He was manic-depressive.
   ❒ He was a man who felt everything deeply.
   ❒ He was the kind of passionate, deeply committed Christian we need more of.
   ❒ He was a master dramatist.
   ❒ He was full of the love of God.
   ❒ other:_____

2. Francis sought to motivate people to repentance by love rather than fear of punishment. Which works better for you as a motivation to change—love or fear? If you can, tell of an example that illustrates your answer.

SCRIPTURE:

 A Universal Verdict. Karl Menninger, in his book *Whatever Became of Sin?*, tells of a man who stood in the streets of downtown Chicago, and every once in a while he would turn and point at a passerby and pronounce the solemn word, "Guilty!" Then he would resume his stance once again. After a while he would turn and point to another person, intoning once again, "Guilty!"—only to return to his motionless position. The most interesting thing was the reactions of the people passing by. Most would look at the man, and then look at each other, and then just hurry on. One man, however, turned to the man with him and said, "Yes, but how did he know?"[2] Of course, the reality is that this man's pronouncement is true of all of us. We are guilty of falling short of the person God calls us to be. The question is, what do we do about it? Some try to ignore their guilt and push it off on someone else—"Society made me this way!" Others wallow in their guilt—"I'm just a worthless worm!" Still others minimize it—"Hey, it's just the way everybody is—no problem!" The biblical way to deal with it, however, is repentance. Repentance is nothing less than seeing your sin, seeing God's offer of forgiveness, and turning your life around in response. It is that response that leads to a healthier, happier life.

Have someone in your group read the following passage out loud. Then go around on each question and let each person share their answer. Take advantage of the Study notes following the questionnaire. Be sure to save the last 20–40 minutes for the Caring time.

19 He entered Jericho and was passing through it. ²A man was there named Zacchaeus; he was a chief tax collector and was rich. ³He was trying to see who Jesus was, but on account of the crowd he could not, because he was short in stature. ⁴So he ran ahead and climbed a sycamore tree to see him, because he was going to pass that way. ⁵When Jesus came to the place, he looked up and said to him, "Zacchaeus, hurry and come down; for I must stay at your house today." ⁶So he hurried down and was happy to welcome him. ⁷All who saw it began to grumble and said, "He has gone to be the guest of one who is a sinner." ⁸Zacchaeus stood there and said to the Lord, "Look, half of my possessions, Lord, I will give to the poor; and if I have defrauded anyone of anything, I will pay back four times as much." ⁹Then Jesus said to him, "Today salvation has come to this house, because he too is a son of Abraham. ¹⁰For the Son of Man came to seek out and to save the lost."

Luke 19:1–10

QUESTIONS:

1. When you were in the seventh grade, which of your physical characteristics were you most self-conscious of around your peers?
   ❒ my weight
   ❒ my height
   ❒ my physical awkwardness
   ❒ my face—pimple city!
   ❒ other:_____

2. How did you restore your self-worth when peers rejected you?
   ❒ I withdrew to my room or my inner thoughts.
   ❒ I laughed it off.
   ❒ I found new friends.
   ❒ I joined them in putting myself down.
   ❒ I found an activity I could excel at to "show them up."
   ❒ I don't remember my peers ever rejecting me.
   ❒ other:_____

3. Finish this sentence: "The most surprising thing to me in this story is ..."
   ❒ that Jesus knew Zacchaeus' name
   ❒ that a person of wealth would climb a tree
   ❒ that Jesus would have the audacity to invite himself over to someone's house
   ❒ that Jesus would go to the house of someone who cheated people
   ❒ that Zacchaeus would change so quickly

4. What about Jesus' gesture contributed most to the change in Zacchaeus?
   ❒ Jesus treated him as a person by using his name.
   ❒ Jesus made him feel needed.
   ❒ Jesus showed that he accepted him enough to eat with him.
   ❒ Jesus ignored the negative talk of the crowd.

5. When was the last time you made a complete change in your behavior, like Zacchaeus did here? What changes could you point to that show how much you changed?

BIBLE STUDY NOTES:

20:27 Sadducees. The Sadducees were a small but highly influential party of Jews composed mainly of wealthy, aristocratic priests. The high priest was often a Sadducee. The Sadducees accepted only the first five books of the Old Testament as authoritative. They also rejected the oral tradition (which put them at odds with the Pharisees). In their leadership roles, they accommodated themselves to the Roman government. This is their first appearance in Luke's narrative because up to this point Jesus has been no threat to the Sadducees. However, his action in the temple (19:45–46) was an invasion of their special sphere of influence and so they became his enemies. **there is no resurrection.** Since the Sadducees accepted only the first five books of the Old Testament, and since resurrection is not taught in those books, they denied its reality.

20:28 Moses wrote for us. Reference here is to what is called levirate marriage (Deut. 25:5–10), which was designed to ensure the continuation of the family name as well as to keep property within a family.

20:29–33 there were seven brothers. This is a hypothetical situation which the Sadducees have concocted to show what they saw as an inherent contradiction between the idea of resurrection and the teaching of Moses.

20:34–36 Marriage is part of the present created order because death necessitates procreation in order to replenish the population. Since there is no death in the afterlife, marriage would not be necessary. This does not mean that there won't be the intimate relationship which marriage represents to us, however. **like angels.** Note that this does not say those who die *become* angels; they are simply *like* angels. Here it also might be noted that the Sadducees also did not believe in angels.

20:37 Moses himself showed. It was vital when talking to the Sadducees to prove something by the teaching of Moses, the only authority they accepted. Jesus here demonstrates the reality of the resurrection in a manner which, though strange to modern ears, would have been seen as a valid argument to a first century rabbi. **in the story about the bush.** At this time, the Scriptures did not have chapter and verse divisions. Passages were located by reference to major events that happened in or near the passage being referred to. This particular text is from Exodus 3:6, a portion of the OT which was accepted by the Sadducees.

CARING TIME and PRAYER REQUESTS:

 This time is for developing and expressing your caring for each other as group members. We do this by sharing our needs and praying for each other's needs.

Each group member should answer the question,

> *How can this group help you in prayer this week?*

Then join together in group prayer.

¹John Pollock, *To All Nations: The Billy Graham Story* (San Francisco: Harper & Row, 1985), pp.68–69.
²Jurgen Moltmann, *Theology of Hope* (New York: Harper & Row, 1967), p. 19.

SERENDIPITY

Small Group
HANDOUT

WEEK 10: PENTECOST 25
Choosing to Hope
Luke 20:27–38

 GATHERING 10 min. **STUDY** 30 min.   **CARING** 20–40 min.

Leader: The agenda has three parts. In the Gathering time you'll be getting to know each other through an "ice-breaker." This will be for your total group. The Study time has two parts: (1) Story and (2) Scripture. If you are short of time, skip the Story and move to the Scripture. Begin by reading out loud the Story or the Scripture to the whole group. Then divide into groups of 4 for the Study time. Finally, regather the total group for the Caring time. Keep to this agenda: (1) Gathering—10 minutes, (2) Study—30 minutes, and (3) Caring—20–40 minutes.

Music in My Life. Put an "**X**" on each of the lines below—somewhere between the two extremes—to indicate how you are feeling right now about each area of your life. If time is limited, choose only two or three.

In my emotional life, I'm feeling like ...
Blues in the Night _____ **Feeling Groovy**

In my family life, I'm feeling like ...
Stormy Weather _____ **The Sound of Music**

In my work, school or career, I'm feeling like ...
Take This Job and Shove It _____ **The Future's So Bright I Gotta Wear 'Shades'**

In my spiritual life, I'm feeling like ...
Sounds of Silence _____ **Hallelujah Chorus**

In my close friendships, I'm feeling ...
Love Is a Battlefield _____ **I'll Be There for You**
(Theme from *Friends*)

As I look at my immediate future, I'm feeling like ...
Yesterday _____ **To Dream the Impossible Dream**

INTRODUCTION STORY:

Billy Graham Teaches Hope in a Hard World. Billy Graham has preached the Gospel to millions of people around the world, filling stadiums to capacity. But sometimes his greatest influence has been when he has witnessed one-on-one to influential world leaders. Such was the case when he met with Winston Churchill during a crusade in England at Wembley. His biographer John Pollock tells the story:

"At the stroke of noon Billy Graham was shown into the Cabinet Room. Sir Winston stood at the centre of the long Cabinet table, an unlighted cigar in his hand. Billy was surprised to see how short a man he was. Sir Winston motioned Billy to be seated and said he had been reading about him and was most happy to have him come, 'because we need this emphasis.' Then he said, 'Do you have any hope? What hope do you have for the world?'

"Billy was naturally overwhelmed at meeting privately the greatest man of the age, but did not forget why he had been allowed the privilege. He took out his little New Testament and answered, 'Mr Prime Minister, I am filled with hope.'

"Sir Winston pointed at the early editions of three London evening papers lying on the empty table, and commented that they were filled with rapes, murders and hate. When he was a boy it was different. If there was a murder it was talked about for fifty years. Everything was so changed now, so noisy and violent. And the Communist menace grew all the time. 'I am an old man,' he said, and repeated the phrase at different points in the conversation nine times. Several times he added, 'without hope for the world.'

"Billy said again that he was filled with hope. 'Life is very exciting even if there's a war, because I know what is going to happen in the future.' Then he spoke about Jesus Christ, and began right at the beginning, turning from place to place in the New Testament and explaining, just as he would to an insignificant inquirer in his hotel room, the meaning of Christ's birth, His death, His resurrection and ascension, and how a man is born again. He moved quickly, inwardly agitated lest he should not put across the essentials in the short time granted him.

"The five minutes which he had scheduled for Graham had become forty, and the clock showed twelve-thirty, when at last Sir Winston stood up. 'I do not see much hope for the future,' he said, 'unless it is the hope you are talking about, young man. We must have a return to God.' "[1]

1. How would you categorize Billy Graham's response to Winston Churchill's question?
   - ❑ stereotypical
   - ❑ simple and direct
   - ❑ positive and biblical
   - ❑ naive
   - ❑ long-winded
   - ❑ inspiring

2. How much hope do you have for the world right now, compared to these well-known figures?

   like Churchill at the beginning _____ **like Billy Graham**

SCRIPTURE:

Keep Hope Alive. When Bill Clinton ran for president the first time in 1992, he did so on the theme, "Keep Hope Alive!" The theme was, of course, a play on Clinton's hometown of Hope, Arkansas, but it struck a responsive strain. People may disagree about Clinton's presidency living up to this theme, but there is no doubt that hope is an important motivator for people. Hope is as essential to our spirit as bread and water are to our bodies. Theologian Jurgen Moltmann has written that because of hope's importance to our spirit, hope should be the "foundation" and "mainspring" of our theological thinking.[2] One of the most important forms which hope takes is the hope in a life after death. Such a hope built the pyramids, and it is on such a hope that Christian faith is built. Still, many people choose not to have such a hope. They choose not to have it because we cannot see beyond the grave, and some people have been disappointed too often to hope in anything they cannot see or touch. Christ sought to be our "eyes," seeing into this uncharted territory for us. If we can but trust in his Word, this vital hope can be ours.

Have someone in your group read the following passage out loud. Then go around on each question and let each person share their answer. Take advantage of the Study notes following the questionnaire. Be sure to save the last 20–40 minutes for the Caring time.

²⁷Some Sadducees, those who say there is no resurrection, came to him ²⁸and asked him a question, "Teacher, Moses wrote for us that if a man's brother dies, leaving a wife but no children, the man shall marry the widow and raise up children for his brother. ²⁹Now there were seven brothers; the first married, and died childless; ³⁰then the second ³¹and the third married her, and so in the same way all seven died childless. ³²Finally the woman also died. ³³In the resurrection, therefore, whose wife will the woman be? For the seven had married her."

³⁴Jesus said to them, "Those who belong to this age marry and are given in marriage; ³⁵but those who are considered worthy of a place in that age and in the resurrection from the dead neither marry nor are given in marriage. ³⁶Indeed they cannot die anymore, because they are like angels and are children of God, being children of the resurrection. ³⁷And the fact that the dead are raised Moses himself showed, in the story about the bush, where he speaks of the Lord as the God of Abraham, the God of Isaac, and the God of Jacob. ³⁸Now he is God not of the dead, but of the living; for to him all of them are alive."

Luke 20:27–38

QUESTIONS:

1. The Jews referred to God as the God of Abraham, Isaac and Jacob. If you could name three great people of faith in your family background, who would they be?

2. Why do you think the Sadducees told this little "riddle" to Jesus?
   - ❑ They honestly wanted to know the answer.
   - ❑ They wanted to embarrass him.
   - ❑ They wanted to prove that there could be no resurrection.
   - ❑ They just liked riddles.
   - ❑ other:_____

3. Why were religious people like the Sadducees so much against the idea of the resurrection?
   - ❑ They just saw no evidence for it.
   - ❑ They were afraid to hope.
   - ❑ They believed in finding your reward in this life.
   - ❑ It was what they had been taught and they didn't question it.
   - ❑ other:_____

4. What do you believe is the most prevalent reason today why people reject the idea of the resurrection?
   - ❑ They see no evidence for it.
   - ❑ They are afraid to hope.
   - ❑ They believe in finding their reward in this life.
   - ❑ It's what they have been taught.
   - ❑ other:_____

5. If you could ask Jesus one question about what life will be like in heaven, what would you ask him?

6. What gives you the most hope when you think about the resurrection?
   - ❑ the anticipation of seeing Jesus
   - ❑ the anticipation of seeing my loved ones
   - ❑ the absence of pain and suffering
   - ❑ the "new body" I will have
   - ❑ finding complete happiness

7. What difference does the resurrection make in your everyday life?
   - ❑ not much
   - ❑ quite a bit
   - ❑ a great deal

BIBLE STUDY NOTES:

21:5 *the temple.* The temple was constructed of huge white stones, some measuring 37 feet long by 12 feet high by 18 feet wide. Josephus, the ancient Jewish historian, described the temple this way: "The outward face ... was covered all over with plates of gold of great weight, and, at the first rising of the sun, reflected back a very fiery splendor. ... The temple appeared ... at a distance, like a mountain covered with snow ... ."

21:6 *not one stone will be left upon another.* Josephus wrote: "Caesar (Titus) ordered the whole city and the temple to be razed to the ground" (A.D. 70).

21:7 *what will be the sign.* The disciples figured that such a cataclysmic event as the destruction of the temple would have to mean the coming of the end times, with other accompanying signs.

21:8 *I am he!* Many others came at the time of Jesus and just after him claiming to be Messiahs. Acts mentions a man named Theudas, a man named Judas the Galilean, and an Egyptian who led 4,000 assassins into the wilderness (Acts 5:36–37; 21:38). In our day we have had people like Jim Jones, Sun Myung Moon and David Koresh.

21:11 *dreadful portents and great signs from heaven.* This is apocalyptic language—graphic, calamitous, cosmic imagery used to describe signs of the end. Such language was used in Isaiah 13:6–22 to describe the judgment of the people of Israel at the hands of the Assyrians. In this context, Jesus may be using it to highlight the significance of God's action in allowing the city of Jerusalem to be destroyed by the Romans.

21:12 *synagogues.* Synagogues served as the Jewish court for trying minor offenses. Offenders could be beaten by synagogue officials. ***kings and governors.*** These would be Gentile courts.

21:15 *I will give you words and a wisdom.* In Acts 6:10 it is said that the members of the synagogue "could not withstand the wisdom and the Spirit" with which Stephen spoke before he was martyred.

21:16 *You will be betrayed.* Such things certainly did happen regularly to the early disciples. In fact, this describes so exactly what happened that some believe these are really the words of an early church writer instead of Jesus himself.

21:18–19 *But not a hair of your head.* This is reminiscent of what Jesus said earlier in Luke 12:7. If taken literally, this contradicts verse 16 where Jesus warns some will be put to death. It also contradicts what was in fact the experience of the early church. What Jesus is saying here is that nothing will threaten their *eternal* security, and by their endurance they would gain their souls.

CARING TIME and PRAYER REQUESTS:

 This time is for developing and expressing your caring for each other as group members. We do this by sharing our needs and praying for each other's needs.

Each group member should answer the question,

> *How can this group help you in prayer this week?*

Then join together in group prayer.

SERENDIPITY

Small Group
H A N D O U T

WEEK 11: PENTECOST 26
A Choice for Persecution
Luke 21:5–19

 **GATHERING**
10 min.

 STUDY
30 min.

 CARING
20–40 min.

Leader: The agenda has three parts. In the Gathering time you'll be getting to know each other through an "ice-breaker." This will be for your total group. The Study time has two parts: (1) Story and (2) Scripture. If you are short of time, skip the Story and move to the Scripture. Begin by reading out loud the Story or the Scripture to the whole group. Then divide into groups of 4 for the Study time. Finally, regather the total group for the Caring time. Keep to this agenda: (1) Gathering—10 minutes, (2) Study—30 minutes, and (3) Caring—20–40 minutes.

Bring Out Your Best. Use the questions below to get acquainted. Go around the group on the first question. Then go around on the next question, etc.

1. Finish this sentence: "If you want to bring out my best, then ..."
   - ❑ feed me!
   - ❑ compliment my appearance.
   - ❑ put me around playful people.
   - ❑ put me in a competitive situation.
   - ❑ give me a charge card and send me to the mall.
   - ❑ give me a challenge.
   - ❑ give me lots of hugs.
   - ❑ other:_____

2. Finish this sentence: "If you want to bring out my worst ..."
   - ❑ put me in a messy room.
   - ❑ try telling me what to do.
   - ❑ try putting me on a committee.
   - ❑ put me in a competitive situation.
   - ❑ give me a charge card and send me to the mall.
   - ❑ criticize me.
   - ❑ make me eat health food.
   - ❑ other:_____

¹Frances Gies, *Joan of Arc: The Legend and the Reality* (New York: Harper & Row, 1981), pp. 2–3, 282–283.

INTRODUCTION STORY:

Joan of Arc Receives Her Reward. Raised a peasant girl, while still in her teens Joan of Arc boldly went to the King of France, who was cowering in fear of the English, and audaciously told him God had sent her to deliver France. Indeed, she led the French army to some unbelievable victories. Later she was arrested by the English and tried as a "witch." Evidence against her was that she had taken to wearing men's clothes, and professed to hear the audible voices of saints who told her God's will. To save her life, she was asked to renounce these voices and the wearing of men's clothing, to show she had renounced her "heresies." She did so. However, she later started wearing men's clothing again, apparently to help fend off the sexual assaults of her male guards. When she did so, she was declared to have "relapsed," and was condemned to be burned at the stake. Her biographer Frances Gies tells what happened:

"As Joan was being chained to the post, she invoked St. Michael in particular. It seems clear that he, who had come to her in the beginning, was also with her at the last. Though she had renounced her voices only a moment before, their hold upon her was too strong to be thus shaken off, and now they returned to her as comforters. ...

"Joan begged Isambard de la Pierre to go to the near-by church of Saint-Sauveur, and to bring the processional cross. She wanted him to hold this before her eyes until she died. He and Massieu went to get it, and Joan embraced it passionately until it was taken from her, and her hands were bound. The fire was lit, and the flames and smoke began to envelop the victim until she was almost hidden from view. Joan took some time to die, so long that the executioner afterwards said to Ladvenu that the execution had been exceptionally cruel. Since the scaffold had been built so high, he could not climb up to dispatch her, as was usual, and he was therefore forced to leave her to the fire. The spectators heard her calling upon God and the saints. ... And at last, as she was released, she uttered a great cry of "Jesus," and then dropped her head."[1]

1. What impression do you get of Joan of Arc from this story?
- ❏ She suffered from hallucinations.
- ❏ She was a women's libber before her time.
- ❏ She was cowardly for renouncing what she thought right to avoid dying.
- ❏ Renouncing nonessentials, like wearing men's clothing, was smart.
- ❏ She was a brave woman who did what she thought God wanted her to do.
- ❏ other:_____

2. What is so important to you that you would be willing to die for it?

SCRIPTURE:

The Price of Faith. Perhaps the greatest evidence for the resurrection of Jesus Christ is the change it made in his disciples. They went from a scared little band, huddled in fear in a locked upper room (John 20:19), to a dynamic troop of witnesses willing to face the most gruesome of deaths—from being crucified upside down, to being mauled by lions, to being beheaded, to just name a few. Jesus, in the passage for this week, warns his followers that these things are coming. He didn't want them to be unprepared. Indeed, the results show that he prepared them well. In the midst of the persecutions described in this passage the church thrived. What about the church today? In modern America there is little persecution of the kind the early church faced. However, while the church grew in the midst of persecution, in the midst of official sanction it often seems to be languishing. Why is that? Perhaps it is because we do not value what has not been dearly earned. But the freedom we have and the faith which has come to us down through history, has been dearly earned, not only by the early church, but by Christian martyrs throughout history. What they have died for, what Christ has died for, we must preserve and value.

Have someone in your group read the following passage out loud. Then go around on each question and let each person share their answer. Take advantage of the Study notes following the questionnaire. Be sure to save the last 20–40 minutes for the Caring time.

⁵*When some were speaking about the temple, how it was adorned with beautiful stones and gifts dedicated to God, he said,* ⁶*"As for these things that you see, the days will come when not one stone will be left upon another; all will be thrown down."*

⁷*They asked him, "Teacher, when will this be, and what will be the sign that this is about to take place?"* ⁸*And he said, "Beware that you are not led astray; for many will come in my name and say, 'I am he!' and, 'The time is near!' Do not go after them.*

⁹*"When you hear of wars and insurrections, do not be terrified; for these things must take place first, but the end will not follow immediately."* ¹⁰*Then he said to them, "Nation will rise against nation, and kingdom against kingdom;* ¹¹*there will be great earthquakes, and in various places famines and plagues; and there will be dreadful portents and great signs from heaven.*

¹²*"But before all this occurs, they will arrest you and persecute you; they will hand you over to synagogues and prisons, and you will be brought before kings and governors because of my name.* ¹³*This will give you an opportunity to testify.* ¹⁴*So make up your minds not to prepare your defense in advance;* ¹⁵*for I will give you words and a wisdom that none of your opponents will be able to withstand or contradict.* ¹⁶*You will be betrayed even by parents and brothers, by relatives and friends; and they will put some of you to death.* ¹⁷*You will be hated by*

SCRIPTURE (cont.) and QUESTIONS:

all because of my name. ¹⁸*But not a hair of your head will perish.* ¹⁹*By your endurance you will gain your souls."*

Luke 21:5–19

1. When you were in junior high, what would you have said was the "absolutely coolest" church or building you were ever in? What did you like about it?

2. Why did Jesus talk about the temple being destroyed, when he saw people admiring it?
- ❏ to show off his psychic powers of prediction
- ❏ to remind people they shouldn't get too attached to the things of this earth
- ❏ to prepare them for what he knew would be an emotional loss
- ❏ to get them thinking about a truly eternal building project—the kingdom of God
- ❏ other:_____

3. Of the things Jesus predicts that his followers would face after his death and resurrection, what would be the hardest for you?
- ❏ going through a natural disaster
- ❏ going through a war
- ❏ being betrayed by family
- ❏ being arrested
- ❏ being hated by people
- ❏ facing execution

4. When in your life have you had to face some modern variety of "persecution"?
- ❏ when, as a teenager, friends made fun of my church-going
- ❏ when I was involved in a protest
- ❏ when I lived in another country
- ❏ when, as an adult, people put me down because of my beliefs
- ❏ when I lost a job because I tried to hold to my principles
- ❏ I don't think this has really happened to me.

5. What do you need to do in order to better stand up in the face of opposition and persecution?
- ❏ to focus more on what God thinks and less on what people think
- ❏ to become more convinced that resurrection is real
- ❏ to pray more for inner spiritual strength
- ❏ to read more inspiring examples of people standing up to such things
- ❏ other:_____

6. Who do you feel God is calling you to share his message with in the coming weeks?

BIBLE STUDY NOTES:

23:33 *The Skull.* In Aramaic, this is *Golgotha,* and in Greek *Calvary.* The name was given because it was a round, bare hill outside Jerusalem, and from a distance it looked like a skull. *they crucified Jesus.* Crucifixion was the most feared of all punishments in the first-century world. It was cruel in the extreme and totally degrading. It is toward this event that Luke has looked throughout his Gospel. When it actually happens, he records it in the simplest, most straightforward way. Josephus, a great Jewish historian of the era, calls it "the most wretched of all ways of dying." The person to be crucified was first stripped. Then his hands were tied or nailed to the cross beam, which was lifted to the upright stake already in place. Typically, it took several hours before death occurred by asphyxiation, loss of blood and shock. *with the criminals.* The crucifixion between criminals was a fulfillment of Isaiah 53:12.

23:34 *Father forgive.* Here Jesus is living out what he had earlier taught his disciples, that they should love their enemies (Luke 6:27–28). This attitude is later emulated by Stephen at his martyrdom (Acts 7:60). *divide his clothing.* The clothes of the condemned person belonged to the four soldiers who carried out the crucifixion (see Psalm 22:18).

23:35 *if he is the Messiah of God.* To the religious leaders, the disgraceful death Jesus was experiencing proved beyond a shadow of a doubt that he could not possibly be the Messiah, who was seen as a figure of power.

23:36 *offering him sour wine.* Offering a "king" such a cheap, bitter drink, especially to quench thirst at a time like this, would be seen as an act of mockery.

23:38 *an inscription.* The crime for which the person was being crucified was specified on a whitened board fastened above the criminal. The charge written here indicates that the "crime" for which Jesus is eventually crucified is not the blasphemy with which the Jews charged him, but sedition, seeking to be king. Pilate probably saw putting up such a sign over a humiliated dying man as an insult to the Jews as well.

23:40–43 This scene is unique to Luke, and is the final example of a string of instances where Jesus reaches out to outcast people with God's grace (see 5:13,31; 7:36ff; 8:26–48; 13:11; 17:16; 18:9–17; 19:1–10).

CARING TIME and PRAYER REQUESTS:

 This time is for developing and expressing your caring for each other as group members. We do this by sharing our needs and praying for each other's needs.

Have each group member answer one or both of the following questions:

❒ What has been the high point of this Pentecost series for you?

❒ What has this group come to mean to you?

Next, have everyone answer the question,

How would you like to be remembered in prayer in the days ahead?

Close by joining hands and praying for each other and thanking God for your time together.

'Corrie ten Boom, *The Hiding Place* (Minneapolis, MN: World Wide Publications, 1971), pp.182–183.

SERENDIPITY
Small Group
HANDOUT

WEEK 12: LAST PENTECOST
Choosing Forgiveness
Luke 23:33–43

 GATHERING 10 min.   **STUDY** 30 min.   **CARING** 20–40 min.

Leader: The agenda has three parts. In the Gathering time you'll be getting to know each other through an "ice-breaker." This will be for your total group. The Study time has two parts: (1) Story and (2) Scripture. If you are short of time, skip the Story and move to the Scripture. Begin by reading out loud the Story or the Scripture to the whole group. Then divide into groups of 4 for the Study time. Finally, regather the total group for the Caring time. Keep to this agenda: (1) Gathering—10 minutes, (2) Study—30 minutes, and (3) Caring—20–40 minutes.

Guardians of the Group. We have a lot of guardians in the world that protect us from many kinds of dangers. This group has had its "guardians" too. In silence decide which person in the group best fulfilled each of the following roles for you. After everyone has made their decisions, focus on one group member at a time, and have the others report the role they chose for that person.

HEART MONITOR: the one who kept the group alive by keeping in touch with the heart

TRAIL GUIDE: the one who brought us back when we wandered from the path

CLASS CLOWN: the one who helped us keep our sense of humor

"CHILD" WHO GUIDES US TO THE KINGDOM: the one who protected our innocence and childlike faith

GUARDIAN ANGEL: the one whose loving protection seemed to come from God

MOTHER HEN: the one whose gift of hospitality made us feel well taken care of

INTRODUCTION STORY:

Corrie ten Boom Learns to Forgive. Corrie ten Boom and other members of her family were sent to prison camps for sheltering Jews from the Nazis during World War II. There they experienced very hard times. The capture of her and her family came in large part because of an act of treachery by a man in a town near theirs. As she discovered the name of this man, Jan Vogel, she struggled with her anger and feelings of hate. She tells of how she faced this issue, with the help of her sister Betsie, in her autobiographical book, *The Hiding Place:*

"Flames of fire seemed to leap around that name in my heart. I thought of Father's final hours, alone and confused, in a hospital corridor. Of the underground work so abruptly halted. I thought of Mary Itallie arrested while walking down a street. And I knew that if Jan Vogel stood in front of me now I could kill him.

"... In the evenings we held a clandestine prayer meeting for as many as could crowd around our bunk.

" 'You lead the prayers tonight, Betsie. I have a headache.'

"More than a headache. All of me ached with the violence of my feelings about the man who had done us so much harm. That night I did not sleep and the next day at my bench scarcely heard the conversation around me. By the end of the week I had worked myself into such a sickness of body and spirit that Mr. Moorman stopped at my bench to ask if something were wrong.

" 'Wrong? Yes, something's wrong!' And I plunged into an account of that morning. I was only too eager to tell Mr. Moorman and all Holland how Jan Vogel had betrayed his country.

"What puzzled me all this time was Betsie. She had suffered everything I had and yet she seemed to carry no burden of rage. 'Betsie!' I hissed one dark night when I knew that my restless tossing must be keeping her awake. ... 'Betsie, don't you feel anything about Jan Vogel? Doesn't it bother you?'

" 'Oh, yes, Corrie! Terribly! I've felt for him ever since I knew—and pray for him whenever his name comes to my mind. How dreadfully he must be suffering!'

"For a long time I lay silent in the huge shadowy barracks restless with the sighs, snores, and stirrings of hundreds of women. Once again I had the feeling that this sister with whom I had spent all my life belonged somehow to another order of beings. Wasn't she telling me in her gentle way that I was as guilty as Jan Vogel? Didn't he and I stand together before an all-seeing God convicted of the same sin of murder? For I had murdered him with my heart and with my tongue.

" 'Lord Jesus,' I whispered into the lumpy ticking of the bed, 'I forgive Jan Vogel as I pray that You will forgive me. I have done him great damage. Bless him now, and his family. ...' That night for the first time since our betrayer had a name I slept deep and dreamlessly until the whistle summoned us to roll call."[1]

STORY (cont.) and SCRIPTURE:

1. What finally motivates Corrie ten Boom to forgive this man?
   - ❏ her desire for sleep
   - ❏ being shamed by her sister's faith
   - ❏ her realization of how much she had been forgiven
   - ❏ being reminded of the teaching of Jesus in the Bible

2. Who in your life have you felt the anger toward that Corrie ten Boom describes in this passage?

A Sharper Focus. Throughout the New Testament we are told that in Jesus Christ we get a picture of what God is like; and if that is true then at no point does that picture get more sharply focused than when he is dying on the cross and says, "Father, forgive them; for they do not know what they are doing." This is the picture, par excellence, of what God is like. This picture tells us many things. It tells us that God is a caring God. Only a caring God would come to earth to suffer when he didn't have to. This tells us that God seeks to win by his love rather than by his power alone. Christ did not come down from that cross and strike his enemies—he stayed there and loved them into submission. This tells us that God is a God who not only demands love and forgiveness, but was willing to model it in the most difficult circumstances. Can we ever again think that God won't forgive our offenses if we but ask?

Have someone in your group read the following passage out loud. Then go around on each question and let each person share their answer. Take advantage of the Study notes following the questionnaire. Be sure to save the last 20–40 minutes for the Caring time.

33When they came to the place that is called The Skull, they crucified Jesus there with the criminals, one on his right and one on his left. 34Then Jesus said, "Father, forgive them; for they do not know what they are doing." And they cast lots to divide his clothing. 35And the people stood by, watching; but the leaders scoffed at him, saying, "He saved others; let him save himself if he is the Messiah of God, his chosen one!" 36The soldiers also mocked him, coming up and offering him sour wine, 37and saying, "If you are the King of the Jews, save yourself!" 38There was also an inscription over him, "This is the King of the Jews."

39One of the criminals who were hanged there kept deriding him and saying, "Are you not the Messiah? Save yourself and us!" 40But the other rebuked him, saying, "Do you not fear God, since you are under the same sentence of condemnation? 41And we indeed have been condemned justly, for we are getting what we deserve for our deeds, but

SCRIPTURE (cont.) and QUESTIONS:

this man has done nothing wrong." 42Then he said, "Jesus, remember me when you come into your kingdom." 43He replied, "Truly I tell you, today you will be with me in Paradise."

Luke 23:33–43

1. The place called "The Skull" was a landmark around Jerusalem. What were some of the landmarks where you grew up? Were there any landmarks with similarly colorful names?

2. What do you think was the predominant feeling in Jesus' heart while he was on the cross?
   - ❏ love
   - ❏ hope
   - ❏ sadness
   - ❏ pity
   - ❏ hurt
   - ❏ rejection
   - ❏ despair
   - ❏ other:_____

3. How do you view Christ's crucifixion?
   - ❏ necessary evil
   - ❏ cruel and unusual punishment
   - ❏ sacrifice for sin
   - ❏ triumph over injustice

4. In the midst of such pain and ridicule, how could Jesus say, "Father, forgive them"? How do these words make you feel?

5. How easy is it for you to forgive people who hurt you?

6. When, and how, did the crucifixion begin to make a difference in your life?
   - ❏ when I understood my sins were forgiven
   - ❏ when I felt peace in my life for the first time
   - ❏ when I committed my life to following Jesus
   - ❏ when I was able to forgive others

7. Is there someone you need to forgive? If so, what is keeping you from forgiving them?